Waltham Forest Libraries

Please return this item by the last date s
renewed unless required by an

D0297975

Jan 18		

Need to renew your books?
http://www.walthamforest.gov.uk/libraries or
Dial 0333 370 4700 for Callpoint – our 24/7 automated telephone renewal
line. You will need your library card number and your PIN. If you do not
know your PIN, contact your local library.

THE

IT'S ALL ABOUT THE URN

ASHES

Also by Graeme Swann

The Breaks Are Off

THE
IT'S ALL ABOUT THE URN
ASHES

ENGLAND VS. AUSTRALIA
ULTIMATE CRICKET RIVALRY

GRAEME SWANN
with Richard Gibson

HODDER &
STOUGHTON

First published in Great Britain in 2017 by Hodder & Stoughton
An Hachette UK company

1

Copyright © Graeme Swann 2017

The right of Graeme Swann to be identified as the
Author of the Work has been asserted by him in accordance
with the Copyright, Designs and Patents Act 1988.

A CIP catalogue record for this title is available from the British Library

ISBN 9781473670839
eBook ISBN 9781473670846
Trade paperback ISBN 9781473670822

Typeset in Adobe Garamond by Palimpsest Book Production Ltd,
Falkirk, Stirlingshire

Printed and bound by CPI Group (UK) Ltd, Croydon CR0 4YY

Hodder & Stoughton policy is to use papers that are natural,
renewable and recyclable products and made from wood grown in sustainable
forests. The logging and manufacturing processes are expected to conform
to the environmental regulations of the country of origin.

Hodder & Stoughton Ltd
Carmelite House
50 Victoria Embankment
London EC4Y 0DZ

www.hodder.co.uk

This book is for my Dad, Ray, whose passion for cricket made me fall in love with this marvellous game.

CONTENTS

1

HOOKED

My personal love affair with the Ashes began on cold winter mornings in late 1986, a time when Europe's 'The Final Countdown' topped the UK music charts, pound notes were still in circulation and *Neighbours* was in its infancy on the BBC.

Yet it wasn't that show that gripped the seven-year-old me. It was the half-an-hour highlights the Beeb would show every night during the 1986–87 series between Australia and England. Due to the fact it was on late, my dad Ray would tape it for my brother Alec and me to watch the following day before school, resulting in the pair of us running downstairs, putting the video on and becoming lost in this magical version of cricket played in some far-off land.

It was an intoxicating experience, charging down the stairs in the dark, not much after 5 a.m. We were so excited, it was like 25 extra Christmas days had been packed into the calendar that year, and each time we would go through the same process, a bit like a pre-match routine. I would fill two bowls with Shredded Wheat or Cornflakes – to be eaten dry as we weren't allowed milk in the front room until Mum and Dad came down, in case we spilled it on the carpet – while Alec set up the VHS. Naturally, I was not allowed to even touch the remote control as the younger brother. He'd shot-gunned that.

Sitting in our dressing gowns, hoods up, we were engrossed watching Ian Botham smash it everywhere. I considered him and others in that England team of 1986–87 to be real-life superheroes. They glorified playing cricket and I wanted to be like them.

Chris Broad, Stuart Broad's dad, scored three hundreds that series and I have vivid memories of him punching back-foot drives through the covers. Then there was little Allan Lamb, my favourite cricketer of all time, looking cool and never getting flustered.

For a boy from Towcester, the fact that Lamb played for Northamptonshire was reason enough for me to idolise him, but my dad also played with him in a benefit cricket match at St Albans, and when he ruffled my hair in the changing room that day it felt like being knighted by the Queen. It makes me laugh whenever I retell him the story these days, and he claims to remember it. Of course he doesn't.

Northamptonshire was my local club and it gave me a way of connecting to that England team. I loved watching him play for Northants, and here he was down under doing the same thing, making things look so easy. He is still one of the most under-rated players to have played for England, I think. Always pugnacious, exceptional against quick bowling and particularly fearless against the short-pitched stuff, he also looked effortlessly cool: the swagger, the smile and the cowboy moustache. Especially the 'tache, you could argue.

Bill Athey wasn't cool, but let's be honest, every team needs its straight man, and so that effectively made him cool by association. Then there were other appealing characters like Gladstone Small, Phil 'Daffy' DeFreitas and the wicketkeeper, Jack Richards, who scored a hundred in the second Test in Perth.

England batsmen seemed to take it in turns to score hundreds from the first day of the series, when Ian Botham smashed 138 in Brisbane. It was the old Gabba ground with the greyhound track running around the outside and it just didn't look like the cricket grounds we had seen over here. The bare-headed Beefy brought added attention to its perimeter by clearing it on several occasions, most memorably a hooked six off Merv Hughes. It was spectacular, sexy, gorgeous cricket.

I had already fallen in love with the game because my big brother played and my dad played, but perhaps because it looked so different from what I had seen here – so other-worldly, being played on the other side of the planet – this was the first series that told me: 'I want to play cricket.' It was just the best game in the world being played in the most magical land – penal colony, call it what you want – and to a young lad it was great.

Watching, I was consumed by thoughts of getting Allan Border out. Suddenly life became about representing the country and winning the Ashes. I wanted to be next in line to join the ranks of Englishmen who were celebrated for coming out on top in the most revered sporting rivalry of them all.

I have no idea how I developed the double loop in my bowling action, but it might not be a complete coincidence that it is reminiscent of Peter Taylor, a bespectacled accountant who briefly bowled off-spin for Australia after being drafted in for the Sydney Test. No one seemed to have seen him bowl before that series, including most of the regular watchers of top-level cricket in Sydney. The rumour that the selectors had meant to call up future Test captain Mark Taylor, his New South Wales team-mate, and got the wrong man was strengthened by the fact that only one recognised opening batsman had been chosen.

There were three other blokes, all capped at international level, ahead of him in the state's spin-bowling pecking order. Yet there he was, a virtually unknown 30-year-old, with just half a dozen first-class appearances to his name, whirling his arms around before delivering the ball, and doing so to great effect.

Perhaps subconsciously his technique had an effect on how I bowled, because I appear to have blatantly copied him. 'Peter Who', as he was dubbed in the build-up, proved the difference between the sides in that fifth Test, taking eight wickets at the Sydney Cricket Ground (SCG) to claim the man-of-the-match award, while a young lad in the Midlands did his best impressions 10,000 miles away in his back garden.

Alec and I were constantly playing in that garden, taking it in turns to be England. Whoever lost the toss had to be Australia, and we would play innings after innings until we got called in for tea. Each team would have five wickets, meaning that five players would be nominated to represent you from each side. I was already patriotic enough to pick the worst possible team I could think of when it was my turn to be Australia.

I would be all the lesser-known names: Dirk Wellham, Tim Zoehrer, Greg Matthews. I simply refused to be Allan Border, Dean Jones and David Boon, preferring to play badly whenever I was the other lot. This doctoring of the game with my substandard efforts was match-fixing in its purest form. Of course, Alec would be trying desperately to win, but I just couldn't stomach winning as Australia, even against my own brother. Yet when he was the Aussies, I wanted him to choose the A-listers, so that winning tasted all the sweeter.

We had bespoke rules for these contests – such as two out of five batsmen having to bat left-handed and every third over having to be sent down left-arm – and we would turn the back-garden tap on to slick up the pitch too. Every day we would be out there, strapping the pads on and bombing the hell out of each other. Our garden had the perfect dimensions for cricket, being about 12 yards wide, and the ball would be flying to all parts.

Only in later years would I come to realise how blessed I had been watching such a successful group of individuals defeating the Australians. I had seen some of the 1985 Ashes, and England had also won that one of course, but I was to come to understand that for an English supporter growing up in the 1990s it was a rite of passage to see your team being hammered by Australia.

People carried on harking back to the marvels of 1981 for the next couple of decades, but that was probably to ease the pain of some horrible thrashings. I reckon the hardest to take was the first in the sequence, in 1989, when the team billed as the worst in Australia's history arrived for a routine defeat. Such forecasts proved extremely foolhardy. To be honest, we got slaughtered. It was absolutely chaotic too, as just about everyone who played county cricket got a Test cap that summer, and not one of them could cope with Terry Alderman, the innocuous-looking swing bowler who wobbled it around a bit and caused mass panic.

Not least for Graham Gooch, our best batsman, who looked like he had homing devices tucked behind the flaps of his one-piece Stuart Surridge pads. Whenever he put them on and walked out to bat Alderman seemed to locate them, yet when he played county cricket Alderman was just an honest pro, a worthy bowler who would hold his own with a few wickets here and there. In the six-Test series in 1989 he got 40-odd. It was just one of those summers when the ball swung round corners, and he was able to get it to talk.

And so my adolescent view of the Ashes was formed. Most of my talking about cricket as a kid was with my geeky older brother, and I owe most of my cricketing knowledge to the fact Alec is such a nerd. I followed him everywhere and became the ideal sounding board for him to show off his extraordinary statistics. He knew everything about everything. He was like a walking *Wisden*. So I always knew the exact margins of England's defeats and the averages of each of the players on either side of the divide.

For when it came to England versus Australia, that was what it was: a divide. From a very young age, you can sense that the competitive rivalry between the two countries is fierce. There is no getting away from the fact it exists, yet if you asked a sports fan from either side they would struggle to explain why. It is there because it always has been, just as night follows day.

Once you have actually played in the games you realise that any sense of hatred between the players is a bit of a myth, but sport at the highest level creates tension, and tension creates occasional flashpoints, and these only serve to fuel that myth. They also help fill time and keep people amused in after-dinner speeches, but they're not truly representative of what happens on the field. From my experience, there is no preconceived nastiness simply because your opponent is Australian. Sure, if someone nicks one and doesn't walk, they are likely to get some stick – but that's because they've got away with one, not because they're playing for Australia.

What is true, however, is that the Ashes as a concept has developed into a huge event over the decades and as players you buy into that when you are selected to play. And the rivalry has perhaps been developed away from the field more than on it. We don't like Australia and they don't like us. Why? It's tradition, isn't it? You don't question it. A game of social one-upmanship exacerbated by the ball-and-chain image, which says we are better than you.

To really get into sport, to really understand the sense of competition in its purest form, to truly understand the highs and lows, you need a diehard rival. Their successes or failures help define those of your own team. Take football, for example. For Newcastle supporters like me there is Sunderland; for Rangers there is Celtic; Man United have got Liverpool – ha ha, that will annoy City fans; Arsenal have got Tottenham. When it comes to international football we all club together and laugh at Scotland, don't we? Or if we're feeling particularly chipper about ourselves, we stoke things up with Germany.

If you ask your average football fan why they hate their

rival team you will get answers like, 'Oh, because they're scum'. You won't actually get a reasoned argument for not liking Rovers if you are a City fan. There is no real substance to any dislike in most cases other than they are not us.

Of course, there are some clubs that have a deep dislike of others for reasons outside of sport. Think of the political backdrop that divides clubs like Nottingham Forest and Leeds United, stretching back to the 1970s and 1980s and the miners' strikes. When one set of fans is crossing a picket line, that's a whole different ball game.

Mostly, though, the ill feeling is not necessarily region to region. It's directed a lot closer to home, and you can't stand the club whose fans live amongst you. They might even be on the same street. Take Newcastle and Sunderland again, for example. Apart from the fact that Sunderland is a complete hole and Newcastle is a fine metropolis – one of the finest on the planet – they sit alongside each other. But there is an historical significance to the cities' rivalry dating to the ship-building era. Everyone assumes that 'Mackem' is a derogatory term for residents of Sunderland. No such thing. There are a couple of takes on the exact origins of the word but they refer to the fact that the ships were built in the city: 'we make them', or to incorporate the north-east dialect, 'we mack 'em'. They would then be sent down the River Wear to sea. Of course, Newcastle fans will provide the variation that before this happened their ancestors would then 'take them', or 'tack 'em', and outfit them. It's important to use anything you can to impose your superiority in these instances, even when the evidence is questionable.

Similarly, the Ashes rivalry has been maintained for the best part of a century and a half because it is so deeply embedded in our country's traditions. It is the way it has always been and it is the way it always will be, I guess, and we don't feel the need to trace its historical origins every time a new series comes around, or to question its significance in the history of the two countries concerned. Because originally the two sides of the contest were symbolic of the Empire and the Colony: the old world versus the new; the elite versus the commoners; the law-abiding citizens versus the law-breakers. And the war between these two contrasting civilisations took place on a sportsfield rather than a battle-field.

It is human nature to look for a rival, to want to engage in a survival-of-the-fittest battle, to compete; and the fact that the Australians are, or more accurately were, descended from the English – albeit biscuit thieves and petty criminals – provided that extra edge to the sporting competition. I have no doubt that during the 1880s there would have been some social malice between the two XIs, but these days when it comes down to it, although there is the odd one you could genuinely make a case for locking up – let's not dwell on David Warner, though – there are some great blokes in either dressing room, and it's the direct one-on-one contest that is so appealing.

There is no doubting that there is something about Ashes cricket that transcends the sport, something that goes beyond the actual match itself and draws in people of all ages, even kids watching for the first time, with its magic dust, making you want to switch places with the bowler or the batsman.

When I was young it was the same with the FA Cup final. It was an all-day event that was screened in its entirety on the TV from early morning, beginning with shots of both teams having breakfast or relaxing in their hotels, then boarding their buses for the trips to Wembley and studying their suits as they walked across the hallowed turf before the match. Watching *Grandstand* on Cup final day was what everyone did. Because of all the hype, it used to feel like the biggest thing in football, even bigger than winning the League. Not these days: it has become nothing more than a sideshow, thanks to emphasis being placed on other things by the authorities. During my youth, though, the fact that the FA Cup finals and the Ashes were on the BBC made everyone talk about them. It was a part of my generation's growing up.

The world was a bigger place then, and seeing cricket played in a far-off land made you take pride in the fact that players in our country were being sent there. To experience it as a player is something else. It is so obviously way bigger than any other series that you play in as an England cricketer. Let's be fair, in a summer when you are up against Bangladesh or New Zealand, no offence to those two teams, but those aren't the kind of challenges you used to fantasise about, in between thinking about one of the cute girls, when you were sitting at the back of the classroom as a 13-year-old.

Of course, every coach says things like 'this is the biggest game you could ever play for your country', because they have to. I have heard that countless times when everyone in the team meeting knows it's a lie. The next game is always the biggest; it's the way sports teams look at things, and I get that. But, come on. Let's have a dose of honesty here. Every player in the room is thinking: 'What a load of rubbish, of course it's not.' It's April, it's Bangladesh, Jimmy is going to get 10 wickets and we will win inside three days. Yes, play the best you can, but let's not pretend it's the Ashes and a game you really dream about.

Touring Australia, I have always felt that it is effectively two countries in one. On one side, there's a fiercely loyal, aggressive, almost redneck kind of society that hates England, and pretty much every other form of outsider, to be honest – a rather misogynistic clan of beer-swigging louts that pronounce their country 'Straya' and sing, 'Aussie, Aussie, Aussie, oi, oi, oi'. Then there is the trendy-lefty, liberal, LGBT-rules-OK crowd who believe everyone should be treated fairly and who tend to be pretty welcoming. It means they've almost got a split personality as a country, which makes for quite a contrasting time while you're there. Things change from week to week, depending on your itinerary.

For example, when the Test series begins, they typically send you to Brisbane first, and as cities around the world go that's about as feral as it gets. Blokes wear the stereotypical cork hats and squeeze themselves into Brisbane Broncos rugby league shorts that barely cover their privates. And they're pretty creative as a welcoming committee, typically introducing themselves with greetings like 'F*** off home, you Pommie bastards.'

I am not sure beginning in Queensland is a tactical thing. It's just an historical one, as they tend to start all home summers there in the modern era, regardless of the opposition. It is perhaps no surprise that Australia have an excellent record of 28 undefeated Test appearances in Brisbane, though, because as soon as you walk into the stadium, you feel the full force of the crowd's hostility.

On day one in 2010–11, Peter Siddle had just taken a hat-trick and I was the next man in. The noise as I walked out to bat, from the moment I left the dressing room, all the way to when he ran in to bowl, was frightening. Absolutely deafening. Like nothing I have experienced in my whole life. The hairs on the back of my neck were literally standing on end. I know you hear that expression from time to time, but it really is the best way to explain the physical feeling I experienced before producing the best forward defence I've ever played. It felt like I had just returned serve from Novak Djokovic and I wanted to scream: 'Yeah, stuff you lot.' I'm glad I didn't, because I was out a few balls later and I'd have looked pretty stupid.

On the bus to the hotel in the evening the chat was all about the atmosphere. 'Could you believe that noise?' That was the general subject. It was like a cauldron. As we were discussing it, one of the guys pointed out a chap waiting alongside us at the traffic lights on a Harley-Davidson – with one of those hats worn by the bikers in the Netflix series *Sons of Anarchy*, the ones that look a bit like a baseball helmet. He had an Australian cricket vest on, some burgundy Queensland or Brisbane shorts, the tightest known to man, and just one flip-flop. He had a can of beer in a home-made holder on the handlebars and he was grinning at us: 'You blokes f***** up? Eh?'

In England, if you go to the cricket you've a good chance of wearing a jacket and even putting a cravat on. Oh, and you might arm yourself with a hamper. You want to get there nice and early to make sure you're guaranteed the best parking position, and you jolly well clap the opposition if they do well. This guy was not one of those chaps. He resembled the kind of beast that would tear down a fence to get in. Throughout our brief encounter he sat swigging from a tin of Castlemaine XXXX, exposing a smile missing one or two teeth here and there – and the fashion sense of Crocodile Dundee.

What a contrast to crowd for the second Test at Adelaide, which has a much stricter dress code, and tends to promote a very refined, antiquated outlook, attracting a more sporting audience willing to applaud good cricket as a result.

Those two first stops in a series provide a real dichotomy at the start of a tour, but it doesn't always work in Australia's favour, as we found when the boguns at Brisbane turned. For the first three days the crowd tore into us and acted as Straya's twelfth man. But by the end of that Test match, after we scored more than 500 for the loss of just one wicket, they were booing their own team. It was like that partisan crowd in *Rocky IV* when they stopped cheering for Ivan Drago and switched allegiances.

Sure, as a rule they love to hate an Englishman down under, but they hate a loser even more, and so when they are dealt a losing team they can't handle it. They just cannot accept being second in any sporting contest, and to be fair they don't try to hide the fact, yet it was still a freaky experience when a proportion of them turned in that way. Suddenly, it was like they were saying: 'Stuff this, this Australian team is embarrassing. I'm going to support the Poms instead.'

We were winning, and playing well, producing exactly the kind of cricket we'd expected to – and this decision by their own supporters only served to put the Australian team under even more pressure. At this time, the Australian players seemed to have it in the back of their minds that their own fans would turn on them, and once they did the negative attitude towards them lasted the entire trip.

During the one-day series that followed the Tests, we were playing in Melbourne and Michael Clarke was getting booed every time he hit the ball. What had started as pockets of disquiet two months earlier had mushroomed into audible, persistent protest.

'Is that because you're a blue bagger?' I asked. 'They're jeering you because you're a New South Welshman, right?'

'No, it's because they think I'm a ****.'

Jesus Christ, this was the way they were reacting to losing the Ashes. They were prepared to jeer a bloke who had won countless matches for them in the past. One of the best players Australia had ever produced.

I can be hyper-patriotic at times, but I have to say that I am pleased to be an Englishman. Let's face it, we have the fairest, most loyal crowds in the world. I think it's because we are the most self-deprecating of nations. We almost like to be rubbish at stuff because it gives us something to whinge about. Equally, it means that when one of our national teams does better than getting walloped, everyone rejoices.

Not that I am your typical England fan. We are a pessimistic country as a rule and there have been countless times when we have been 50 for no wickets chasing 120 and the default position around the stands is that we're going to lose. But I've always felt like a square peg in a round hole because I'm an eternal optimist. 'Win from any position' – that's my mantra. From the sofa, I always cheer until the bitter end. As a player, I always felt that there was a chance until the scoreboard told us otherwise.

Ahead of one Ashes series the England players were asked

to consider contingency plans if things didn't go as we had envisaged. We had to write down all the what-ifs and think about how we would cope with them as a team. Some of my team-mates came up with things like 'What if they are six down at lunch, then put on a partnership of 100?' Or 'What if we are six down at lunch?' My thoughts tended to be the complete opposite: 'What if we're bloody not six down? What if we bowl them out for next to nothing?'

We have this doom-and-gloom outlook, that a huge kick in the biffs awaits us – it means that when we do win we celebrate feverishly, and I've always liked that too. It's why when moments such as the 2005 Ashes victory come around the whole country joins together and celebrates properly. The players got MBEs, for Christ's sake! Even Paul Collingwood, although it is rumoured in cricket circles that Her Majesty the Queen gave him one just to wind up Shane Warne.

It felt like everyone was united in their belief during those crazy six weeks that this was the best thing ever. Of course it was a brilliant achievement, but was it really the greatest performance by an England team ever? No, probably not. It was blown up in part because we'd been hammered for years and years, and winning in those circumstances felt all the better. We had got used to losing to the degree that when we actually won, all sense of perspective went out of the window, and in a perverse kind of way it felt like normality was restored when the England team went to Australia 14 months later and lost 5–0.

In football, in every build-up to a World Cup we are all desperate for England to win and, no matter how positive we are as a nation about the prospect, there is always that caveat: 'Oh, we won't win it; I just hope we have a good run.' Why won't we win it? We certainly won't if we go in with an attitude like that. I don't believe that anyone in Germany thinks they're going to lose a semi-final on penalties.

England supporters are extremely loyal, though, and the Barmy Army in particular – simply because there is a core of them that watched England around the world for 20 years when they had little or no chance of winning, especially when it came to the Ashes. Yet there they would be in the stands, shouting for their team, spending their life savings, in high spirits. It was almost like a perverse badge of honour: 'Look at just how bad we are. We've spent everything to follow this shower.'

They'd found meaning in their lives, and those of us in cricket know lots of people like this, or people who want to be that kind of person. Every Englishman wants to do something slightly mad. We don't want to be brash, like the Australians, or like the Americans, going around pumping each other's tyres up. We want to celebrate from positions of adversity. At least this attitude taught us how to deal with defeat after defeat.

Since England got that urn back after 16 years in 2005 it has been the Australians who've had that extra pressure heaped on them. I am surprised Ricky Ponting kept his passport, to be honest, after overseeing three Ashes losses. Yes, he might have been the best Australian batsman since Don Bradman, but it's a wonder they didn't force him to live back in Tasmania at the very least. Or even dispatch him to New Zealand.

I am sure both Joe Root and Steve Smith have already thought about the risks and rewards that go with leading their countries into this winter's Ashes, because it is not a series that creeps up on you. Nowadays, in the age of 24/7 sports news, every major sporting event is built up to the *n*th degree, and for the Ashes that means a countdown clock. We'll all be ticking off the days to the tenth such series of the 21st century whether we like it or not, and then the coverage of the series itself will boot everything else into touch.

Before a day's play in a Test match against South Africa – which is a big deal for an England player, a series I always looked forward to and always wanted to do well in – you know it's going to be tough and that you'll have to play well to come out on top. There will be three camera crews out on the field – Sky Sports and Channel 5 amongst them – and a few radio reporters milling about from *Test Match Special*. All in all, there will be around 50 people out there. In contrast, before an Ashes Test there is barely a blade of grass to be seen. Take Cardiff in 2009 as an example: it felt like there were hundreds out there as we practised ahead of the toss. Every media organisation you could think of seemed to be around with their own crew, and there was even one from

Japan. That made me chuckle. I assume Monty Panesar is a big draw in Tokyo.

It was a similar story after the game. If you get the man-of-the-match award in a one-day international against New Zealand at Lord's, that's quite an achievement. New Zealand are a very good side. You're wheeled into a press conference with three cameras and two dozen journalists dotted around the room. But if you are man of the match against Australia, everything is multiplied by four. There's a big microphone on the desk and everyone's eyes are focused on what you are about to say. It feels like you're addressing the world, and that's the kind of situation you dream about as a kid. It's your superstar moment, surrounded by the bright lights. The world is there to hear you sing and so you sing as loud as you can.

2
GRACE AND FAVOURS

So what is it about the Ashes – that most symbolic of sporting trophies – that gets the beans going for English and Australian cricketers? When all is said and done, it is effectively worthless – a handful of dust contained in a tiny terracotta urn that no one ever gets their hands on. How did something so small mushroom into something so . . . well, not to put too fine a point on it . . . er, big?

It is pretty easy to understand why boxers occasionally lose all sense of perspective before world-title fights. Undoubtedly, it has something to do with the size of the bounty. How can you expect anyone to avoid acting like a pork chop when the reward for winning is a mythical purse stuffed with Benjamin Franklins? Yet historically, the quest for this earthy-coloured urn has featured some win-at-all-costs actions, as if the burnt cinders inside were actually the elixir of life.

Its precise origins remain a matter of debate 135 years after the first known reference relating to England matches versus Australia. But they can be dated back to The Oval in 1882 and England's second home Test against the Australians. For it was this match that contained the first widely reported antagonism between two international cricket teams. And the individual at the centre of it all remains one of cricket's household names all these decades on. A man so famous he is recognisable by his initials, and one who acted as though he was bigger than the game itself. On this occasion, however, W.G. Grace's flouting of the spirit of the game was to back-fire in spectacular fashion.

The incident at The Oval that so incensed the Australians came when Grace took advantage of their late-order batsman Sammy Jones wandering out of his ground to carry out some gardening mid-pitch. Grace whipped off the bails and appealed for a run-out, which the umpire – somewhat aghast at the gamesmanship, it was later suggested – felt obliged to answer in the affirmative in the absence of a withdrawal by the home team. Despite already being in command of the contest – Australia were the equivalent of 76–6 second time around, after conceding a deficit on first innings – England stuck by their guns to claim another wicket.

Yet Grace's action only served to further demonise the demon in Australia's ranks. For it was the fast bowler Freddie 'the Demon' Spofforth who was so upset by this particular act of skulduggery that he burst into the home dressing room to read Grace his fortune. No doubt warning him: 'B'gad, Grace, that's just not cricket; we will make you pay for this, just see if we don't.' Or some Antipodean-tinged 19th-century equivalent, spoken with fist shaking from within a white glove, dressed and ready for a duel. It was the kind of act to make any competitor want to take his own retribution. And so it came to pass. England were later dismissed for 77, chasing a target of just 85. Fourteen of the 20 wickets Australia claimed for victory went to their attack spearhead Spofforth.

Pulling off such a plainly wrong act will not have done W.G.'s team-mates any favours. You can imagine it would have made life difficult for some of them, but he was the dominant personality and as such the outcome was delivered on his watch. He might have top-scored with 32, but Grace could rightly be held to account for one of the biggest embarrassments Victorian society could suffer. Defeat to Australia was the equivalent of a national-security breach. It was like having the crown jewels stolen by a bunch of convicted petty thieves on release from their lock-up at the ends of the earth. Good Lord. It constituted a political loss of face. A national crisis, no less.

It did not go down well with the national press either, particularly the *Sporting Times*, whose mock obituary of English cricket gave the unheralded journalist Reginald Shirley Brooks an unlikely place in the history of English sport.

In Affectionate Remembrance

OF

ENGLISH CRICKET,

WHICH DIED AT THE OVAL

ON

29th AUGUST, 1882,

Deeply lamented by a large circle of sorrowing
friends and acquaintances.

———

R.I.P.

———

*N.B.—The body will be cremated and the
ashes taken to Australia.*

With these words Brooks, a typical Fleet Street hack, could hardly have known what he had started. Whether or not the Ashes tradition began with his pen remains a moot point, but what is utterly undeniable is that it was at the very least partly responsible, setting in motion a chain of events that led to the urn becoming one of the most famous pieces of sporting memorabilia across the globe.

During the following winter of 1882–83, the Hon. Ivo Bligh led England on tour and used his official arrival oration – following the customary two-month voyage by ship – to announce that his team were there to try to recover 'those Ashes'. And those Ashes were given further substance when, at one of the regular gatherings at the family estate of Sir

William Clarke, president of the Melbourne Cricket Club, the Clarke family's music teacher, Florence Morphy, and other women within the entourage presented Bligh with a keepsake.

Some people will suggest the red clay urn they passed over is not much to look at, standing just six inches in height, and containing the ashes of a bail, ball or veil depending on the version of the story you prefer. It's a rather condescending trophy too, isn't it? Representing a one-off defeat as an act of finality simply because of the characteristics of the opposition. A permanent reminder of when England were really bad, and arguably of the start of Australia's devotion to winning. Its value has been maintained because of what it stands for rather than its size or contents.

Bligh was true to his word that winter. England did recover those ashes, and they were to remain in English hands for the next decade, metaphorically at least. Physically, the urn stayed in his possession until his death in 1927, when it was donated to the MCC's cricket museum by his widow – a certain Florence Morphy.

Deemed too delicate to be transported, it has been kept behind glass since the 1950s and so replicas have been used for on-field presentations. I know this only too well, as when we won in 2009, Andrew Strauss was handed an urn with a £9.99 price tag stuck on the bottom. It had been purchased from the Lord's shop for use at the presentation across London at The Oval.

* * *

Early on there was a strong class aspect running through the Ashes. Over here in England, cricket was the game of choice for those with wealth and power, and they made sure it was played properly by people with plummy voices who were only too happy to reiterate: 'This is the way to play the game.' At least that was the stereotype they adhered to.

The Australians? Well, they were quite simply uncouth. They had derived from the dregs of society and they needed to be kept in their place. They hated us because we were elitist, and we detested them because of their backgrounds, looking down our noses at them and treating them with disdain. Our predecessors would have wanted to play the game with style, while you can imagine the early Australians showing a bit of mongrel to knock some of their top hats off. The cricket sounds a great deal feistier than anything I ever experienced, and all the animosity stemmed from one England defeat to the underclass.

Grace certainly didn't take it sitting down. What a character he was. Who can forget his infamous comment to an opponent in a charity match when, having been bowled first ball, he simply replaced the bails and chimed, 'My dear thing, they've come to watch me bat, not you bowl.'

Without the Ashes, certain players might not have enjoyed the fame and notoriety that came their way. Take 2005, for example, when Andrew Flintoff became a national hero and 13 million people cheered on the England team from their living rooms. Now that's a proper TV audience. That series reached out to the entire population, to the extent that kids became obsessed with cricket and got involved with the game, wanting to replicate what their heroes like Freddie were doing. Obviously the teams in subsequent England wins were not to become as immediately recognisable, as the audiences dropped to 3.5 million and one million, but back in 2005 you would have struggled to find anyone in the country that didn't know who Flintoff was and what he'd been up to that summer.

TV wasn't even a twinkle in John Logie Baird's eye when Grace was in his pomp, of course, but consider where the Gloucestershire man stood in the nation's consciousness. During the 1880s, he was probably more famous than the Queen. He was certainly this country's, and perhaps even the world's, first sporting superstar, and everyone would know what he looked like through his depiction on cigarette cards and advertisements.

Yet there was a real dastardly side to him, as we have seen with that Oval incident, and he would go to great lengths to try to win. To run someone out while they pat down a divot really is the lowest of the low. One of the things I love about cricket and its devotion to tradition is that it has retained a gentlemanly code at its core. There is a certain way to play, a certain way to prosper, and I would be appalled to think that any England player would replicate those actions today. The more I consider Grace's exploits, the more turned off I get. Yes, he was revered for his record, and cricket is all about statistical achievements on the field, but we shouldn't forget the journey that led him to such heights.

No one can deny the talent of someone like Luis Suárez on the football field, but he's always bent the rules to his advantage. He cheats, he dives, he bites. Sure, he's one of the most talented footballers that's ever lived, but he just sounds like an average bloke. You wouldn't want your kids to spend five minutes with him. Gary Lineker possesses an inferior goal-scoring record, albeit that he was a fine player, but he was a fine man as well and there is something in that. I am sure he didn't want to win any less, but he still spent an entire career out of referees' notebooks. Now, he's the kind of guy you'd stick up for in a bar fight. If it all kicked off, you'd have Gary Lineker's back, wouldn't you?

To me, Mankading, running down the middle of a pitch, diving, keeping the ball from a throw-in after one of your team's gone down injured – it's all the same. No, it's not illegal, but you are getting away with something that you shouldn't. For years there has been nothing in the laws of cricket and football to punish you for these acts but, as the South African saying goes, it is a little bit like kissing your sister. You just don't do it.

Winning is always important in an Ashes series, but there are ways to win, and you don't want to achieve it with a sense of injustice hanging over you. For instance, there was one regrettable occasion when Ryan Sidebottom barged Grant Elliott over in a one-day international at The Oval in the summer of 2008 and he was then run out. Of course, as a team we should have withdrawn our appeal, but in the heat of the moment we didn't see that it was wrong. Paul Collingwood, in his role as captain, asked whether Sid was going for the ball and he said, 'Hundred per cent I was.' Elliott was knocked to the floor as he ran across the ball's path, and the wrong call was made. We were absolutely wrong to uphold the appeal, but there had been no underhand tactics at play.

In the decade after the events at The Oval in 1882, England did win, as Grace atoned for that shock defeat by any means he could. England dominated the Ashes series of the 1880s and early 1890s, winning eight in a row. Neither team has bettered such a stretch, but it was matched by the Australians of more than a century later, and it took the once-in-a-lifetime performance of Michael Vaughan's team to derail the 2005 Australians and prevent them returning home with a ninth.

There is no denying that cricket is a batsman's game, but it wasn't much of one in the penultimate decade of the 19th century. Bowlers completely dominated the Ashes during this period, and although Grace was the star attraction, scoring a maiden hundred in such contests in the whitewash-completing win of 1886, the efforts of an attack comprising slow left-armers Johnny Briggs and Bobby Peel plus those of George Lohmann were greatly responsible for an overall score-line of 16–4 in England's favour in 'live' matches between

1882–83 and 1890. (A flick through the record books reveals that England were pegged back to 2–2 in the first of those eight series but were declared winners of the Ashes at 2–1 up as the original scheduling had incorporated only three Test matches.)

Lohmann, a seamer only a tad brisker than medium pace, took 25 wickets in three Tests in consecutive winters down under at a cost of 7.56 runs apiece, aided by some substandard surfaces, a tally bettered by Peel, whose 101 wickets versus Australia included a sequence of 33 at 7.24 between 1887–88 and 1888. Briggs and Peel would later endure unusual endings to their careers: the former after suffering an epileptic fit at Headingley, and the latter sacked by Lord Hawke at Yorkshire after turning up drunk for the umpteenth time. That was not the sackable offence, however. It was peeing on the pitch before the start of the match that did for him. At least the England team of which I was a part in 2013 had the decency to wait until twilight, and the completion of a 3–0 series victory at The Oval.

Grace's standards of poor behaviour were sandwiched somewhere in the middle of these bookends to a day's play, such as the occasion during the 1891–92 tour that he fronted when he denied Harry Moses a fielding substitute during the match at the Sydney Cricket Ground. He became more irascible as the tour progressed, losing his temper on the field during the two defeats that meant Australia won back the urn and sent him packing as England's first defeated captain since Florence Morphy's gift to her future hubby nine years earlier.

Even England's dead-rubber win in Adelaide was tainted by a row over the umpires, and the 1891–92 series loss was an expensive one. The £3,000 tour fee Grace charged was comparable to a decent Indian Premier League contract in modern terms, during an era in which sportsmen did not command huge fees. In a results-based business it did not appear to be money well spent.

The home crowds certainly enjoyed his demise. Grace was not a fan of Australia and the contempt he felt for it was mutual. Perhaps best summarised by the howling and yelling that greeted each wicket in the pivotal success at Sydney when England squandered a 163-run advantage on first innings.

The home barrackers also had a new hero akin to Spofforth to do their bidding – Ernie Jones, a fast bowler from a mining background, whose reputation as a chucker saw him no-balled in separate matches. He achieved further notoriety in 1896 by sending down a chin-high delivery to Grace – the first recorded beamer in international cricket history.

It may well have been one of the most popular deliveries of the age, for the uncompromising Grace was a divisive figure even in his own dressing room, regularly cutting down team-mates with his razor-like quips. None better than during the Old Trafford Test of 1896 when, after springing a surprise by inviting wicketkeeper Dick Lilley to have a bowl, he yanked the part-timer down from cloud nine following the capture of Australia captain Harry Trott's prized wicket: 'You must have been bowling with the wrong arm.' Lilley was promptly dispatched behind the stumps once more.

Times were a-changing as the century came to its end. Previously dominated, Australia were becoming more and more competitive, arguably at a time when England were also gaining strength. The opening Test of 1894–95 in Sydney highlighted the intensity of the play. It would be the first and – for some 86 years, until a bloke with the Christian names 'Ian Terence' came along and had a knees-up in Leeds – the only instance of a team winning an international cricket match after being asked to follow on.

The completion of this turnaround sounds like an episode that might have taken place on a club tour. Tests were timeless in those days, of course, and at the end of day five Australia were just 64 runs shy of their 177-run target, with eight wickets standing. Resigned to their fate, the touring Englishmen sought solace in the bottom of their glasses that evening, drinking into the early hours.

Water was to prove their saviour, however. Lots of water.

The first of it was a deluge from the heavens that transformed the pitch into an old-school sticky dog. The second was the volume that was poured over the badly hung-over Bobby Peel's head by his captain, Andrew Stoddart. The dual soakings had their desired effects on proceedings: the England bowlers got the ball to misbehave and Peel was the most effective of the lot, taking four of the final half a dozen wickets to fall as Australia were dismissed for 166.

England went on to triumph in the series 3–2 and as a result of the competitive nature of the matches, the Ashes came to be seen as the definitive sporting contest of its era. Not that in those days there were pre-series predictions of what one team was going to do to the other via carrier pigeon or anything like that. In fact, the symbolism of the urn had – if anything – been forgotten during the period of English dominance. It was arguably the de-bearding of Grace and his team in 1891–92 that reminded the populations of both countries what was at stake. How a pantomime villain stokes up interest, eh?

Date	Venue	Team	Scores	Team	Scores	Result
30/12/1882	Melbourne	Australia	291 & 58-1	England	177 & 169	Australia won by 9 wickets
19/01/1883	Melbourne	England	294	Australia	114 & 153	England won by an innings and 27 runs
26/01/1883	Sydney	England	247 & 123	Australia	218 & 83	England won by 69 runs
10/07/1884	Manchester	England	95 & 180-9	Australia	182	Drawn
21/07/1884	Lord's	Australia	229 & 145	England	379	England won by an innings and 5 runs
11/08/1884	The Oval	Australia	551	England	346 & 85-2	Drawn
12/12/1884	Adelaide	Australia	243 & 191	England	369 & 67-2	England won by 8 wickets
01/01/1885	Melbourne	England	401 & 7-0	Australia	279 & 126	England won by 10 wickets
20/02/1885	Sydney	Australia	181 & 165	England	133 & 207	Australia won by 6 runs
14/03/1885	Sydney	England	269 & 77	Australia	309 & 38-2	Australia won by 8 wickets
21/03/1885	Melbourne	Australia	163 & 125	England	386	England won by an innings and 98 runs
05/07/1886	Manchester	Australia	205 & 123	England	223 & 107-6	England won by 4 wickets
19/07/1886	Lord's	England	353	Australia	121 & 126	England won by an innings and 106 runs
12/08/1886	The Oval	England	434	Australia	68 & 149	England won by an innings and 217 runs
28/01/1887	Sydney	England	45 & 184	Australia	119 & 97	England won by 13 runs
25/02/1887	Sydney	England	151 & 154	Australia	84 & 150	England won by 71 runs
10/02/1888	Sydney	England	113 & 137	Australia	42 & 82	England won by 126 runs
16/07/1888	Lord's	Australia	116 & 60	England	53 & 62	Australia won by 61 runs
13/08/1888	The Oval	Australia	80 & 100	England	317	England won by an innings and 137 runs
30/08/1888	Manchester	England	172	Australia	81 & 70	England won by an innings and 21 runs
21/07/1890	Lord's	Australia	132 & 176	England	173 & 137-3	England won by 7 wickets
11/08/1890	The Oval	Australia	92 & 102	England	100 & 95-8	England won by 2 wickets
25/08/1890	Manchester					Match abandoned without a ball bowled
01/01/1892	Melbourne	Australia	240 & 236	England	264 & 158	Australia won by 54 runs
29/01/1892	Sydney	Australia	144 & 391	England	307 & 156	Australia won by 72 runs
24/03/1892	Adelaide	England	499	Australia	100 & 169	England won by an innings and 230 runs
17/07/1893	Lord's	England	334 & 234-8	Australia	269	Drawn
14/08/1893	The Oval	England	483	Australia	91 & 349	England won by an innings and 43 runs
24/08/1893	Manchester	Australia	204 & 236	England	243 & 118-4	Drawn
14/12/1894	Sydney	Australia	586 & 166	England	325 & 437	England won by 10 runs
29/12/1894	Melbourne	England	75 & 475	Australia	123 & 333	England won by 94 runs
11/01/1895	Adelaide	Australia	238 & 411	England	124 & 143	Australia won by 382 runs
01/02/1895	Sydney	Australia	284	England	65 & 72	Australia won by an innings and 147 runs
01/03/1895	Melbourne	Australia	414 & 267	England	385 & 298-4	England won by 6 wickets

3

THE GOLDEN AGE
OF GOOGLIES

I F Grace was the figurehead of the first generation of England's Ashes cricketers, his characteristics stood in contrast to the free-spirited gang that were to be his immediate successors. Throughout history there have been periods in which the England team were unimaginative and workmanlike. Thankfully, in most cases this has encouraged more attacking players to emerge as a reaction to the boring cricket. And so it was as the 19th century turned into a more beautiful butterfly called the 20th. On the Australian side was the aesthetically pleasing Victor Trumper; on the English, a raft of elegant strokemakers who would ensure that the diligently brilliant Grace, the most prolific batsman the game had seen, was consigned to the archives.

The most audacious of this new breed was not even English by birth. Yes, long before England's native dressing-room tongue was Afrikaans, we were welcoming imports into our XI. For the 1896 series, the selection of Kumar Shri Ranjitsinhji – born in India but educated at Cambridge University – was resisted initially by Lord Harris, the man responsible for such matters. But the wristy flicks to leg, viewed by Harris as possessing the potential to have a bad influence on the batting of others, were not kept off the international stage for long. Just one match, in fact, due to the pressure building for Ranji's inclusion within the England XI.

Ranji, spry and alert at the crease, represented the unorthodox more than 100 years before it became trendy, improvising his strokes on a whim, and often walking across his stumps to open up shots to the leg side. Footage of him on his first England tour of 1897–98 is amongst the first recorded in the sport, and reveals a series of languid caresses of the ball on the move. The grumbling around the county game suggested that such a style was simply not cricket, that one should drive the ball on the off side like a gentleman, and Lord Harris was amongst the detractors. Goodness only knows what he and they would have made of all the reverse sweeps, switch hits and ramps that proliferate in the modern game.

An unbeaten second-innings hundred on debut at Old Trafford more than justified the inclusion of a man who claimed to be a prince, and in later life would actually become one. But in Victorian Britain Ranji also had to overcome prejudices relating to his background and colour, and even a motion for his exclusion from the England team. He did so by wooing the spectators with his magic from the East, often in tandem with his close friend and Sussex team-mate Charles Fry.

Fry, another of those cricketers whose initials went before him, and therefore equally familiar as 'C.B.' (middle name Burgess), was an all-rounder in life not just cricket. He would play in Ashes series for 13 years but never toured. Rumour had it that he refused to venture out of his ground for fear that it would lead to further dalliance between his wife, Beatrice (10 years his senior), and Fry's former mentor, Charles Hoare (15 years her senior).

Equally, however, Fry had lots of other pursuits that demanded his attention at home. In addition to being a batsman of great repute – one who reeled off a record six consecutive first-class hundreds – he played full-back for England at football, served the clubs of Southampton and Portsmouth, and held the world long-jump record. At rugby union, he was proficient enough to represent the Barbarians. His agility matched his versatility, and there can be no sportsman to have been so outstanding at so many sports. Roy Race, eat your heart out.

The larger-than-life Fry was equally prolific away from the playing fields, listing public-school teacher, journalist, nude model and Royal Navy captain amongst his lifetime of professions. Although his attempts to become a Liberal MP did not come to fruition, he did serve as a public figure, embarking on missions such as the one to meet Adolf Hitler. His idea? To persuade the Nazis to take up Test cricket! Can you imagine, if they had taken him up? The Germans would have beaten us on bowl-outs as well as penalties.

During the League of Nations meeting in Geneva in 1920, for which he was present as secretary to his great friend Ranjitsinhji, by then Jamsahib of Nawanagar and one of India's delegates, he was supposedly offered the throne of Albania. Ranji had been involved in the negotiations and although there has been some scepticism about the whole episode, given his friend's affection for wind-ups, there is evidence to suggest that Albania was seeking an Englishman with an independent annual income in excess of £10,000, and that would have ruled out Fry despite his multifarious pursuits.

Instead, he had to settle for England captain as his official title. Fry was put in charge for the summer of 1912 after the 1911–12 tourists returned from Australia with a 4–1 win under their belts. Undefeated in seven Tests in charge – three of them against South Africa during a failed triangular experiment – he retained the Ashes 1–0 after an extra day was added to the third Test at The Oval.

Unsurprising, really, since the Golden Age team Fry fronted included all-time greats like Jack Hobbs, Wilfred Rhodes, Frank Woolley and Sydney Barnes, men whose classical abilities we still laud a full century on.

Jack Hobbs who collected records like the opening batsman that he was, would tuck singles to fine leg. He made more first-class hundreds (197) than any other player in history, shredding W.G.'s mark of 126 – and legend has it that he would have made more but for the fact he would often give his wicket away to allow others to bat. The Great War also took out four prime years for a man who would become Test cricket's oldest centurion and the sport's first knight.

Born in Cambridge, 'the Master' spent his youth watching Ranjitsinhji practise, and the first half of a career split by service as a mechanic in the Royal Flying Corps was befitting of Ranji's style: light on the feet and rapier of stroke. When it resumed, he had to adapt to reflect his increased years. With experience came a more rounded, classic technique. In middle age, his hundreds were compiled primarily off the back foot.

There was a cricketer like Yorkshire's Wilfred Rhodes at every cricket club up and down the country in the 1980s, when I would travel to see my dad play on Saturdays. You probably know the type: started out down the bottom of the order and worked his way to the top by making the most of his opportunities. Could bowl all day too, and give the opposition nowt. The difference being that Rhodes did it at international level, and against the Aussies.

In Sydney in 1903–04, he went in last and took part in the most dogged and ultimately most prolific tenth-wicket alliance in Ashes Tests for 110 years. His 130 share with

R.E. Foster was not bettered until Ashton Agar and the late Phillip Hughes combined at Trent Bridge in 2013. Eight years later, he went in first for England versus the Australians at Melbourne, partnering Hobbs in the record first-wicket stand of 323, one that lasted until the Mark Taylor/Geoff Marsh effort in Nottingham in 1989.

All this was supplemented by his left-arm spin, of course. Although the bowling did take a back seat when he moved to the summit of the batting card.

Frank Woolley, the great Kent all-rounder, was second only to Hobbs in terms of run mass, and across 32 years of first-class cricket struck 145 hundreds, took more than 2,000 wickets and caught pigeons at slip. Similarly to Hobbs, as a youth he had watched established players train, at Canterbury, and he would later join the Kent ground staff.

None of this particular quartet played the game as a social pursuit, in fact. To them cricket was not a pastime but a chosen profession. They were the pioneers in the era when teams were routinely a mixture of gentlemen and players, and the hired hands would be held responsible for the upkeep, or otherwise, of the amateur captains of the England team. In general, the split followed the same course: the gentlemen were the batsmen; the players, the labourers doing the hard yards, were the bowlers.

No one, however, was run into the ground as much as Sydney Barnes, the fast bowler plucked from Lancashire League cricket by Archie MacLaren for the 1901–02 tour of

Australia. One of the reasons for his selection was that Lord Hawke had insisted that the exertions of Rhodes and George Hirst in winning the Championship with Yorkshire made them unavailable for the tour. And to think that everyone suggested it was revolutionary when Andy Flower began a resting policy with England, leaving players out of one-day cricket from 2009 onwards.

Barnes was a hostile bowler whose slippery menace and ability to get the ball to leap off a length was allied to an acidic tongue. Despite not emerging onto the national scene until the age of 28, he was the bowler that had everything, able to bowl pace, swing or spin depending on match and atmospheric conditions. He also had a considerable amount of that bowler's gold dust in his personality: a fiery temper.

Presumably there was a good deal of cursing when, just two matches into his debut Test series, this bowling machine on legs malfunctioned. In the absence of the Yorkshire duo, MacLaren had bowled him into the ground. His return of 19 wickets was pretty healthy, his body considerably less so, and as he hobbled off at Adelaide, with him went English hopes. In his absence, Australia cruised to a 4–1 success.

Barnes showed himself to be the man for all seasons – not to mention venues – when, upon recall in the summer of 1902, he claimed six wickets in the first innings of the only Test match ever to be played at Sheffield's Bramall Lane, swinging the ball prodigiously through the city's smoggy, industrial air. However, in the second innings Australia's Victor Trumper, whose greatest skill was to eschew a free-spirited nature to triumph in the most testing conditions, struck 62 and Clem Hill, the captain, a hundred, to wrest back the initiative. England were left too far adrift and with defeat came a 1–0 deficit in a series that was – for several decades at least – acknowledged as the best ever played between the two countries.

At the time, England's greatest strength also proved to be their greatest weakness. Their depth of talent, augmented by the rise of the professionals, was incomparable to that of previous generations and it was said that during 1902 they fielded arguably their strongest ever XI – with Rhodes walking in at jack. Perhaps it was this embarrassment of riches that caused the apparently blasé attitude towards selection by Lord Hawke for the fourth match at Old Trafford. Revolving doors were slowly becoming fashionable in the United States following a patent secured by Theo van Kannel in Pennsylvania in 1888. But they were not successful when applied by Hawke and his panel to England's selection policy.

Out for Manchester went Barnes, Fry, Hirst and Gloucestershire's Gilbert Jessop. Under-strength England lost a nail-biter, and although Jessop hit the fastest Ashes hundred on his return at The Oval to make sure the thriller went the home side's way on this occasion – his 104 spanning just 77 minutes – he later wrote: 'It was in the selection room that the rubber was lost.'

From a second-innings position of 48–5, Jessop's counter-attacking brilliance took yet another contest down to the wire – following the Aussies' three-run win in the north-west – although his departure set up both a tense finish and an enduring myth. With 15 runs required, the last-wicket pair of Hirst and Rhodes were discussing the equation when the former is reported to have said, 'We'll get 'em in singles, Wilfred.'

It's a much-borrowed phrase these days when chases bubble towards a tension-filled climax. Unfortunately, though, according to Rhodes, just as Arthur Conan Doyle never penned the phrase 'Elementary, my dear Watson' for Sherlock Holmes in any of his works, so those words never left his partner Hirst's mouth. Somebody, somewhere, added them for effect as an afterthought.

However, it is true that Albert Einstein once said: 'The most beautiful thing we can experience is the mysterious. It is the source of all true art and science.' And the mysterious was at the heart of England's plot to pour hot oil over Australia's grip on the urn when they ventured to the southern hemisphere for the 1903–04 series. Something of the other was required, it was thought, to prevent a sequence of five consecutive defeats.

And how it worked. The Australians were mesmerised by a man who could lay claim to be the first innovator amongst international bowlers. We'd have probably never seen Bernard

Bosanquet but for the fact he was good friends with the England captain Pelham Warner, a Middlesex and Oxford University team-mate.

Most within English cricket's establishment would have dismissed Bosanquet's credentials as a bowler, not least because no one could be certain how many times his deliveries would bounce once they pitched. But Warner had seen him more than most and knew that in the form of one Bosanquet delivery in particular, England had an ace up their sleeve.

The googly was new, and carried all the intrigue of a Charles Dickens novel. If the Australians hadn't seen it before, how were they going to react?

The googly was conceived while Bosanquet – whose multifarious sporting abilities resulted in him throwing the hammer for Oxford University in addition to being a member of its billiard team – played the Victorian game of Twisti-Twosti. It involved bouncing a tennis ball on a table in such a way that your opponent – sitting on the other side – could not catch it. By changing the angle of his hand, and the release point of the ball, he was able to con his adversaries that it was travelling on one path when it was actually on quite another.

Bosanquet himself explained in an article written for the *Morning Post* during the 1920s:

> After a little experimenting I managed to pitch the ball which
> broke in a certain direction; then with more or less the same

delivery make the next ball go in the opposite direction! I practised the same thing with a soft ball at 'Stump-cricket'. From this I progressed to the cricket ball . . . The method of delivery is the secret of its difficulty, and this merely consisted in turning the wrist over at the moment of delivery far enough to alter the axis of spin.

To an opposing batsman, the googly looked like a leg-break but turned in the opposite direction, and with the bowler himself never truly leaving the experimental phase – despite the fact he'd first plucked up the courage to transfer it from the nets to a county match three years earlier – no wonder the Australians were struck by a debilitating fear of the unknown. They already had the unerringly accurate left-arm spin of Wilfred Rhodes to contend with at one end, without having to counter a leg-spinner with a wicked trick in his armoury. With no experience of facing a delivery that defied all perceived cricket wisdom, they were forced to learn on the job.

The fact that Bosanquet wasn't in complete control only added to the difficulty of picking his sleight of hand. Let's face it, if the bowler didn't know where the ball was landing and which way it would subsequently dart, how the devil were they to know? When confronted with newfangled methods of attack, the challenge for the opposition is to unearth an antidote, and to do so as quickly as possible.

Of course, this uncertainty only retained its effect if he

was pitching the ball in a dangerous part of the pitch. It certainly wouldn't apply if the ball in question was a waist-high full toss or a triple bouncer. Or at least it shouldn't work. Dean Elgar, the left-handed South African opening batsman, did his best to disprove this theory during a County Championship match in 2017 when he was bowled by a delivery from Hampshire's young leg-spinner Mason Crane that pitched halfway down and very nearly bounced twice, the off stump being yorked on the second. Crane's celebration suggested embarrassment, but with Elgar in rich form ahead of the Test series against England, I would have been milking the moment, saying: 'Just because I've seen his weakness and you lot haven't . . .'

Like many changes, the googly was met with cynicism. The MCC were lobbied to ban it as it was felt its presence within the common game was stymieing the stroke play of the age. No longer could a batsman stand tall and drive through the off side with great certainty. To me, such tripe proves beyond doubt that batsmen have always been spoilt beggars likely to ruck at the slightest hint of not getting their own way. Like a child who wants crisps for dinner.

As Bosanquet went on to say in that newspaper article, published in the 1925 edition of *Wisden*: 'Poor old googly! It has been subjected to ridicule, abuse, contempt, incredulity, and survived them all. Deficiencies existing at the present day are attributed to [its] influence . . . But, after all, what is the googly? It is merely a ball with an ordinary break produced by an extra-ordinary method. It is not difficult to detect, and, once detected, there is no reason why it should not be treated as an ordinary break-back. However, it is not for me to defend it. If I appear too much in the role of the proud parent I ask forgiveness.'

Thankfully it survived, yet it still struggled to shake off the accusation that it was somehow bending the rules, that it didn't have a place in decent company. In Australia, it attracted a derogatory nickname: the 'wrong 'un'. Although now common in cricket parlance, and diluted by the ages, at the time the phrase was also used for members of society viewed as possessing bad character – criminals, philanderers, divorcees and homosexuals.

Bosanquet, who as a schoolboy at Eton bowled medium pace, shrugged off the suspicions to play the decisive hand in a 3–2 victory in the 1903–04 series. True enough, he didn't really know how to land it with regularity, but amongst the grubbers and full tosses were hot spells. Seriously hot spells. In the pivotal match at Sydney, having sent down just two fruitless overs in the first innings, he claimed six wickets in an hour during the second, to hasten England to a 157-run win. As Pelham Warner knew, when Bosanquet landed it on a good length, on a hard pitch, the bounce made him the most difficult bowler to face on either side.

This series stands out for being one in which spin reigned as king. It had the potential to be a sign of things to come in the tussles between the two countries. Bosanquet, an amateur, forged a fine partnership with Rhodes and possessed the all-round game to hint at a longer international career. An upright batsman standing six foot tall, he scored 21 first-class centuries in addition to his revolutionising of bowling, registering one in either innings for Middlesex versus Sussex at Lord's in 1905, a match in which he also bagged 11 victims with the ball. He claimed 132 first-class victims in the summer of 1904 at a cost of under 22 runs apiece.

Yet he was to disappear from international cricket with the speed at which he entered, after the limited control he had over his bowling became increasingly erratic. Although he continued to play sporadically after 1908, due to business interests, he did not bowl, and like those of the best magicians his tricks disappeared in a puff of smoke.

To think that some bloke just thought 'what if?' and ended up with 25 wickets in seven Test appearances. I cannot tell you how much his backstory appeals to me. If you are going to be a star, why not burn quickly and brightly like a supernova, then fade out to nothing? What a way to leave your mark.

Arguably, he became more famous in Australia – where, courtesy of its place in Richie Benaud's commentary lexicon, they still refer to the delivery as a 'Bosie' – than in England. But the global game has been richer for people like the unusually named Bosanquet. Without the innovators, the challengers of normality, the game would go stale, wouldn't it? These days we are quite accustomed to the innovation of new shots, like Tillakaratne Dilshan's 'Dilscoop' and the newest of them all – England World Cup winner Natalie Sciver's 'Natmeg', in which she squeezes out yorkers for runs by jabbing down on them, propelling the ball between her feet. And it's very natural for other players to try to emulate particular skills for personal profit.

It has always been this way. What happened when word got round about the googly? Global rivals tried to copy Bosie's baby. On the 1907 tour to England, South Africa dispatched not one, not two, not three, but four mystery spinners. As the saying goes, imitation truly is the purest form of flattery.

On a similar note but slightly different tangent, I picked the number 66 shirt when I played one-day cricket for England, primarily because I thought it would be unique. That is, until Joe Root came along and laid claim to it for obvious reasons. Others have started using it since, though, and to see a couple of guys around the world with '66' on their backs – essentially in recognition that I did well – is a nice feeling. It's not much of a legacy to the game, but I will take it. It certainly beats the feeling I had back in 2000 when I thought I would never wear an England shirt again.

Bosanquet had very much been Warner's pick, but the captain did not always get the team he wanted during this era. In fact, England and Australia rarely managed to get their first-choice XIs out on the paddock. On some occasions, as we have already seen when so many players were inexplicably rested in 1902, they picked plain stupidly.

Take the 1909 series, for example, when England went into a Test match with just one fast bowler in their party. That was a summer when they used 25 different players. Some habits die hard, I guess, because 80 years later we were still chopping and changing teams from one match to the next and somehow expecting to achieve positive results. Talk about the lunatics running the asylum.

Date	Venue	Team	Scores	Team	Scores	Result
22/06/1896	Lord's	Australia	53 & 347	England	292 & 111-4	England won by 6 wickets
16/07/1896	Manchester	Australia	412 & 125-7	England	231 & 305	Australia won by 3 wickets
10/08/1896	The Oval	England	145 & 84	Australia	119 & 44	England won by 66 runs
13/12/1897	Sydney	England	551 & 96-1	Australia	237 & 408	England won by 9 wickets
01/01/1898	Melbourne	Australia	520	England	315 & 150	Australia won by an innings and 55 runs
14/01/1898	Adelaide	Australia	573	England	278 & 282	Australia won by an innings and 13 runs
29/01/1898	Melbourne	Australia	323 & 115-2	England	174 & 263	Australia won by 8 wickets
26/02/1898	Sydney	England	335 & 178	Australia	239 & 276-4	Australia won by 6 wickets
01/06/1899	Nottingham	Australia	252 & 230-8d	England	193 & 155-7	Drawn
15/06/1899	Lord's	England	206 & 240	Australia	421 & 28-0	Australia won by 10 wickets
29/06/1899	Leeds	Australia	172 & 224	England	220 & 19-0	Drawn
17/07/1899	Manchester	England	372 & 94-3	Australia	196 & 346-7d	Drawn
14/08/1899	The Oval	England	576	Australia	352 & 254-5	Drawn
13/12/1901	Sydney	England	464	Australia	168 & 172	England won by an innings and 124 runs
01/01/1902	Melbourne	Australia	112 & 353	England	61 & 175	Australia won by 229 runs
17/01/1902	Adelaide	Australia	388 & 247	England	321 & 315-6	Australia won by 4 wickets
14/02/1902	Sydney	England	317 & 99	Australia	299 & 121-3	Australia won by 7 wickets
28/02/1902	Melbourne	Australia	144 & 255	England	189 & 178	Australia won by 32 runs
29/05/1902	Birmingham	England	376-9d	Australia	36 & 46-2	Drawn
12/06/1902	Lord's	England	102-2	Australia	did not bat	Drawn
03/07/1902	Sheffield-BL	Australia	194 & 289	England	145 & 195	Australia won by 143 runs
24/07/1902	Manchester	Australia	299 & 86	England	262 & 120	Australia won by 3 runs
11/08/1902	The Oval	Australia	324 & 121	England	183 & 263-9	England won by 1 wicket
11/12/1903	Sydney	Australia	285 & 485	England	577 & 194-5	England won by 5 wickets
01/01/1904	Melbourne	England	315 & 103	Australia	122 & 111	England won by 185 runs
15/01/1904	Adelaide	Australia	388 & 351	England	245 & 278	Australia won by 216 runs
26/02/1904	Sydney	England	249 & 210	Australia	131 & 171	England won by 157 runs
05/03/1904	Melbourne	Australia	247 & 133	England	61 & 101	Australia won by 218 runs
29/05/1905	Nottingham	England	196 & 426-5d	Australia	221 & 188	England won by 213 runs
15/06/1905	Lord's	England	282 & 151-5	Australia	181	Drawn
03/07/1905	Leeds	England	301 & 295-5d	Australia	195 & 224-7	Drawn
24/07/1905	Manchester	England	446	Australia	197 & 169	England won by an innings and 80 runs
14/08/1905	The Oval	England	430 & 261-6d	Australia	363 & 124-4	Drawn
13/12/1907	Sydney	England	273 & 300	Australia	300 & 275-8	Australia won by 2 wickets
01/01/1908	Melbourne	Australia	266 & 397	England	382 & 282-9	England won by 1 wicket
10/01/1908	Adelaide	Australia	285 & 506	England	363 & 183	Australia won by 245 runs
07/02/1908	Melbourne	Australia	214 & 385	England	105 & 186	Australia won by 308 runs
21/02/1908	Sydney	Australia	137 & 422	England	281 & 229	Australia won by 49 runs
27/05/1909	Birmingham	Australia	74 & 151	England	121 & 105-0	England won by 10 wickets
14/06/1909	Lord's	England	269 & 121	Australia	350 & 41-1	Australia won by 9 wickets
01/07/1909	Leeds	Australia	188 & 207	England	182 & 87	Australia won by 126 runs
26/07/1909	Manchester	Australia	147 & 279-9d	England	119 & 108-3	Drawn
09/08/1909	The Oval	Australia	325 & 339-5d	England	352 & 104-3	Drawn
15/12/1911	Sydney	Australia	447 & 308	England	318 & 291	Australia won by 146 runs
30/12/1911	Melbourne	Australia	184 & 299	England	265 & 219-2	England won by 8 wickets
12/01/1912	Adelaide	Australia	133 & 476	England	501 & 112-3	England won by 7 wickets
09/02/1912	Melbourne	Australia	191 & 173	England	589	England won by an innings and 225 runs
23/02/1912	Sydney	England	324 & 214	Australia	176 & 292	England won by 70 runs
24/06/1912	Lord's	England	310-7d	Australia	282-7	Drawn
29/07/1912	Manchester	England	203	Australia	14-0	Drawn
19/08/1912	The Oval	England	245 & 175	Australia	111 & 65	England won by 244 runs

4

THE MASTER, THE BIG SHIP AND THE DON

THERE were mitigating circumstances for the first whitewash in Ashes history, and Englishmen of the 1920s weren't afraid to let them be known. It had, according to their parochial defence, more than a little to do with the advent of the First World War. It had taken the lives of five dozen first-class cricketers, weakening the pool of English talent, and therefore creating an imbalance between the old foes.

'I doubt whether English cricket has really recovered from the effects of the War,' said Frank Woolley, one of those to feature for England before 1914 and from 1919 onwards. 'You see, we missed half a generation and since then young men have found many other ways of occupying their leisure hours. Still, I believe it is only a passing phase and cricket will one day produce an abundance of great players.'

Even accounting for such affliction, it should have been possible to avoid a scoreline like the one of 1920–21:

Australia 5 England 0. There are normally a few players able to put in performances to check the other team's momentum. However, on this occasion, as in the modern series of 2006–07 and 2013–14, they were not forthcoming. On paper, Australia were as much a team thrown together as England – nine debutants on either side across the five matches tells the story – while the tourists' batting still had the serene presence of Hobbs at the top and the debonair Woolley in the middle.

What England lacked, though, were bowlers: those that bring home the corn. The hired hands were the ones who would arguably have made a difference because, as we all know, bowlers win matches. As bowlers tended to be from manual backgrounds, indulging in cricket to increase their income, they were also the species most greatly hit during the war. They were the ones in the trenches. The gentlemen batsmen made for officers of rank.

By this stage, the atmosphere during Test cricket in Australia could be quite intimidating. While crowds in England were still mostly genteel gatherings – the smattering of spectators that did turn up showing an appreciation for good sport – fanaticism had been spawned down under. The majority of those in attendance were farm workers and labourers, unafraid to show their support for those on the Australian side of the fight, or to let the Poms have it if they displayed the temerity to put up a fight.

One notable example of this partisan attitude had resulted in the booing and jeering of Sydney Barnes in Melbourne during England's comprehensive away win of 1911–12. Barnes, in the middle of an hour-long spell that yielded five wickets, got so fed up with his treatment by the locals that he simply threw the ball to the turf and stood at the end of his mark in protest, arms folded, refusing to run in again until the cacophony ceased.

That is exactly the kind of thing my dad Ray would have done. When we played together for Northampton Saints he would sometimes act extremely childishly – until he got his own way. For example, on one occasion he was captain in a match at Birchfield Road, our home ground, and found himself in a big argument with our wicketkeeper, Nick Francis, who was repeatedly moving the field.

'Nick, I am captain, leave the field placings to me,' he said.

'Oh, come on, Ray. It's obvious we needed someone at extra cover.'

With that, Dad stormed off the field and sat on a bench beyond the boundary line at fine leg. Standing at slip, I was mortified. Dying with embarrassment.

'Come on, Dad. Get back on.'

'No, I am staying here,' he sulked.

As luck would have it, next ball, the batsman had a bit of a swipe and Chinese-cut it straight to my dad's feet. He picked it up, almost triumphantly, and declared: 'Right, shall we do it properly then?'

He's always had that streak in him. Apparently, the reason he was dropped from the England Over-60s team was that he was proving too difficult to manage. At least he has stayed true to himself – it's no good getting to your sixties and then pretending to be a nice bloke.

Barnes, the scourge of Australian batsmen during a career that reaped 189 Test wickets in 27 appearances, can lay claim to have been England's first champagne cricketer. Because during lunch and tea breaks he used to sip bubbly, believing it was the done thing. His new-ball partner Frank Foster also developed the taste for it, and they were good for 66 scalps between them in 1911–12's 4–1 success.

Taking alcohol on board certainly did not detract from Barnes's skill. As Clem Hill, the Australian batsman, recalled of his own dismissal during that damaging spell in Melbourne: 'The ball pitched outside my leg stump, safe to the push off my pads, I thought. Before I could "pick up" my bat, my off stump was knocked silly.'

The great Harold Larwood was said to have been a yard or so more slippery after taking ale on board, and it was a practice maintained by many until the 1990s.

Incidentally, the first couple of times I played for the MCC, there was a bottle of red wine at the lunch table. I thought it was just wonderful. In previous generations at Northants there would be a tray of beers at lunchtime and players would routinely have a pint each. I champion the idea because everyone plays sport better when they're drunk, don't they? Medical science might suggest otherwise, but I don't believe I've ever played any sport badly after two or three pints. In fact, like most people after two or three pints I begin to feel like Superman.

During my international career I was a strictly water man, and used to down litres of the stuff. Being in more advanced years compared to the majority of my colleagues, I was more susceptible to extra calories, and had to work hard to keep my amazing figure, so I didn't bother with any of the so-called sports drinks doing the rounds. When you look at Gatorade – and other isotonic products – how can anyone be stupid enough to believe that they can enhance your body's performance?

As far as I understand, it is basically water with a load of sugar dumped into it. Now, if you are Jimmy Anderson or Stuart Broad covering 30 km an innings by running in from halfway to the boundary, then fine. But if you're bowling spin and standing at second slip for seven hours a day, covering a total distance of around 300 metres, and your biggest exertion is a walk between overs, drinking four litres of highly sucrosed liquid – we are talking half a dozen teaspoons of sugar per 330 ml can – that's a lot of weight you are putting on. Seeing as my rival for the England spinner's spot was Samit Patel for a while, I couldn't afford to let myself go any more.

Talking of body shape, there was a huge figure, quite literally, at the heart of Australia's historic 5–0 victory at the start of the 1920s. Warwick Armstrong's giant frame – he stood 6 foot 3 inches tall and weighed 21 stone – earned him the nickname 'the Big Ship'. I imagine that four years of inactivity during the war can only have increased the size of the timber. I have always been drawn towards obvious characters of the game and he seemed to be one. He played with a smile on his face, but off the field he constantly rucked with authority – partly because he began playing in an era in which players were in greater control when it came to running the game. Sounds like my favourite kind of cricketer, to be fair.

Armstrong's popularity with ordinary Australians was attributable to his long service to the sport. He was, after all, one of the few cricketers in the country whose Test career straddled the Great War. Equally, he possessed a mighty record. Everyone likes a winner, and here was a guy who pursued success in the most uncompromising manner imaginable. It was an attitude at the very heart of his clean-sweep series in 1920–21.

In his use of gamesmanship, Armstrong is comparable to Grace. He would openly challenge umpires' decisions and make his own case known in the most vociferous, and occasionally uncouth, manner. Unsurprisingly for a man with such a physique, he imposed himself on those in his 'working' environment. He developed a reputation amongst the England team for being unsportsmanlike and aggressive, not that he appeared to care a jot.

In addition to his visual impressiveness, the Big Ship also docked in people's heads. In one of the Ashes' weirdest episodes, Frank Woolley, on debut at The Oval in 1909, was made to wait nearly 20 minutes to face his first ball in Test cricket despite coming in to bat at number six midway through a session. Armstrong did not feign injury or illness. Instead, he partook in a series of warm-up deliveries that kept evading team-mates. Woolley survived his first ball, but his trying time did not last a great deal longer, as he departed for eight runs.

In summary, Armstrong was a right pain to play against, doing everything he could to make life difficult for those that crossed his path. A wrist-spinner, he bowled his toppies down a negative leg-side line to frustrate batsmen half a century before it became fashionable to do so in limited-overs cricket. As a batsman he eliminated risk and focused on crease occupation – to maximum effect in that 1920–21 series, when he stacked up 464 runs, finishing as the leading run-scorer on either team.

Not only did he defy the English bowlers to do so. He also had to overcome one of his periodic bouts of malaria, for which he prescribed himself nips of whisky (outside of cricket, he sold the stuff), and on top of that he had to deal with his nemesis Ernie Bean, the administrator who ran cricket in Victoria. Bean had been angered when Armstrong pulled out of state duty with a bruised leg sustained in Ashes combat. His crime: not being unavailable, but breaking protocol by telling playing colleagues of his situation ahead of informing the suits. Bean was onto a loser, however, when he tried to drum up support for action against Armstrong. His big-hearted displays made him untouchable when it came to team selection.

Whatever England threw at Australia during a run of eight consecutive Baggy Green wins, it was repelled by Armstrong's army, an army with two fast-bowling generals: Jack Gregory and Ted McDonald. In a precursor to the bodyline tactics of the following decade, they turned batting into a physical as well as mental challenge with their blows to batsmen's bodies.

To withstand their barrage was a triumph of courage and application, as Woolley acknowledged when reflecting on his personal efforts at Lord's: 'As a matter of fact I consider the two finest innings I ever played were in the second Test against Australia in 1921 when I was out for 95 and 93. I don't think I ever worked harder at any match during my career to get runs as I did then, nor did I ever have to face in one game such consistently fast bowlers as the Australian pair, Gregory and McDonald. Square cuts which ordinarily would have flashed to the boundary earned only two, and I believe that those two innings would have been worth 150 apiece in a county match.'

This pair were the first to give opponents what is known in the fast-bowling trade as 'the treatment'. They would look to strike their target – batsmen not stumps – following it up with a word or two. It struck fear into England, not least the Lord's debutant Johnny Evans, a player who had resumed his career after escaping from a German prisoner-of-war camp.

Although the individual accolades went to touring players during the 1924–25 series, Australia continued to dominate. Herbert Sutcliffe, of Yorkshire, struck 734 runs at an average in excess of 80 and Maurice Tate was prolific with the ball, snaring 38 wickets, yet the Australians still completed a 4–1 victory.

He might not have had his name added to the annals of spin bowling like Bosanquet, but Clarrie Grimmett did contribute to its variety with the invention of the flipper – effectively a back-spinner with a tendency to keep low. He didn't play that many matches but he had a phenomenal record. He was the quickest to 200 in Tests and he dealt in five-wicket and ten-wicket hauls – all down to this new delivery he had brought to the world stage.

The tide was to turn in 1925, however, a significant year for first-class cricket. That August, Jack Hobbs made history. Everyone knows he is the answer to Jamal's 20 million rupee question in *Slumdog Millionaire*: who has scored the most first-class hundreds? It was in Surrey's match versus Somerset at Taunton that summer that Hobbs equalled and then surpassed W.G. Grace's total of 126.

Wally Hammond was equally prolific, and particularly after

hours, away from the field. England were in need of a hero and Hammond fitted the bill. If Hobbs was Niki Lauda, the functional multi-world champion, Hammond was James Hunt, the talented playboy. It really depends on your personality which one you'd rather be. Would you like to be remembered by your peers as being the best your country has produced? Or for being a prolific swordsman? I know which one I would plump for.

Hammond was cricket's version of that Hollywood Lothario Errol Flynn. They were both men of many talents, the one in common being attracting the company of women. Hammond was said to have missed matches because of his affairs, and his outside pursuits were well known within the dressing rooms he frequented.

One can only speculate as to what illness he had picked up on a tour of the Caribbean, having returned home with a fever and septic swellings in the groin area. It was claimed a mosquito had bitten him during the team's stay in Guyana. Gravely ill in a private Bristol hospital, womanising was off the agenda for a while. In fact, his cricket career was even under threat. Recovery was hastened by the visits of the then chairman of selectors.

As Hammond himself recounts in *Cricket My Destiny*: 'Plum Warner came to see me and has said since that I was in the valley of the shadow of death . . . It is absolutely true to say that his visits put new heart into me, and perhaps provided me with just sufficient strength to turn the dark corner. He would not hear complaints but reassured me with such utter confidence that I should get better and make hundreds for England against Australia and other opponents that in the end I was given courage and resistance enough to pull through. If there is such a thing as faith healing in the world, I can recommend with all my heart Dr Warner.'

Fortified by these words, Hammond scaled the heights in his debut Ashes series of 1928–29, overshadowing the other significant newbie, Donald Bradman, by obliterating Sutcliffe's record run haul of 734 in a series, and raising the bar to an eye-watering 905. On the back of this mountain of orthodoxly compiled runs, England won 4–1. The efforts of Bradman, for one of the few times in his professional life, were eclipsed. His contribution represented just 52 per cent of Hammond's volume.

One of cricket's most veiled statistics is that Bradman's Australian career began with a defeat of gargantuan proportions. And, after contributing scores of 18 and one in what was a record 675-run Test loss at Brisbane, he was dropped for the next match. He returned in the third Test to become, at 20 years of age, Australia's youngest centurion, but there were few other challenges to England's might in that series.

In triumphing in Australia for the first time in 17 years, prestige had been returned to English cricket. 'A happy family off the field, they pulled together in every match like a well-oiled machine,' according to *Wisden*'s overview of the tour. Percy Chapman's team also came as close as any England team to completing the Australian preserve of the whitewash, having gone into the final match with four wins out of four.

Chapman's leadership drew high praise, not least with regard to his handling of Harold Larwood, who would be used in a very different guise on the following trip. On one memorable afternoon at Brisbane when Australia lost four wickets for 40 runs, Larwood was said to be faster than his usual self, and he also contributed to the win in Sydney, more than making up for the fact that his candle appeared to have burnt out by the penultimate match. Douglas Jardine also displayed his lust for defeating the Aussies in their own backyard, four years before the pair would take the starring roles.

Beyond question, though, the batting success of the tour was Hammond, whose double hundreds at Sydney and Melbourne, plus twin centuries at Adelaide, suggested something of a playboy streak. Yet his batting drew the highest praise for a quality Hammond could rarely be accused of displaying in other spheres – restraint.

The public interest in the series was incredible too, contrary to the theory that the one-eyed home support would only turn out en masse to barrack for a winning team. The five Tests drew a combined attendance in excess of 850,000 people, and raised profits estimated at £20,000, moving cricket into a more commercial environment. Each of the English first-class counties was given £500, as was the Minor Counties association.

Hammond and England did not reign for long, however. If the 1928–29 series belonged to the Gloucestershire man, the one that followed 18 months later was indisputably Bradman's. At the peak of his powers in the 1930 series in England, the boy from Bowral feasted to the tune of 974 runs, scoring 309 of them in a day at Headingley. The year proved to be a microcosm of the parallel careers of Hammond and Bradman, with the former left in the latter's slipstream.

Despite his grand entrance to the Ashes stage, the Englishman's average of 113.12 versus the Australians in his debut series dropped to 51.85 over the course of his career, considerably down on his mark of 58.45 against all-comers – by the mid-1930s New Zealand, India and West Indies had joined South Africa in playing regular Tests. Hammond scored four hundreds in his first four Ashes appearances; only five more in the following 29.

In contrast, Bradman's record versus England was other-worldly. His career average of 99.94 is arguably the most famous incomplete number in the history of sport, and his return of 89.78 in Ashes matches wasn't too shabby, either. His ratio of hundreds in these matches was better than one in two (19 in 37).

After play Bradman would retire to his hotel room, quite

the recluse, and pen letters to his wife. We can all have a stab at what Hammond might have been up to. With one man overshadowing his entire professional career, there must have been a lot of frustration to release in other pursuits.

Date	Venue	Team	Scores	Team	Scores	Result
17/12/1920	Sydney	Australia	267 & 581	England	190 & 281	Australia won by 377 runs
31/12/1920	Melbourne	Australia	499	England	251 & 157	Australia won by an innings and 91 runs
14/01/1921	Adelaide	Australia	354 & 582	England	447 & 370	Australia won by 119 runs
11/02/1921	Melbourne	England	284 & 315	Australia	389 & 211-2	Australia won by 8 wickets
25/02/1921	Sydney	England	204 & 280	Australia	392 & 93-1	Australia won by 9 wickets
28/05/1921	Nottingham	England	112 & 147	Australia	232 & 30-0	Australia won by 10 wickets
11/06/1921	Lord's	England	187 & 283	Australia	342 & 131-2	Australia won by 8 wickets
02/07/1921	Leeds	Australia	407 & 273-7d	England	259 & 202	Australia won by 219 runs
23/07/1921	Manchester	England	362-4d & 44-1	Australia	175	Drawn
13/08/1921	The Oval	England	403-8d & 244-2	Australia	389	Drawn
19/12/1924	Sydney	Australia	450 & 452	England	298 & 411	Australia won by 193 runs
01/01/1925	Melbourne	Australia	600 & 250	England	479 & 290	Australia won by 81 runs
16/01/1925	Adelaide	Australia	489 & 250	England	365 & 363	Australia won by 11 runs
13/02/1925	Melbourne	England	548	Australia	269 & 250	England won by an innings and 29 runs
27/02/1925	Sydney	Australia	295 & 325	England	167 & 146	Australia won by 307 runs
12/06/1926	Nottingham	England	32-0	Australia	did not bat	Drawn
26/06/1926	Lord's	Australia	383 & 194-5	England	475-3d	Drawn
10/07/1926	Leeds	Australia	494	England	294 & 254-3	Drawn
24/07/1926	Manchester	Australia	335	England	305-5	Drawn
14/08/1926	The Oval	England	280 & 436	Australia	302 & 125	England won by 289 runs
30/11/1928	Brisbane-E	England	521 & 342-8d	Australia	122 & 66	England won by 675 runs
14/12/1928	Sydney	Australia	253 & 397	England	636 & 16-2	England won by 8 wickets
29/12/1928	Melbourne	Australia	397 & 351	England	417 & 332-7	England won by 3 wickets
01/02/1929	Adelaide	England	334 & 383	Australia	369 & 336	England won by 12 runs
08/03/1929	Melbourne	England	519 & 257	Australia	491 & 287-5	Australia won by 5 wickets
13/06/1930	Nottingham	England	270 & 302	Australia	144 & 335	England won by 93 runs
27/06/1930	Lord's	England	425 & 375	Australia	729-6d & 72-3	Australia won by 7 wickets
11/07/1930	Leeds	Australia	566	England	391 & 95-3	Drawn
25/07/1930	Manchester	Australia	345	England	251-8	Drawn
16/08/1930	The Oval	England	405 & 251	Australia	695	Australia won by an innings and 39 runs

5

THE MOST UNPLEASANT TEST EVER PLAYED

IF you could live through one Ashes series again, which one would it be? For me, it would have to be 1932–33 and bodyline.

For a start, it was a rare example of England possessing the quickest bowler, and it would have given me indescribable pleasure to have been tucked in at short leg chirping at the Australian batsmen as Harold Larwood charged in. Of course, I would time-travel back with every single one of the best sledges used in the following 85 years, to make me look like the father of cricketing wit.

But there was a serious, undeniably sinister side to this particular episode in Anglo-Aussie relations. England had arrived on Australian shores that winter as the best-planned touring team ever, and the plan revolved around stopping one man. The man? Bradman. The plan? To nullify run-scoring by the use of intimidatory short-pitched bowling, delivered at the line of the body. Or, as it has been recorded in the annals for short: bodyline.

The individual who devised it was Douglas Jardine, a scheming tactician, who knew what everyone else did at that time, that the way to stop Australia was to stop Bradman – part human, part machine when it came to batting. It was not a plan hatched overnight, either. Jardine, born in India but with Scottish heritage, was appointed England captain in July 1931, giving him 15 months to scheme. As we have already seen, he had witnessed Bradman's developing talents on the previous tour of Australia.

What he came up with shook the party line because it occurred during such a genteel age. Cricket had obviously evolved in the 50 years since the start of the Ashes matches, but generally it was still about which team scored the most runs. It was one's duty to bowl nicely, and whichever XI totted up the highest total was declared the winner. However, Jardine realised that not bowling nicely not only challenged tradition but also offered the key to altering results. By this stage, professionals, like the great Jack Hobbs, were well and truly established in the game, following decades of resistance to any individual profiting from their actions on a cricket field. Bodyline, I would argue, was the first instance of professionalism being applied on a tactical level.

No wonder its instigator was viewed with such suspicion. Douglas Jardine lived up to his cold-hearted, James Bond-villain image, and was clearly not in the job to win friends

– either in his own team or in the opponents' dressing room. He was an extremely clinical captain who took emotion out of the decision-making process. Of course, it might have been an aid that he did not seem to possess any of the softer ones such as sympathy and empathy. He saw a way to stop Don Bradman and simply told his team: 'This is the way we're going to do it.'

Credit to him for this, as he exploited a weakness in Bradman's game that no one else had found, albeit by pushing the boundaries of fair play to the limits. On instructing his fast bowlers to aim for his chest rather than the stumps, Jardine was able to reduce the Don to mortal levels of performance.

Although it was widely viewed as being unsporting, you have to remember firstly how highly skilled Bradman was, and secondly the fact he still had a bat in his hand. England were trying to restrict their opponents by challenging normal practice. And while their approach may have been unethical in the eyes of 1930s Australia, it was not illegal.

Digesting the series in the second decade of the 21st century, it just sounds like part of the game and certainly not comparable to Australia's Chappell brothers, who conspired for Trevor Chappell to bowl underarm to close out a one-day international against New Zealand in 1981 when a six was required for victory. That really is testing the limits of fair play.

What West Indies did to the world, and for the good of world cricket in the long run, with their hostile bowling attacks of the 1970s and 1980s was celebrated. Their pace and power were admired, yet bodyline was arguably the forerunner of their tactics. The 1930s version was frowned upon mainly because nobody knew how to deal with it. Although Bradman still averaged 56.57 in the series, that represented only just over half of his career return, and so what Jardine implemented has to be viewed as being incredibly successful.

Undoubtedly, a proportion of its impact was down to shock factor. These days, as a matter of routine, batsmen wear helmets and chest pads, a real armoury of protection, whereas the threat posed by the leather ball in those days must have felt all the greater for the lack of it. There was much more personal risk involved batting in the 1930s against these new, shocking tactics.

What I can't comprehend, knowing the Australians as I do from several series of experience, is that almost their entire nation, to a man, viewed bodyline as unsporting – as a challenge to the authenticity of the game. Yes, the same nation that has no problem with batsmen edging the ball and standing their ground. To my mind, when you know you're out and you choose to try to get away with it by placing the responsibility on someone else to make a decision, surely that is cheating in its purest form?

Yet in Australia, if you get away with it, somehow that's

considered OK – to the point that it caused outrage when, during the 2003 World Cup semi-final, Adam Gilchrist walked after clearly being given not out by umpire Rudi Koertzen. Gilchrist knew he had got a feather on an attempted sweep, and after a brief pause, he tucked his bat under his arm and headed for the St George's Park pavilion. For Australia, the Gilchrist incident was a huge thing, front-page news. Of course, the two events are decades apart, but for a country to think bodyline so wrong and living on your luck by heaping the pressure on the umpire to make a decision is so right does seem a tad hypocritical.

I am not trying to say that England players all walk; very few of us have done so over the years. I am just trying to emphasise that you cannot paint yourself whiter than white and then move the goalposts when it suits. As it happens, I am all for retrospectively banning people who don't walk. Draconian, I know, but if you edge the ball you should shuffle off back to the dressing room and allow the game to continue. As a deterrent, something like a five-year ban should suffice. Or perhaps the culprit should be forced to watch a DVD of *Mrs Brown's Boys* on repeat for 24 hours.

Sure, Douglas Jardine was a pretty joyless character, by all accounts. But while I can accept people not liking him for his personality, or lack of it, to vilify him for what was the first example of modern-day specialism, formulating plans to stop a particular individual, is poppycock. If he had been around these days we would probably consider him to be a leading tactician, applauded for his cricket brain and creativity. Not that the tactics stretched much beyond damaging the fulcrum in the Baggy Green machine with a bombardment of the upper body. To limit Bradman was to reduce the effectiveness of the Australian team.

The most obvious comparison that comes to mind when I think of teams trying to stop one individual is the way opponents tried to nullify the late New Zealand rugby union player Jonah Lomu. Other wingers have had similar physical attributes since – for example, George North, of Wales, is half an inch smaller than the 6 foot 5 inches that Lomu stood, and although not as heavy as his 120 kg frame, is still big enough and yet can sprint 40 metres in 4.97 seconds. But when Lomu emerged on the wing in the mid-1990s, he was an absolute giant, someone who defined the description 'game-changer'. No one could believe the sheer size of this bloke and what he was doing out wide. He was so powerful and difficult to stop when in full flow that teams would double or treble up on him in defence, though usually to no avail.

Teams were abandoning their established preparation methods, just to counter only one member of the opposition. He was so good, so far ahead of his time, that it changed the way opponents thought about playing, and in this regard he and Bradman were streets ahead of their contemporaries. They effectively rewrote whole textbooks for their sports. Lomu recast what was possible for a winger and what they should look like. Suddenly, wide men could be selected to dominate with their physicality, and not have to be elusive, nimble runners aiming to round opponents' back lines on the outside.

Equally, Bradman was able to set the bar at previously unheard-of levels when it came to scoring runs. Cricket is a numbers game and he simply took the numbers to new levels. There was no physicality to his batsmanship. In fact, at 5 foot 7 inches there wasn't much to him at all. But in terms of hand–eye coordination and ability to time a cricket ball he was supremely talented. I've heard some modern players argue that the game is so much faster now that he would not have prospered in the same way, but to me that's a load of baloney. If the Don had been around these days he would have adapted to his surroundings to stand at the summit of the sport.

As a sportsman you can only truly be compared with those of your own generation, but surely the best players of any generation would be able to prosper if displaced to another. These days Bradman would be equipped with a helmet and be playing on truer wickets, so that would help to combat what people perceive as a harder challenge against faster, more aggressive bowlers. His extraordinary eye, coordination and lightness on his feet were gifts that would have surpassed those of his peers in any period you wish to choose. There is also an argument to say he would be better than any modern batsman simply because he could play spin – although he did rather let this theory down by famously getting done through the gate by Eric Hollies in his final

Test, allowing his career average to finish in double rather than triple digits.

It grinds my gears to hear people suggesting that great talents like him would not have been able to transcend their time. Those of us involved in cricket, in whatever guise, should pay deference to those who played the game before us. Even if deep down you think that the modern era is tougher, perhaps keep it to yourself. Don't be so arrogant that you think that the time you live in is superior to any time that has gone before.

There is always another side to the argument. Just think of all the aids a modern-day batsman has: the size of the bat and the power it can generate, the smaller grounds, and the quicker outfields. Not to mention a much greater knowledge of diet, nutrition and weight-training for strengthening. Yet no one has come near to matching the numbers of the boy from Bowral. Even the great Adam Voges only managed 61.87 in 20 Tests before calling it quits. My old Nottinghamshire team-mate has a cherished place in Test cricket history as number two to Bradman. No wonder he got out when he did.

If Jardine were any other nationality we would be calling him every name under the sun. That we do not is simply because he did something worthwhile for our country. What is undeniable, though, is that he was not a figure you could easily warm to. You were just glad he was on the English team.

In those days, he would have been viewed as perfect

captaincy material: of the right stock, from a family of doctors, with a good education and having seen something of the world, after being raised in India. His wearing of a Harlequin cap marked him out from the common herd, in case anyone was uncertain about that.

This cold, calculating character wasn't looking for brownie points. He didn't have the common touch. He was no man of the people. He just wanted to get the job done, and in one way I admire that, as when it comes to being successful on the sports field who cares what people really think of you?

I'm in awe of his tactical acumen. He was way ahead of his time and didn't give a toss what anyone else thought of him or his on-field decisions. That's one of the greatest traits you can have as a sportsman – to be clinical in your thinking when out on the field of play. It was by sticking to his principles and following them through that he completed his task of bringing those Ashes home.

Triumphing in Australia became an obsession for Jardine, who spent the two-month sea voyage watching film of Bradman batting on the 1930 tour to England. He had no first-hand experience of it, as one of those out of favour for that series. The footage was all fairly repetitive, of course, as this Fred Astaire armed with a wand of willow danced down the pitch to hit the ball to his chosen destination – all along the carpet of course, as he seldom took the aerial route. But amongst the montage of boundaries, the eagle-eyed Jardine spotted a snag in the cloak of invincibility.

It was action from the final Test at The Oval that revealed
Bradman did not get into line when Larwood was getting
the ball to rear up on a dry pitch. Whereas others did so,
and took the blow, most notably Archie Jackson, the brilliant
Bradman did not, weaving out of the way. He notched a
double hundred but Jardine was not about to let the facts
get in the way of a good theory. 'He's yellow,' he proclaimed.

And so, over dinner in a Piccadilly restaurant in August
1932, Jardine discussed the observations with Larwood and
two other Nottinghamshire cricketers, the county captain,
Arthur Carr, and Larwood's new-ball partner, the left-armer
Bill Voce.

Larwood's extra pace would be crucial in getting bodyline
to work effectively, tucking Bradman up, denying him width
and forcing him to play on the leg side rather than on the
off. Carr had a belief that fast bowlers were physically bolstered
by a couple of lunchtime pints, and swore that the former
miner grew stronger in the afternoon as a result. None of
my captains ever recommended such an action, but if it had
meant going that extra yard for the team, I might have been
persuaded.

With his bowling attack briefed, the next stage for Jardine
was to indoctrinate the rest of his team, and he didn't miss
a beat in this regard, using the long journey over water to
create the collective frame of mind for the hostile series he
anticipated. Tactically, he wanted the competition to have a
real us-and-them edge. So he reinforced a dislike for all things

Australian on the boat journey, then rejected gifts and refused to cooperate with the local press on arrival.

Australia were given notice of the war about to break out during England's final warm-up match versus New South Wales when Bradman took evasive action and was bowled middle stump. Their 24-year-old batting star then opted out of the first Test in Sydney at the beginning of December 1932 due to ill health, and in his absence Stan McCabe's unbeaten 187 – an innings hot on cross-batted shots – proved futile. In the second innings, Larwood scythed through the batting with a five-wicket haul, and Jardine's team were 1–0 up before Bradman had contributed a run.

That equation did not change immediately when he returned at the end of the month for the second Test at Melbourne, where, greeted upon his arrival at the crease by Bill Bowes rather than the fire-breathing, beer-swilling Larwood, he somehow contrived to redirect a gentle lifter into his stumps from an attempted hook. The Don was dismissed first ball for the only time in his international career. Naturally, he made amends with a match-winning unbeaten hundred in the second innings in front of a 60,000 crowd.

England were undeterred by the riposte and stuck to their guns – by selecting their four-man pace battery of Larwood, Voce, Bowes and Gubby Allen for the third Test in Adelaide, ten days later. In their first innings, England recovered from a stodgy beginning to post 341. But the real drama unfolded in Australia's first innings of what *Wisden* called 'probably the most unpleasant Test ever played'.

Batting was treacherous on a sporting Adelaide Oval surface and contributed to the Australian captain Bill Woodfull taking the impact of a Larwood exocet above the heart, causing consternation in the stands, and rendering Woodfull unable to continue until medical attention was provided on the side of the pitch.

The hefty blow drew praise from one fielder in particular. 'Well bowled, Harold,' chimed Jardine.

The Adelaide Oval had been transformed into a cauldron of animosity, but it was the words that followed, uttered by Woodfull on a treatment table in the home dressing room an hour or so later, that were to prove the most incendiary. To this day, they are perhaps the most famous spoken during an Ashes series.

'There are two teams out there on the oval. One is playing cricket, the other is not.'

They were directed towards the England tour manager, Pelham 'Plum' Warner, and his assistant, Dick Palairet, after the pair knocked on the home dressing-room door to enquire after the health of the felled Australian captain, dismissed shortly after his bruising. Woodfull, a man of robust moral fibre, first instructed them that he did not wish to discuss the situation and only provided his judgement when asked what the matter was.

'This sort of thing is ruining the game, which is too good to be spoiled, and it is time some men got out of it,' he concluded, before turning his back, signalling it was time for the visitors to leave.

Jardine had exacerbated the situation by swinging his field round to the bodyline positions immediately after Woodfull had been pinged. More than one Australian player later wrote in their autobiographies that they feared a riot in the stands – in Christian Adelaide, the City of Churches, of all places. The locals might have been brought up to turn the other cheek, but they did not take to English provocation kindly. It was also said that Jardine, the Dick Dastardly in whites, repositioned himself to be closer to the hisses and jeers of the crowd. Inside, he was probably sniggering like Muttley.

Shortly after the match's resumption, which took place with a ring of police around the oval's perimeter, following Sunday's rest day, came an incident that increased the threat of a riot scenario. Abetted by a top edge, Australian wicketkeeper Bert Oldfield was struck on the head by a ball from Larwood. Although the popular Oldfield exonerated the bowler of blame immediately – it left him sidelined for a month with a stress fracture across his temple – the paying public were not so forgiving.

Just think about what it would have taken for a mob to storm the field in the 1930s. Crowds have definitely evolved and become more animated, and perhaps this was the era when they started to become more involved in the game. Nowadays it doesn't take much for some crowds. Take Edgbaston, for example, which houses a support that can be very judgemental about what happens in the middle, or even what has been said in the build-up to a match. Say something out of turn, gesticulate at the wrong time or generally act grumpy, and you can find yourself on the hitlist of the Eric Hollies Stand. Especially if the clock has ticked past four o'clock and they've all been oiled.

Aaron Finch was their plaything for an hour during the 2017 Champions Trophy defeat to England. Stationed on the boundary by his captain Steve Smith, he failed to allow his guard to drop, maintaining an unusually stern demeanour – and because of this they toyed with him, singing 'Finchy's going home', to the tune of the Lightning Seeds' Euro '96 anthem, between jeers every time he fielded the ball.

As Justin Langer learned during the 2005 Ashes, the way to deal with such a crowd is to apply the old adage about not beating them but joining them. After numerous slights about his stature or lack of it, Langer – whose default position is completely humourless, in my experience – removed his boots and knelt on them, shuffling along to fit in with the dwarf image. From that moment, they were putty in his hands. Suddenly, he was an honorary Pom and could do no wrong.

English supporters are quite witty both with what they sing and with the clever one-liners they come up with. In contrast, the Australians don't seem to have any creativity in this regard, and I am yet to meet one that can get the tune to any song. Even something so simple as 'When the Saints go Marching in' totally throws them. The tradition of terrace singing in England and Wales is very strong, and that has undoubtedly contributed to crowd behaviour over the years.

The era in which the controversial Adelaide Test took place, the 1930s, was a time when people generally did what they were told. You followed the demands of those above you in the hierarchy. You thought twice about speaking out of turn, let alone bellowing a ditty heavy with profanities at the top of your voice. So it must have taken a lot for a public gathering to become so restless at the actions taking place on a cricket field. The Australian batsman Stan McCabe reportedly instructed his team-mates to prevent his mum leapfrogging the picket fence in the event of him being knocked off his feet, while Larwood was said to have discussed potential weapons in the event of a pitch invasion, telling Les Ames: 'You can take the leg stump for protection. I'll take the middle.'

Jardine was there to control the working-class boys in his charge, to instruct them, to guide them, to govern them. People will question why they subserviently followed orders, but this was a very different time and you did what your superiors told you to do. There was an air of servitude, a sense that your country expected, and you would fulfil your duty.

* * *

Of course, one of the fast bowlers, Gubby Allen, simply refused, a diplomatic decision that left him well placed to be captain for the MCC's next visit to Australia. He was powerful enough at Lord's to say no – he was on the committee by the summer of 1933 – whereas the others were not. He still managed 21 wickets by orthodox methods, while there were 11 successes for the left-arm spin of Hedley Verity too, statistical evidence that bodyline was not a blanket attack.

In fact, bodyline was only used for periods amounting to between one third and a quarter of an innings. This, though, simply increased its potency. If England had sent down over after over with their physical intimidation, it would merely have given the Australians more practice against it. This way, it was effectively a dose of shock treatment.

It remains so even now, and we accept that being struck by short deliveries is part and parcel of the game. I know what it's like to be hit during a good bumper barrage because Peter Siddle thwacked me more than once in the 2009 Test match at Cardiff. And I was well protected with armguards and chest pads. It makes me think how horrible it must have been to face a bowler of Larwood's class when he had been told to 'kill, kill, kill'. No matter how much practice you put in and no matter whether you believe you're a good short-ball player or not, no one really likes to face bowling that's flying around your lugholes, especially without a helmet. It must have felt like being stood against a wall faced by five rifles.

Bodyline was an effective tactic because it maintained its fear factor, and it maintained its fear factor because Larwood bowled it with such unerring accuracy. Had his spells been erratic, it would have allowed occasional respite and lessened the chances of a batsman being dismissed. But in continuing to threaten life and limb as well as the stumps, he prevailed.

Larwood didn't need the reaction of a crowd – one that could only have been more enraged if he had started to barbecue koalas and kangaroos in front of their eyes – to tell him he was getting to the Australians, and Bradman in particular, by making the ball rise up awkwardly into the ribcage. He could see as much from Bradman's awkward movement at the crease.

'As soon as Don started darting to and fro across the wicket, I knew I had him,' Larwood wrote in his autobiography.

Leg theory gave a batsman multiple choices: move out of line with the stumps and risk exposing them; attempt to flick the ball away but keep it out of the reaches of the on-side fielding trap; or accept the blows to the body. Bruises were as common as boundaries.

Retaliation did not come in the form of tit-for-tat tactics, as although Australia were a fine team, and had gone into Adelaide with the score at 1–1, their Achilles heel was a chronic lack of quality pace bowlers. Instead, they reckoned the pen mightier than the sword and, bypassing the England manager Warner, sent a cable direct to the MCC.

What was said in their correspondence could not have been more inflammatory. Bodyline, they argued, was challenging the best interests of the game of cricket. 'In our opinion, it is most unsportsmanlike. Unless stopped at once it is likely to upset the friendly relations that exist between Australia and England.'

Imagine the severity of such an accusation. It might as well have been an expletive-laden rant, questioning the parentage of the entire English tour party. Unsportsmanlike – anything other than the U-word! As bastions of the game, the upholders of the spirit of cricket, it was quite an accusation to make against a team representing the MCC. The phrase 'it's just not cricket' was born, and the threat to the future of the tour was tangible. Vic Richardson was in a club of one amongst the Australians, believing that the telegram should not have been dispatched. He viewed the wording as a red rag to a bull, and of course, coming after the home side went 2–1 down, it looked like snivelling.

Historically, the Ashes pushes teams to their competitive limits, but these days we find it hard to fathom how pushing those limits could end up with governmental intervention. Nevertheless it certainly threatened civility between the two nations at the time, to the point that the Australian prime minister, Joseph Lyons, feared a British boycott of his country's goods. Such an action had the potential to cripple the Australian economy.

The sport of cricket played a much bigger part in people's

everyday lives then than it does now. There weren't the other distractions so prevalent in the 21st century. (I couldn't believe it recently when I went on a sponsor's golf day during the 2017 summer and found that I was the only person in a hundred, the majority of whom were cricket followers, who had any idea that the Australians might pull out of the 2017–18 Ashes over an unseemly pay dispute.)

After a tactical pause occupying the best part of a week, MCC hit back with a recipe of utter indignation and double bluff. Their response read:

We, Marylebone Cricket Club, deplore your cable. We deprecate your opinion that there has been unsportsmanlike play. We have fullest confidence in captain, team and managers, and are convinced that they would do nothing to infringe either the Laws of Cricket or the spirit of the game. We have no evidence that our confidence has been misplaced. Much as we regret accidents to Woodfull and Oldfield, we understand that in neither case was the bowler to blame. If the Australian Board of Control wish to propose a new law or rule it shall receive our careful consideration in due course. We hope the situation is not now as serious as your cable would seem to indicate, but if it is such as to jeopardise the good relations between English and Australian cricketers, and you consider it desirable to cancel remainder of programme, we would consent with great reluctance.

Only following the exoneration of Jardine and his team did the tour continue. Despite all the talk of damage to the Empire, it would undoubtedly have struck the Australian board that there was no such thing as bad publicity. The gate receipts had never been so good, even surpassing those of England's 1928–29 visit. Jardine's men matched that tour's scoreline with two more victories, but the clinically executed plans came at a cost to its two great protagonists.

The establishment never fully pardoned Jardine for his bodyline methodology, and Larwood was blackballed as its chief practitioner. When Australia suggested that neither man be selected for the 1934 series, the bigwigs at Lord's acquiesced. The captaincy was stripped from Jardine well in advance of it, while Larwood was also disowned.

Despite standing up for their men under provocation – no one likes to be accused of cheating, do they? – the MCC altered their opinion when they saw bodyline for themselves. It was later considered a breach of fair play and was outlawed, with limits placed on the number of fielders allowed behind square on the leg side.

With his England days now behind him, Nottinghamshire bowler Larwood – who had returned home to a hero's welcome – sought a future in, of all places, Australia. There is a lovely story that shows beneath his Machiavellian exterior Jardine did indeed possess a heart, in addition to deep-rooted loyalty. Jardine sent Larwood an ashtray as a gift, with the message 'To Harold for the Ashes – 1932–33 – From a grateful Skipper' inscribed on it. He was also the one notable figure to provide a 'bon voyage' to his former team-mate when Larwood boarded the ship from Liverpool to Sydney in 1950 to begin a new life amongst those he used to torment.

Date	Venue	Team	Scores	Team	Scores	Result
02/12/1932	Sydney	Australia	360 & 164	England	524 & 1-0	England won by 10 wickets
30/12/1932	Melbourne	Australia	228 & 191	England	169 & 139	Australia won by 111 runs
13/01/1933	Adelaide	England	341 & 412	Australia	222 & 193	England won by 338 runs
10/02/1933	Brisbane	Australia	340 & 175	England	356 & 162-4	England won by 6 wickets
23/02/1933	Sydney	Australia	435 & 182	England	454 & 168-2	England won by 8 wickets

Who, me? W.G. Grace's flouting of the spirit of the game at The Oval in 1882 led to the creation of the Ashes and the intensity of the rivalry between England and Australia. He was a dominant figure in Ashes series for two decades.

Above left: At the end of the 19th century, England were blessed with larger-than-life characters such as the unorthodox Ranjitsinhji, left, and the multi-talented C.B. Fry, right.

Above right: A touch of class – the Hon. F.S. Jackson, victorious England captain in 1905, is followed out of the Lord's Pavilion by, from left to right, A.O. Jones, C.B. Fry and Archie MacLaren.

Left: The distinctive strokemaker Victor Trumper, here at The Oval in 1905, played in eight Ashes series from 1899 to 1911–12. In 1902, his uncharacteristically dogged second-innings 62 helped Australia to victory in the only Test played at Sheffield's Bramall Lane.

Pelham 'Plum' Warner's faith in Bernard Bosanquet's newfangled googly brought him a 3–2 Ashes victory as captain in 1903–04.

Bosanquet's time at the top was brief, playing in only seven Tests from 1903 to 1905, but what a legacy!

A team from England's Golden Age. The 1911–12 tourists featured not only Frank Woolley and Sydney Barnes (back row, third and fourth from the left), but also Wilfred Rhodes and Jack Hobbs (middle row, far left and second from the right).

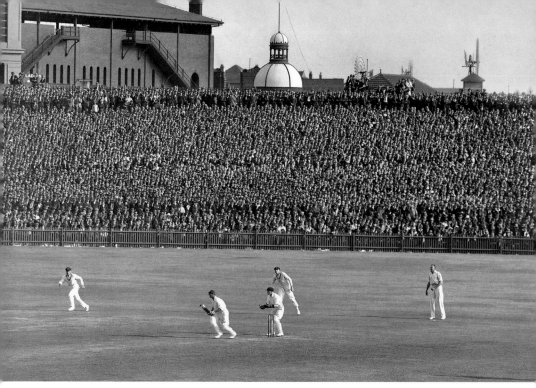

A packed crowd but not a beer snake in sight, as Jack Hobbs bats at the SCG in 1928–29. This time the Master was bowled by Clarrie Grimmett for 40, but England won the Test and went on to take the series 4–1.

At The Oval in 1930, the Australian team acclaim Hobbs – second only to Donald Bradman as an Ashes run-scorer – at the start of his final Test innings, aged 47.

C.V.GRIMMETT
(SOUTH AUSTRALIA)

Four bowlers who played a part in famous Ashes battles. Left-arm spinner Hedley Verity, left, took 15 Australian wickets on a sticky dog at Lord's in 1934, in England's last Ashes win there until 2009. Clarrie Grimmett, right, played his first Test in 1925 aged 33, yet remains the fastest to take 200 Test wickets.

Slow left-armer Wilfred Rhodes, left, became a more-than-useful batsman in a 30-year Test career. New-ball bowler Sydney Barnes, above, took 189 Test wickets in 27 Tests from 1901 to 1914 and was a great believer in the benefits of mid-match champagne.

The man with a plan. Douglas Jardine had spotted a weakness in Don Bradman's game, but his ruthless tactics for the 1932–33 series would not win him many friends.

Lord Hawke was part of the MCC committee involved in an exchange of indignant telegrams with the Australian Board over England's bodyline tactics.

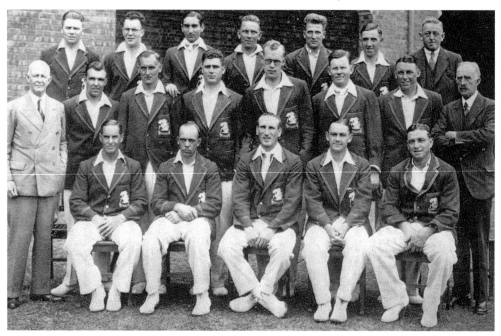

England's 1932–33 squad. Back: George Duckworth, Tommy Mitchell, the Nawab of Pataudi, Maurice Leyland, Harold Larwood, Eddie Paynter, Bill Ferguson (scorer). Middle: Plum Warner (manager), Les Ames, Hedley Verity, Bill Voce, Bill Bowes, Freddie Brown, Maurice Tate, Dick Palairet (asst. manager). Front: Herbert Sutcliffe, Bob Wyatt, Douglas Jardine (captain), Gubby Allen, Wally Hammond.

Harold Larwood, the key bowler in Jardine's scheme. How I would love to have been tucked in at short leg as Larwood charged in.

Batsman Bert Oldfield was hit later by a Larwood short delivery in the 3rd Test in Adelaide, described by *Wisden* as 'probably the most unpleasant Test ever played'.

The man they were trying to stop – Don Bradman slips as he avoids a short ball from Bill Voce in a tour match two weeks before the 1st Test of the 1932–33 series.

Vol. CXXVII. No. 1645. London, January 4, 1933.   POSTAGE: Inland, 1½d.; Canada and Newfoundland, 1½d.; Foreign, 2d.   Price One Shilling

SUTCLIFFE   D. R. JARDINE   HAMMOND

BOWES   G. O. ALLEN   VOCE

WARRIORS OF THE TEST WAR

At the time of writing England has commenced the great match in victorious fashion, the outstanding feature being Bradman's dramatic first-ball exit due to Bowes. To all cricket lovers some of the special report merchants have done much to harm the intrinsic spirit of the game. Shakespeare's saying in "Hamlet," "Bring me to the test and I the matter will re-word," seems particularly applicable to-day

a

Hold the front page – six of the England team who featured in the most acrimonious Ashes series of them all. Clockwise, from top left, Herbert Sutcliffe, Douglas Jardine, Wally Hammond, Bill Voce, Gubby Allen and Bill Bowes.

6

THE INVINCIBLES

W HILE England's success in 1932–33 was based on pace and hostility, Australia relied on spin bowling in 1934 to shift the Ashes pendulum in the other direction once more, as Bill 'Tiger' O'Reilly and Clarence 'Clarrie' Grimmett double-wristedly grabbed the opportunity to put the green and gold ribbons back on the trophy.

Sir Donald Bradman reckoned O'Reilly to be the finest bowler he ever faced, while the other man in this leg-spinning duo, Grimmett, was statistically the best. No other bowler in the history of Test cricket can match the speed with which he reached the 200-wicket mark, although India's Ravichandran Ashwin was only one behind his 36-match achievement in getting to the double hundred in 2016.

Both had enjoyed success against England in the not-so-distant past. Grimmett had finished leading wicket-taker with 29 on Australia's triumphant 1930 tour, while O'Reilly roared between the boos of bodyline to make 27 unheralded incisions into the tourists' batting. In tandem, they shared a half-century – Tiger taking that other big cat's proverbial share with 28 of the 53.

Their backgrounds were contrasting. While O'Reilly was of Irish extraction – one of the team's Catholic core, also including Stan McCabe, Jack Fingleton and Chuck Fleetwood-Smith, that did not rub along with Bradman – Grimmett was essentially an outsider who worked his way in.

To me, Grimmett's appeal is increased by the fact that he was not even a true-blue Aussie. He was a Kiwi. Born in Dunedin, he was dissuaded from fast-bowling by a school coach, and set off on a journey to become an international spin bowler.

Because they didn't have first-class cricket in New Zealand, he was forced to head to Australia in search of furthering his aims, first playing club cricket in Sydney, then moving on to Melbourne, briefly, for a stint with Victoria, before putting his roots down in Adelaide for a career with South Australia. With Test cricket not coming to find him as a young man, he went to find it, much like the South Africans that flitted to England during the apartheid era did.

There is limited footage, but the prospect of watching more footage of him and O'Reilly bowling in partnership gets me all nostalgic. Sure, they bowled on uncovered pitches, which theoretically made it easier for spinners to prosper, but I have always liked the thought of cricket when the slow bowlers are on top.

And in English conditions he was terrific. Of his 216 Test wickets, 67 came over here, a good proportion as the result of his trademark flipper. Just as Bernard Bosanquet gave world cricket the Bosie, the leg-spinner's delivery that went the other way, Grimmett – or Grum, as he was better known, not for the way the first two syllables of his surname sounded in a Kiwi accent but because when O'Reilly first watched him in an upstate game as a teenage fan the scoreboard erroneously read 'Grummett' – introduced another variation on the orthodox.

When I used to bowl leg-spin, messing about in the nets as a kid, I was pretty average at it, yet I could bowl a near-perfect flipper. I'm not sure why this was – perhaps just because of the way I held the ball in my hand and the fact that it has a similar release point to that of off-spin. The action of the ball coming out of the hand is the same, but when delivered with a leg-spinner's action you just flip it out of the front using your thumb.

So, while I couldn't bowl a genuine leg-spinner for love nor money, I managed to get the perfect drift and the ball to skip off the pitch. It's amazing when you get it right. During a net session in Bristol ahead of a one-day international I bowled Paul Collingwood with a flipper once, impressing him sufficiently for him to try to persuade me to bowl it in a match scenario. But I lacked the bottle.

Grimmett's farewell to Test cricket was as dramatic as his start. Having been plucked from Sheffield Shield cricket at the age of 33 to face England in the final match at Sydney in 1924–25, he responded with 11 wickets. A late developer primarily because of the hurdles he had to clear as an outsider, he was clearly in a rush to make an impression. The end was astonishingly abrupt. Having taken 44 wickets in five Tests against South Africa in the winter of 1935–36, including ten-wicket hauls in each of his last three appearances, he was never selected again after the final of the trio in Durban.

There was never any real explanation given as to why he had been dropped. Had he lost it? There was no evidence to suggest so on the basis of his statistics. Did everyone start picking the flipper? Not likely. The fact that he was at times unplayable, and then disappeared, the flipper going with him into retirement, is one of cricket's great mysteries. This variation in a leggie's repertoire didn't reappear until Shane Warne made it fashionable again in the 1990s.

No one could fathom the decision to overlook Grimmett. As his sidekick O'Reilly pointed out in his *Wisden* obituary: 'It was illogical to assume that age was the reason for his discard. He was 47, it is true, when the touring side was chosen, yet two years later, at the age of 49, he established an Australian record of 73 wickets for a domestic first-class season. Which raises, rather pointedly, the question of why the hell was he dropped?'

Oddly, Bradman was by this juncture not only his state

captain but also Australia captain, meaning he had a decisive influence on national selection. O'Reilly reckoned in losing faith in Grimmett, Bradman had lost faith in the best spin bowler to have graced the global game.

And not only that: 'Grum's departure was a punishing blow to me and to my plans of attack. His diagnostic type of probing spin buttressed my own methods to such a degree that my reaction to his dismissal was one of infinite loss and loneliness.'

It was an omission comparable to those made by England in the past, such as in 1902 when Lord Hawke opted to overlook Sydney Barnes, plus George Hirst and the all-rounder Gilbert Jessop for the Old Trafford Test, or another unexplained absence for Barnes at the start of the 1909 series. I am not sure how you could ever justify leaving out your most prolific bowler.

During 1934, in perfect unison, Grimmett and O'Reilly supplemented the batting efforts of Bradman, Bill Ponsford and McCabe to set up match-winning positions. Both were, above all, masters of length, and the contrast in their bounce and speed caused all sorts of problems. Despite being his change bowlers, these two spinners were Bill Woodfull's main artillery.

While Grimmett's round-arm action produced low bounce, and only served to make his flipper an even more dangerous proposition, the taller O'Reilly bounded in to the crease and sent the ball down from a stooping position at a quicker speed. And the ball that rushed on low was the prime source of his multitude of lbw dismissals. Grimmett was also much more likely to vary his flight. When the pitches were unresponsive, he played a holding role, limiting England's scoring rate against him to 1.68 runs per over.

O'Reilly, whose attacking instinct saw him bowl perennially with a short leg in place, edged the wickets column in 1934. In the first Test match at Nottingham in June, O'Reilly took 11–129 to Grimmett's 8–120; in the third Test at Manchester there were seven wickets in the first innings for 189 runs for O'Reilly; at Leeds, in the fourth Test, Grimmett won 7–5, and in the final Test at The Oval Grimmett had 8–167 and O'Reilly 8–151.

What a contrast a wet Lord's offered as, in the one match Australia lost, England's bowlers feasted on a pudding pitch while Grimmett and O'Reilly managed two wickets between them. It was Hedley Verity, the Yorkshire left-arm spinner, who caught the Australians out in that second Test with his ability to get purchase from the sticky dog in St John's Wood, taking 15 wickets in what was to be the last Ashes win at the ground for England for 75 years.

Bradman started that 1934 summer with illness and although his innings of 304 at one of his favourite haunts, Headingley, and 244 at The Oval indicated a resumption of normal service, his health deteriorated when a complicated appendicitis delayed his return home until 1935. Talk about overstaying your welcome. All Englishmen were sick of the sight of the great Don by the mid-1930s. There was no foreigner they would rather have seen the back of. Yet here he stayed recuperating, as if to rub their noses in it.

The next time the England team saw Bradman, in 1936–37, he was Australian captain. His opposite number? That man Gubby Allen, the conscientious objector to bodyline warfare from four years previously. Yet Allen was not himself averse to a trick that was to all intents and purposes a circumvention of the rules of fair play.

After Bradman reacted to the latest in a selection of glue-pot surfaces – the Australian summer of 1936–37 was a particularly wet one – by altering the usual batting order and sacrificing tail-enders O'Reilly and Fleetwood-Smith one evening of the third Test at Melbourne while it dried out, Allen schemed another short-ball welcome for the Australian great. When he arrived at the crease next morning with half his team dismissed for 97 runs, Bradman was served up a bumper by Bill Voce. This time England's pre-planning involved the changing of the field as Voce began his run-up. Walter Robins, stationed at square leg, had been instructed to backpedal to deep square in anticipation of a hook. The theory was sound; unfortunately, the catching was not.

An apology from Robins at the end of the over to his captain drew a measured sting in return: 'Oh, don't give it another thought, old boy. You've just cost us the Ashes, that's all.'

Of course, they turned out to be prophetic words. Bradman made the most of his early life, struck 270 and Australia won their first match of the series, having lost the first two.

Despite this turnaround in fortunes, it was not necessarily the happiest of times for the new captain. Four players were summoned by Australia's Board of Control – the Blarney Army of O'Brien, O'Reilly, Fleetwood-Smith and McCabe – to a brief meeting at which they were read an inconclusive statement. The implication was that there was indiscipline within the Australian camp, and that they were at its heart. There were insinuations of a lack of fitness, poor timekeeping and excessive drinking.

All this was done without Bradman's knowledge, although the Board were clearly fighting the new captain's corner. Even decades later, O'Reilly said he could not forgive Bradman for this episode. Despite the disharmony, however, the team's performance was not affected, demonstrating that you do not all have to be mates to enjoy collective success.

Australia were 2–0 down in the series when Bradman was spared by Robins's fielding gaffe, but they went on to become the only team to win an Ashes from such a scoreline. No matter their differences, O'Reilly and Bradman remained essential components of a winning formula.

This was further emphasised in 1938 in England when it took a win in the final Test match before the Second World War for Wally Hammond's team – he took the England captaincy after relinquishing his professional status (except in cases of emergency caused by injury or illness, only amateurs could be placed in charge) – to gain a share of the series. A raft of records tumbled at The Oval in the process, most notably Len Hutton registering Test cricket's then highest score of 364, and Hammond's first victory coming by the biggest ever margin of an innings and 579 runs. But Australia had already retained the Ashes courtesy of their two major match-winners.

As we have seen already, Bradman, for all his greatness, did have that habit of rubbing people up the wrong way. And when the two teams resumed hostilities in Australia after the war, under the same captains, there was another incident akin – or Ikin – to Bill Woodfull being struck above the heart in Adelaide 14 years earlier.

Bradman had fought off ill health to play in that 1946–47 series – gastritis had left him underweight, in direct contrast to Hammond, who at 43 was now fighting a burgeoning waistline. Bradman won the toss and batted at Brisbane, and soon found himself in action following an inauspicious start. There was little of the fluency associated with his batsman-ship early in his innings, according to the reports, but he appeared to be turning the corner when England believed they'd got him.

An attempted guide to third man, off the bowling of Bill Voce, did not take the thickness of the bat Bradman anticipated and flew to second slip, where Jack Ikin took a comfortable catch. It was one of those occasions when the fielding side were so confident of it being out that they neglected to appeal. Only when they saw Bradman rooted to the crease, staring into the distance, did they bother. The umpire, George Borwick, was equally unmoved and Bradman, insistent he had jabbed the delivery in question down into the turf on impact, continued his innings.

England paused in collective incredulity and Hammond declared: 'A fine way to start a series.'

As I mentioned previously, the Australians can be a funny bunch at times, harping on about a challenge to sportsmanship at one moment and then immersing themselves in the gamesmanship of failing to walk the next. England were in no doubt that it had been a fair-cop dismissal, while the actions of one of Bradman's team-mates told its own tale. Keith Miller, on debut, immediately reached for his batting gloves. O'Reilly, perhaps not surprisingly, also fell short of backing his captain.

As usual, the devil of the story is in the detail. Bradman, on 28 at the time, was a revitalised force after lunch and ploughed on to one of his customary big hundreds. His final tally reached 187; Australia were exhausted for 645. Then a Brisbane storm spiced up the pitch. Had Hammond's team claimed the prized scalp of Australia's best player to Ikin's catch, they could have been batting for the best part of a day before the change in the weather. Instead, they were faced with a pitch spicier than your average Bombay curry house.

It was the start of an unhappy tour for Hammond, who proved as aloof as his opposite number Bradman. In the age of gentlemen and players it was common for grounds to have different changing rooms for each, but the 43-year-old batting great took this a stage further by travelling around the country alone in a Jag donated to him by an admirer. And to rub further salt into this gaping sore, his old adversary Bradman this time racked up 680 runs in five matches, demonstrating that despite the lull between 1939 and 1945 and his sickly resumption, there was still plenty left in the tank. Australia eased to a 3–0 win, and the gulf between the two teams was growing.

The fact that Bradman's men were getting stronger came down in part to the emergence of one of their first rapid pace-bowling duos. Ray Lindwall and Keith Miller were the forefathers of Lillee and Thomson when it came to dishing out the chin music to England batsmen. The emergence of Lindwall was interesting, though, as he was a clone of Harold Larwood, having witnessed him bowl as a kid and tried to copy his action. Miller, a fighter pilot in the war, was an indestructible all-rounder, the kind of bloke who would have made a fine comic-book character to maintain morale amongst the Allied Forces, and whose good looks, dynamic style and jack-the-lad off-field image earned a big Brylcreem sponsorship deal.

'Pressure is a Messerschmitt up your arse,' he was fond of saying. 'Playing cricket is not.'

With a hostile new-ball pairing, Australia were quite literally unbeatable, their strength only increasing through a new regulation for the 1948 season that allowed the taking of the new ball every 55 overs. Not much encouragement for the development of spinners there, eh? If the ball left the hands of Lindwall and Miller, it tended to fall into those of the left-arm quick Alan Davidson.

It had been Bradman's final career ambition to complete his last tour of England without losing a match. Like most things he set out to achieve on a cricket field, he accomplished it. The 1948 side he captained would go down in cricket folklore as the Invincibles. They came, they saw, they conquered. Not just England but all-comers, their refuse-to-lose policy matching that of Vic Richardson's Aussies of 1935–36, who went unblemished on a tour of South Africa.

It's amazing when you consider modern scheduling that touring Australian teams used to play so many fixtures. Bradman's last stand featured 34 first-class matches – they came up against all the counties, and it makes you wonder how the seamers kept their pace above 60 miles per hour with that kind of workload.

Their impregnable run included 25 wins. Opponents were mown down as if caught in machine-gun fire in no-man's-land. Only the courageously heroic Denis Compton, who was floored when top-edging a bouncer in the third Test at Old Trafford, in a carbon copy of the Bert Oldfield incident in the 1932–33 tour of Australia, prevented a whitewash.

Returning to the field following a nip or two of brandy, having left it some time earlier dripping blood, he struck an unbeaten 145. A cocktail of Compton bravery and Manchester rain was enough to keep the Australians out of range, and Bradman missed the opportunity to round things off perfectly.

The same could be said of his personal quest, of course, when – via his second-ball duck at The Oval, beaten by an Eric Hollies googly through the gate – his career average dipped to 99.94. He had required only four runs in that innings for the 100 mark, and after failing to make them was reported to have said: 'It's not easy to bat with tears in your eyes.' Sentimental claptrap denied by England's close fielders in the aftermath, and by Bradman, who dismissed the attribution of the quote to him in later life.

Date	Venue	Team	Scores	Team	Scores	Result
08/06/1934	Nottingham	Australia	374 & 273-8d	England	268 & 141	Australia won by 238 runs
22/06/1934	Lord's	England	440	Australia	284 & 118	England won by an innings and 38 runs
06/07/1934	Manchester	England	627-9d &	Australia	491 & 66-1	Drawn
20/07/1934	Leeds	England	123-0d	Australia	584	Drawn
18/08/1934	The Oval	Australia	200 & 229-6 701 & 327	England	321 & 145	Australia won by 562 runs
04/12/1936	Brisbane	England	358 & 256	Australia	234 & 58	England won by 322 runs
18/12/1936	Sydney	England	426-6d	Australia	80 & 324	England won by an innings and 22 runs
01/01/1937	Melbourne	Australia	200-9d & 564	England	76-9d & 323	Australia won by 365 runs
29/01/1937	Adelaide	Australia	288 & 433	England	330 & 243	Australia won by 148 runs
26/02/1937	Melbourne	Australia	604	England	239 & 165	Australia won by an innings and 200 runs
10/06/1938	Nottingham	England	658-8d	Australia	411 & 427-6d	Drawn
24/06/1938	Lord's	England	494 & 242-8d	Australia	422 & 204-6	Drawn
08/07/1938	Manchester					Match abandoned without a ball bowled
22/07/1938	Leeds	England	223 & 123	Australia	242 & 107-5	Australia won by 5 wickets
20/08/1938	The Oval	England	903-7d	Australia	201 & 123	England won by an innings and 579 runs
29/11/1946	Brisbane	Australia	645	England	141 & 172	Australia won by an innings and 332 runs
13/12/1946	Sydney	England	255 & 371	Australia	659-8d	Australia won by an innings and 33 runs
01/01/1947	Melbourne	Australia	365 & 536	England	351 & 310-7	Drawn
31/01/1947	Adelaide	England	460 & 340-8d	Australia	487 & 215-1	Drawn
28/02/1947	Sydney	England	280 & 186	Australia	253 & 214-5	Australia won by 5 wickets
10/06/1948	Nottingham	England	165 & 441	Australia	509 & 98-2	Australia won by 8 wickets
24/06/1948	Lord's	Australia	350 & 460-7d	England	215 & 186	Australia won by 409 runs
08/07/1948	Manchester	England	363 & 174-3d	Australia	221 & 92-1	Drawn
22/07/1948	Leeds	England	496 & 365-8d	Australia	458 & 404-3	Australia won by 7 wickets
14/08/1948	The Oval	England	52 & 188	Australia	389	Australia won by an innings and 149 runs

7

N-N-N-N-NINETEEN

THIS was an age of near-perfection. After Bradman's flirtation with a three-figure career average in 1948 came Jim Laker's 19 out of 20 in 1956, a performance that has come to mean more to me as a result of my own England career. For when I went past Laker's career Test wicket tally of 193 on the opening day of the Test series in India in 2012–13, my mum Mavis called me and got very emotional. Now, she's not generally an emotional person, but my achievement had touched her because Laker was her father's hero.

My grandad Les lived in Warrington and was a regular watcher of cricket at Old Trafford. And he liked northern cricketers, so Laker's Yorkshire roots appealed to him. Whenever Laker was due to play in Manchester, for Surrey or England, he'd be there, and would wax lyrical about him to my mum. She was an only child and he used to tell her about what a fantastic bowler he was. My grandad was there for the Ashes match in 1956 when Laker took his 19 wickets. Naturally, my mum had little idea and less interest in what he was going on about, and she didn't think much about it until years later when she met my dad and therefore married into a cricket family. So it was a special moment for me when she got so tearful during that phone call, telling me how proud she was.

As a player, when you go past landmarks and break records they don't tend to mean much at the time. It is only later, when you have finished playing, that you take stock of your achievements, and so latterly I recognise that it was quite a big thing in the history of the game to surpass Laker's haul. His was one of the famous names when I grew up. Not surprising, I guess, given that he held the record as England's most prolific off-spinner in Tests for 60 years. So it was different from a couple of the records that I claimed, which were arguably anomalies of the time – such as being the first England spinner to take 50 Test wickets in a calendar year in 2010. Looking into that one further, you find that Derek Underwood took 41 in 1977 but only got to play 10 matches, while he had 30 in just five appearances in 1969. My 64 had come in 14 matches. Achievements based on consistent performances over long periods of time give you a much greater feeling of satisfaction.

Of all the individual performance records in Test cricket, if you wanted a bet on the one to last the test of time, the safest would be that of Laker. The highest score by a batsman fell several times in my own career, for example, passing from Brian Lara to Matthew Hayden and then back again. But no one has come near taking 19 wickets in a Test match. In fact, no one has even come close to emulating it in first-class cricket, the closest being 17.

Just imagine what it would take to claim 10 in an innings: a bowler would have to be in the best of form, conditions would have to be favourable, and the opposition would have to avoid mix-ups in their running. Oh, and however well you bowl, the bloke at the other end has to go for a blank. What are the odds of all that coming together?

Actually, I reckon Tony Lock must have had a really decent PR company, because several England cricketers of bygone generations have told me that the left-arm spinner bowled better than Laker. He just couldn't pick up the wickets, apparently. You can imagine it, can't you? 'I'm bowling better than him – he's having all the luck.'

Laker had offered a foretaste of what was to come when he took a ten-for in the first innings of Surrey's meeting with the Australians at The Oval earlier that summer. This was not a vintage Australian batting unit, but it had been on the winning side of the equation in the second Test at Lord's, one dominated by pace bowling, and that of Keith Miller in particular, who took 10 wickets in the match.

One–nil down, Peter May, England's newly appointed captain, decided spin should hold sway for the rest of the series, and set Laker and Lock, his Surrey spin twins, in motion. His masterstroke was to recognise that it was in this department that England were undoubtedly superior. But the Aussies kicked up a fuss when the surfaces sported less grass than the North African desert, where Laker served in the Second World War. For it was in a match between the Servicemen of the Ashes rivals in Cairo in 1944 that he developed a taste for Antipodeans on toast. He took 6–10, which of course were remarkably modest figures given what he would go on to achieve.

What I admire most in Laker, though, was the reaction of others to his off-spin. Sir Garfield Sobers, the great West Indies all-rounder, commented in his autobiography that: 'When you batted against Laker you could hear the ball fizz as he spun it.' His methods are the ones that I always adhered to as I came through the system at Northamptonshire – if you are going to be a spinner, spin it hard. As John Arlott, in his role as *Guardian* cricket correspondent, reflected in Laker's obituary: 'He paid the price for the terrific tweak he gave to the ball by eternally massaging his cruelly bowed spinning finger with ointment.' Ted Dexter, one of those with the confidence to stand at short leg while he whirled away, later wrote: 'When you saw him bowl you wondered why any off-spinner would contemplate bowling in a different fashion. He made it all look simple.'

In the 1956 series, Australia were yet to beat one of the counties when they turned up in Leeds in July, although they held the advantage after two Tests. The Ashes were arguably within their grasp when England lost their first three wickets for 17 runs. The door was ajar for the Australians, but with Keith Miller unable to bowl due to a sore knee, and therefore playing as a specialist batsman, May and Cyril Washbrook slammed it shut with a 187-run partnership.

When Australia batted, the pitch was first dusty, then, following a deluge, sticky. Laker and Lock shared 18 wickets – Laker, brought up by his aunts in nearby Bradford before relocating south in wartime, edging the split 11–7 – as England levelled things with victory by an innings.

Then came the most freakish bowling performance in history, once the series had headed across the Pennines. This time England built a more stable platform, and a score of 459 gave their bowlers plenty to work with. As did the dusty pitch.

Laker's use of variation was not limited to flight. He also altered his release points, and even the length of his run-up. But what remained consistent was his accuracy. Bowling round the wicket – complementing the very different angle of attack the slow-left-arm orthodox of Lock offered – he looked to pitch the ball on an off-stump line and beat the right-handed batsmen through the gate. Australia's attempts to hit him off his length in their first innings were disastrous. They were dismissed for just 84.

Further rain delayed Australia's follow-on until the fifth day, but even when applying a more circumspect approach, they could not extract his venom. Having taken 9–37 in the first innings, this time he went one better, rushing through the lot for 53 runs, as the ball curved in to beat defensive lunges or fly off the inside edge to leg slip or short leg.

The Australians cried foul at the Old Trafford pitch and Bert Flack, the groundsman, later confessed: 'Thank God Nasser has taken over the Suez Canal. Otherwise, I'd be plastered over every front page like Marilyn Monroe.' No, not that Nasser. This one was Egyptian president Gamal Abdel Nasser, who nationalised the canal company after nearly a century of British-French control.

Laker's reaction to the adulation, as he walked off, high-lighted his self-effacing attitude. He didn't even raise a smile. The headlines next day were similarly restrained. 'Laker Takes 19 Wickets', read the *Daily Sketch*.

By the end of 1956, the Aussies must have seen Laker in their most disturbed nights of sleep. In seven matches against them, including two for Surrey, he claimed 63 wickets. In the only summer in which England selected him for every single one of their home Tests, he claimed 46 victims, a record for a bilateral series.

In the final match, at his home ground of The Oval, Australia did all they could to stave off defeat, crawling to 27–5 in their second innings, from an astonishing 38.1 overs, before weather curtailed things, leaving England with a 2–1 series win. Laker finished with the ridiculous second-innings figures of 18–14–8–3.

* * *

This exposure of Australia's weakness against off-spinners – they were a rare breed back home as the drier surfaces had encouraged fast bowlers and wrist-spinners for half a century – helped redress the balance of Ashes confrontations. England had completed three consecutive series victories for the first time in 60 years.

Fred Trueman, omitted for Old Trafford despite contributing the two non-spin wickets in Leeds, recognised it as a watershed moment, writing in his memoirs *As It Was*: 'Jim Laker's feat helped further the renaissance of English cricket in the Fifties.'

England had selected their pre-war players when cricket resumed post-war. However, rather like we would see half a century later when there was another sea change under Michael Vaughan, it was only when selectors plumped for the new breed of cricketer – one that did not carry the mental baggage that went with losing regularly to those in green and gold – that fortunes changed.

England's regaining of the Ashes in 1953 under Len Hutton's captaincy had delivered an equally historic blow. The Ashes had been in Australian possession for 19 years and such a result was worthy of a knees-up. Not as lavish as that thrown by Elton John following the Mike Gatting-fronted England team's series win in 1986–87, nor the very public celebration of 2005 with its open-top bus and use of Downing Street's gardens as public toilets. No, Len Hutton's team were recognised at a much more austere setting – their reception was held at the Albert Hall, Pudsey, West Yorkshire. Sounds like a case of no expense dared.

It had been pretty obvious that the first Bradman-less series for 24 years – in Australia in 1950–51 – had left Ashes cricket in need of a hook to re-engage dwindling audiences. Ashes cricket was just not Ashes cricket without the Special Don. Crowds were down by a quarter on those of the 1930s. To no great fanfare, Australia breezed to a 4–1 win that winter.

But with a change of captain for England, and the appointment of a Yorkshire captain at that, came a change of fortune. Len Hutton was England's first professional to be awarded the position on a permanent basis, and he set about making them a tougher proposition. The give-'em-nowt approach seemed to work wonders. Under Hutton, the team's over rate dropped, as did their run rate, but resilience increased and the win percentage went north.

At home in 1953, England played like George Graham's Arsenal of the 1990s, maintaining a deadlock until the fifth and final Test and then nabbing one from what was to become their set piece. Yep, they paired Laker and Lock together, Australia's batsmen struggled, and supporters streamed out of The Oval singing: 'One–nil to the Eng-er-land, one–nil to the Eng-er-land.' OK, I made that bit up, but you get my drift.

At the end-of-series presentation on the pavilion balcony, perched above the masses of people on the outfield, the Australian captain Lindsay Hassett quipped: 'England deserved to win. If not from the first ball, at least from the second-last over.' Perhaps an attempt to make light of the fact that his team were the first from an Australian perspective to be blanked in the Ashes since 1926.

For a first away win since the bodyline series, England reverted to type once more through the emergence of an unknown fast bowler. As the great Richie Benaud later said: 'For a short time, Frank Tyson blasted all comers.' He certainly blasted them in Australia in 1954–55. Tyson, a 24-year-old with only a single season of county cricket behind him, had developed a reputation for blowing teams away. Hence 'Typhoon', the nickname he inherited. Certainly beats 'Tyse'.

During the first Test in Brisbane, however, he displayed none of the ferocity that had seen him break Bill Edrich's jaw with a bouncer the previous summer, as the humidity and heat quickly sapped his energy. The masterstroke came in shortening his run-up in the second Test at Sydney; the focus to use it with purpose was provided by a personal bumper barrage from Ray Lindwall that resulted in Tyson receiving a knockout blow to the back of his head. Climbing off the canvas proved to be his Devon Malcolm moment. Those Australian guys were history. After Tyson came round, Hutton remarked: 'I swear there was a new light in his eyes, as if a spark had been kindled deep down inside him.' The human twister caused complete devastation to Australia's prospects, conjuring wins for the tourists in both the second and third matches of the series, resulting in a 3–1 win for England.

With three England Ashes victories in a row completed in 1956, Australia's response to Laker was to unearth some match-winning spinners of their own. It is a fairly natural reaction to copy successful opponents, rather than creating a particular form of attack yourself. For example in 2000, Chris Schofield got one of England's central contracts because he had blond hair and bowled leg-spin, albeit not quite to the same level as Shane Warne. Some of the attributes were there, so it appeared they gave him one by way of encouragement.

The new breed of spinner lacked orthodoxy. Jack Iverson had been the forerunner in the early post-war meetings between the foes, pushing the ball out of the front of his hand to create its fizz. While Bradman famously practised batting by hitting a golf ball with a stick, Iverson, a 35-year-old debutant, developed his bowling technique by squeezing a ping-pong ball through his fingers while playing French cricket on army service in New Guinea. His ability to transfer the skill smoothly to cricket earned him the nickname 'Freak'.

I've always liked bowlers that buck the trend and challenge the way things have traditionally been done. Just because bowling techniques have worked for someone else it doesn't necessarily follow they will work for everyone, so why not try something new? Putting two fingers up to the system has always appealed to me, and in my case this took the form of bowling a very traditional kind of off-spin at a time when finger-spinners weren't being considered unless they housed a doosra in their armoury.

Of course, it's human nature for people to copy and so Iverson, a bowler who claimed 21 wickets at an expense of 15.24 runs each in a fleeting international career – he never appeared outside of that 1950–51 series – did not remain unique for long. Suddenly, everyone was looking for a different way to get the ball to misbehave off the pitch. As a journeyman bowler whose candle flickered for the briefest of stints, his was a brilliant story, but, through no fault of his own, Iverson spawned world cricket's first great chucking debate.

In 1958–59 suspicion fell on the left-arm fast bowler Ian Meckiff and on Keith Slater, who alternated between pace and spin. However, there was no debate necessary over Jimmy Burke's off-breaks – he openly admitted his elbow straightened and bent in delivery.

All I know from playing over a long period of time is that throwing has remained prevalent in cricket. I always maintained that it was not the fault of those bowlers called for 'chucking' but the fault of the authorities for not stamping out the practice more effectively. They could have eradicated it in the first place, but they were only too happy to encourage spinners of the modern era, especially those exponents of the doosra, despite the fact I am still yet to see anyone who can bowl a legitimate one at a speed of anything more than 30 miles per hour.

To bowl one any quicker, in my mind, would result in your arm snapping off, as you are forcing it through a motion against its natural flex and putting extreme force through your shoulder and your elbow in the process. Science might prove otherwise, but I am confident there is no way that the pace and power required can be achieved with an arm that stays within the permitted 15 degrees of flexion. My efforts resulted in a severely sore elbow, and I have heard of other people with orthodox bowling actions trying it and they haven't succeeded. All they have managed to do is knacker their arms up.

The giant fast bowler Gordon Rorke completed a renegade quartet in Australia's 1958–59 team, although his rangy legs offered another problem altogether. In those days, it was the back not front foot that had to be behind the line in the cases of no-balls, allowing the process of dragging to take place. It meant bowlers like the six-and-a-half-foot Rorke delivered the ball from about 18 yards, and I know what tough work it is to face someone of that height from so close, as Stuart Broad had a generous interpretation of what represented 22 yards in practice!

The fear for England in Australia in 1958–59 was being viewed as Whingeing Poms if they complained. Peter May as captain opted for the stiff upper lip rather than protest in the knowledge that the Australians, for all their quibbling about the pitches of Leeds and Manchester in 1956, had stopped short of making any official complaints. Instead, he waited for the end of a 4–0 series thrashing before signalling an intention to bring up the issue with the MCC. For various reasons, none of the crooked crew played again in Tests against England, and Meckiff suffered the ignominy of being no-balled for throwing four times in his one and only over in a Test against South Africa in Brisbane in December 1963.

With an overall scoreline of 6–4 from 25 Tests, Australia held the Ashes throughout the Swinging Sixties. It was an era in which the commentators of my childhood were pitched against each other. Richie Benaud was the soothing voice of summers on the BBC, with his 'Morning, everyone' welcome and economy of words at the microphone. As a player he was the man whose captaincy turned the Australian team back around after those three straight series defeats in the 1950s, and he was also the first to 2,000 runs and 200 wickets in international cricket, five of which, during the second innings at Old Trafford in 1961, secured bowling leg-spin around the wicket, proved decisive in the series.

Benaud was also responsible in part for the term 'sledging' entering cricket's lexicon. Fast bowler Grahame Corling – parents couldn't spell, obviously – played for Australia throughout the 1964 Ashes. But according to Benaud it was for an incident while playing for New South Wales three years later that Corling, wonderfully dubbed 'I'll be' by his team-mates, made his mark on the game. Apparently, he was caught swearing in front of a woman and one of his team-mates responded: 'Aargh, "I'll be", you're as subtle as a sledgehammer.' From then on, anyone lacking subtlety on the field was said to be sledging.

And that is where Fred Trueman – who provided proof of the old maxim that you can always tell a Yorkshireman, but you can't tell him much – comes in. Fiery Fred was one of those cricketers who always knew best, and was unafraid to let others know exactly where they were going wrong. As one of the best fast bowlers the world has seen, he would use intimidation as one of his main weapons, telling one of the Australian batsmen who shaped to close the gate on his way out from the Lord's Pavilion: 'Don't bother shutting it, son, you won't be out there long enough.' One of his best barbs to opponents he considered to be riding their luck was, 'You've got more edges than a broken piss pot'.

Even his own team-mates were not safe. In Australia in 1962–63, he rebuked two of them for missing chances off his bowling. When the Reverend David Sheppard dropped one in the slips, he barked: 'Kid yerself it's a Sunday, Rev, and put your hands together.' Then in response to an apology of 'Sorry, Fred, I should have crossed my legs', after an edge flew through another member of the cordon, Colin Cowdrey, Trueman weighed in with 'No. But your mother should have.'

It's fair to say Trueman went against the grain, directly challenging the captain, Ted Dexter, throughout that particular trip and criticising selection in public. He also told a tale of how that winter began on the wrong foot. During the 1962 season, he had bowled more than 1,100 overs, and was intent on resting up on the voyage to Australia. However, two days into the trip, Dexter informed the touring party that Gordon Pirie, a British Olympic athlete, was aboard and had agreed to take regimented daily training.

In keeping with the image I have of him – derived from visits from grandad Les, who would insist on watching *The Indoor League*, in which Fred gave expert analysis on shove ha'penny and bar billiards before closing with 'Ah'll sithee', as well as his guest appearance in *Dad's Army* – Fred would have had his pipe in his mouth and a pint to hand on deck. Instead, Pirie wanted him running up and down it, and to cut out certain food. His favourite steak should be ditched and replaced by fruit, salad and nuts.

'Apparently he knew a man in the Arctic who kept to such a diet,' Trueman recalled in *As It Was*, 'and was still chasing reindeer at the age of 95. I told him he'd find there were very few, if any, reindeer in Australia and even if there were some, I had no desire whatsoever to chase them. I was only interested in chasing Australian batsmen – back to the pavilion – and I needed steaks to do that.'

Unconvinced by the newly imposed regime and worried that running on hard surfaces would tighten the calf muscles,

Trueman was determined to slip these compulsory fitness sessions and undermined Pirie's methods.

"'Have you ever run against a guy called Vladimir Kuts?' I asked. Pirie told me he had. "Yes," I replied, "and if I remember correctly, Kuts was on his lap of honour before you crossed the finishing line. So if that's what your regimented training does for you, then you can count me out. I'm at the top of my profession. I aim to stay there for as long as possible."'

Trueman had a great Test record, of course, with his 307 wickets costing 21.5 runs each. Oddly, though, his career didn't incorporate any fulsome Ashes success. He was a bit-part player in the home wins of 1953 and 1956, and his one significant personal contribution – the eight wickets at Melbourne that helped put England ahead in 1962–63 – was followed by his criticism of Dexter for failing to pick a second spinner in Sydney in the match that followed. Fred Titmus took seven wickets from one end, but the pace bowlers had little joy from the other, and Australia drew level.

In 1964 the failure of Lord Ted and Trueman to agree on anything had disastrous effects in the third Test at Headingley. Dexter wanted his fast bowler to pitch the ball up; Trueman wanted to bounce the Aussies out. The consequences of this were short-pitched bowling to a full-length field – Peter Burge hooked and pulled his way to 160, taking advantage of the gaping acreage through square leg, and Australia, on the ropes at 178–7, finished with a match-winning 389.

But this series, which Australia won 1–0, did include an historic Trueman moment – when, in having Neil Hawke swallowed at slip by Colin Cowdrey in the final Test at The Oval, he became the first bowler in Test history to reach 300 wickets. Not one to talk down his own achievements, when asked whether he foresaw anyone breaking his career tally, he replied: 'Aye, but whoever does will be bloody tired.'

Date	Venue	Team	Scores	Team	Scores	Result
01/12/1950	Brisbane	Australia	228 & 32-7d	England	68-7d & 122	Australia won by 70 runs
22/12/1950	Melbourne	Australia	194 & 181	England	197 & 150	Australia won by 28 runs
05/01/1951	Sydney	England	290 & 123	Australia	426	Australia won by an innings and 13 runs
02/02/1951	Adelaide	Australia	371 & 403-8d	England	272 & 228	Australia won by 274 runs
23/02/1951	Melbourne	Australia	217 & 197	England	320 & 95-2	England won by 8 wickets
11/06/1953	Nottingham	Australia	249 & 123	England	144 & 120-1	Drawn
25/06/1953	Lord's	Australia	346 & 368	England	372 & 282-7	Drawn
09/07/1953	Manchester	Australia	318 & 35-8	England	276	Drawn
23/07/1953	Leeds	England	167 & 275	Australia	266 & 147-4	Drawn
15/08/1953	The Oval	Australia	275 & 162	England	306 & 132-2	England won by 8 wickets
26/11/1954	Brisbane	Australia	601-8d	England	190 & 257	Australia won by an innings and 154 runs
17/12/1954	Sydney	England	154 & 296	Australia	228 & 184	England won by 38 runs
31/12/1954	Melbourne	England	191 & 279	Australia	231 & 111	England won by 128 runs
28/01/1955	Adelaide	Australia	323 & 111	England	341 & 97-5	England won by 5 wickets
25/02/1955	Sydney	England	371-7d	Australia	221 & 118-6	Drawn
07/06/1956	Nottingham	England	217-8d & 188-3d	Australia	148 & 120-3	Drawn
21/06/1956	Lord's	Australia	285 & 257	England	171 & 186	Australia won by 185 runs
12/07/1956	Leeds	England	325	Australia	143 & 140	England won by an innings and 42 runs
26/07/1956	Manchester	England	459	Australia	84 & 205	England won by an innings and 170 runs
23/08/1956	The Oval	England	247 & 182-3d	Australia	202 & 27-5	Drawn
05/12/1958	Brisbane	England	134 & 198	Australia	186 & 147-2	Australia won by 8 wickets
31/12/1958	Melbourne	England	259 & 87	Australia	308 & 42-2	Australia won by 8 wickets
09/01/1959	Sydney	England	219 & 287-7d	Australia	357 & 54-2	Drawn
30/01/1959	Adelaide	Australia	476 & 36-0	England	240 & 270	Australia won by 10 wickets
13/02/1959	Melbourne	England	205 & 214	Australia	351 & 69-1	Australia won by 9 wickets
08/06/1961	Birmingham	England	195 & 401-4	Australia	516-9d	Drawn
22/06/1961	Lord's	England	206 & 202	Australia	340 & 71-5	Australia won by 5 wickets
06/07/1961	Leeds	Australia	237 & 120	England	299 & 62-2	England won by 8 wickets
27/07/1961	Manchester	Australia	190 & 432	England	367 & 201	Australia won by 54 runs
17/08/1961	The Oval	England	256 & 370-8	Australia	494	Drawn
30/11/1962	Brisbane	Australia	404 & 362-4d	England	389 & 278-6	Drawn
29/12/1962	Melbourne	Australia	316 & 248	England	331 & 237-3	England won by 7 wickets
11/01/1963	Sydney	England	279 & 104	Australia	319 & 67-2	Australia won by 8 wickets
25/01/1963	Adelaide	Australia	393 & 293	England	331 & 223-4	Drawn
15/02/1963	Sydney	England	321 & 268-8d	Australia	349 & 152-4	Drawn
04/06/1964	Nottingham	England	216-8d & 193-9d	Australia	168 & 40-2	Drawn
18/06/1964	Lord's	Australia	176 & 168-4	England	246	Drawn
02/07/1964	Leeds	England	268 & 229	Australia	389 & 111-3	Australia won by 7 wickets
23/07/1964	Manchester	Australia	656-8d & 4-0	England	611	Drawn
13/08/1964	The Oval	England	182 & 381-4	Australia	379	Drawn
10/12/1965	Brisbane	Australia	443-6d	England	280 & 186-3	Drawn
30/12/1965	Melbourne	Australia	358 & 426	England	558 & 5-0	Drawn
07/01/1966	Sydney	England	488	Australia	221 & 174	England won by an innings and 93 runs
28/01/1966	Adelaide	England	241 & 266	Australia	516	Australia won by an innings and 9 runs
11/02/1966	Melbourne	England	485-9d & 69-3	Australia	543-8d	Drawn
06/06/1968	Manchester	Australia	357 & 220	England	165 & 253	Australia won by 159 runs
20/06/1968	Lord's	England	351-7d	Australia	78 & 127-4	Drawn
11/07/1968	Birmingham	England	409 & 142-3d	Australia	222 & 68-1	Drawn
25/07/1968	Leeds	Australia	315 & 312	England	302 & 230-4	Drawn
22/08/1968	The Oval	England	494 & 181	Australia	324 & 125	England won by 226 runs

8

MOUSTACHES AND MEDALLIONS

O N the one hand, the 1960s could be considered as the
era in which Ashes series were most keenly contested.
On the other, it was arguably home to the dullest cricket on
the planet. Thank goodness that the 1970s put up a serious
form of rebellion.

An example of the conservatism that it kicked into touch
came in the final Test at Sydney in 1962–63 when Australia
held the urn and defended it so resolutely that they would not
be drawn into a chase of 241 in more than 80 overs. England
dangled a carrot, yet the reaction suggested they had offered
some left-over Christmas sprouts. Successful completion would
have delivered a 2–1 series victory, but Richie Benaud was for
sticking not twisting, proving that Ted Dexter was not the only
ultra-conservative captain of the decade. With the two countries
so well matched, they effectively tried to bore the other to death.
It wasn't so much a case of last man standing as last man awake.

Ted didn't seem to be a great fan of the maverick or even anything that went slightly against the grain as far as I could see. He famously blamed England's 3–0 defeat by India in 1992–93 on captain Graham Gooch and some of the other players' designer stubble, saying, 'We will be looking at the whole issue of people's facial hair'. I wonder how he'd have liked my Pat Sharp haircut circa 2005?

Heaven only knows what our Ted made of the hirsute Australian bunch marshalled from first slip by Ian Chappell in the 1970s. Chappell's style of cricket was like the gunfight at the O.K. Corral, and in the Zapata-moustached Dennis Lillee he had his Wyatt Earp. Anyone who ran into town was to be run straight back out again under the heaviest of assaults. Australia's new breed of cricketer looked like rock stars, and partied like them too – they were even known to party with them.

So what a great twist to the story that the hairy bikers were scalped in 1970–71 by an England team whose primary attacking weapon was the softly spoken John Snow, a parson's son fond of poetry. Appearances have rarely been more decep-tive than with the meanest English fast bowler of his time. Gentle off the field; Godzilla on it.

Snow's speciality was to challenge the interpretation of what constituted a bouncer by perfecting the delivery that rose to an awkward height but still passed below the shoulder – the kind that would have been given the nod of approval by Harold Larwood. This particular delivery, however, was the source of an ongoing dispute between Snow and the home umpire Lou Rowan during a series that was littered with more short stuff than a mini-skirt convention. Snow indignantly argued that these armpit ticklers were not the head-high bouncers that constituted intimidatory bowling. Rowan, who Snow later lambasted in his autobiography *Cricket Rebel* for possessing an unflinching stubborn streak, argued otherwise.

Snow explained that he did not set out to hurt opponents, but that dishing out the fractures simply went with the job specification. His aim with each delivery was to promote anxiety and uncertainty in the Australian batsmen. Nothing eroded confidence more comprehensively, though, than a blow to the body. Anyone who says they enjoy facing genuinely fast stuff with the potential to floor you has a problem with the truth. Some play it better than others, but no one really enjoys it.

It was one of the blows he landed in the final Test of the 1970–71 series that escalated into a full-on Sydney riot and threatened the first forfeiture in Test cricket – 35 years before Inzamam-ul-Haq claimed that unwanted accolade when he walked Pakistan off at The Oval under ball-tampering allegations, never to return. In a moment of misjudgement, Australia's number nine, Terry Jenner, tried to duck his third delivery in the first innings but effectively headed it straight to cover. Jenner, who gained greater notoriety as Shane

Warne's mentor than for his own leg-spin, was helped off the field bloodied, triggering a response from Rowan at the bowler's end.

Rowan was not having it, and issued a warning. Snow presented a case that the Australians were liberally sprinkling their own eight-ball overs with genuine bumpers, and yet he was being spoken to for a more modest use. When Ray Illingworth, the captain, joined in it could be termed a full-on row.

The over recommenced, and the outfield took a gentle peppering of beer cans. That was the calm. The storm broke seconds later when Snow trudged down to fine leg. He could hear some booing and hissing as he approached the picket fences.

'As I was wandering down I saw three English guys in the second row of the bleachers, nodded to them, and then I saw this figure beetling around the footpath with his head down,' he recalled. 'Suddenly there was a hand on my shoulder, and then the cans started.'

Unsurprisingly, those gathered on the Hill at Sydney were inebriated. Snow later claimed his half-cut assailant could not communicate because he was 'stoned'. Snow stood back out of range and responded to those providing a verbal volley by mimicking an orchestra conductor. Elsewhere on the boundary tin-can alley, Derek Underwood became a target for the yobs' lobs, and one of the sightscreen operators received a blow from a can and was carted off to hospital.

As the missiles rained down, Illingworth waded in, sleeves rolled up, a lock of hair draped across his forehead, looking like he was ready to knock some heads together, and signalled to his men to leave the field. Illingworth was a no-nonsense Yorkshireman, and his message here was clear. Up yours, Australia. You don't treat us like that. We're English, you know. Seven minutes they spent in the dressing room, before a visit from Rowan – the Shakoor Rana of his day – smoked them out.

'What's going on, Mr Illingworth?' he said. 'Is your team coming back on the field or are you forfeiting the match?'

It was effectively a rhetorical question. England, 1–0 up in that 1970–71 series after winning on their previous visit to Sydney, were dominating the seventh – yes, seventh – Test too. The beer cans and stubbies were swept up, as was Australia's tail and a 62-run win provided a 2–0 away win and the first change in the balance of power since the 1950s.

Illingworth possessed a sharp cricket brain and his pragmatism made the Leicestershire one-day teams he captained the most feared for a while. You could argue that he held back off-spin bowling in this country by appearing on TV bowling these darts at leg stump with a packed on-side field. Kids always try to replicate those they see on the telly, and this was unadulterated negativity at a time when it was not the done thing to use the width of the crease to cut off the stumps. Nevertheless, I have always liked Ray Illingworth because I grew up with him on the Beeb commentary. Then he became England manager. He was like all the other author-itarian figures in my life: northern, steeped in cricket and he didn't smile very often.

If one Yorkshireman united this England team, another threatened to tear them apart with his self-indulgence at the crease. While Snow took 31 wickets to win the bragging rights amongst bowlers, Geoff Boycott top-scored in that 1970–71 series in Australia, but showed the selfish streak that was to make him such a Marmite character.

Boycott batted magnificently and unlike some of his team-mates was relatively untroubled by Australia's finger-flick bowler John Gleeson. Although most deliveries zipped straight off the turf, some spun, causing consternation amongst the tourists' ranks. Boycott's comment about being able to read the Australian mystery spinner – reports vary as to whether the conversation took place with Basil D'Oliveira or John Edrich – is top-notch, old-school Yorkshire gold. Had Boycott differentiated between the off-break and the leggie? 'Oh, aye. I worked that out a fortnight ago,' Boycott is alleged to have said. 'Just don't tell those buggers up there,' he added, with a nudge towards the visitors' dressing room.

Overall, though, the sum of England's parts had Australia covered in that tour, and for the 1972 series in England too, thanks to another Yorkshire match-winner – a fungus called fusarium that played its part in denying Ian Chappell's rapidly improving team in its quest to take back the crown.

Heading into the final two Tests in 1972, the scoreline stood at 1–1. England victory in Leeds rendered the Oval match that followed academic. The series was to finish 2–2. However, the circumstances around the Headingley Test aroused suspicions everywhere. Australia's pace bowlers Lillee and Bob Massie, who had bagged an incredible 16 wickets on his Test debut at Lord's, posed a serious threat. So the conspiracy theorists tracked back to the moment Derek Underwood was called up as a second spinner. He had not played in the previous three Tests but came to the fore at Headingley on a pitch that, according to John Woodcock, writing in *The Times*, 'might have been made for Underwood . . . it does no one any credit'.

Then came that pesky fusarium – a fungus carried in the water – that killed off all the grass. According to Ian Chappell, the day before the match Keith Stackpole hurled a cricket ball into the pitch and it rebounded no higher than his toes. In contrast, a throw of the same velocity further along the square was bouncing chest high.

Skulduggery, cried Australia, who struggled on a surface devoid of pace and bounce. Illingworth's half-century in a low-scoring match proved crucial – although it would have been painful work to transform into a highlights reel, his strike rate just 22 runs per 100 balls. England's captain conceded that the pitch was undoubtedly poor, but said it was a classic case of *force majeure*.

While we are on the subject of pitch preparation, I must

say I have absolutely no problem doing so with the home team in mind. What I would, add, however, is that ideally every venue should have its own unique pitch, something a bit different within its characteristics that presents a challenge to both sets of players that is not replicated in entirety else-where. Perth should be rapid, Brisbane should bounce and seam, Sydney should spin, Lord's should be a batter's paradise, Trent Bridge should promote the art of swing.

I love the variation of challenges presented as you travel from ground to ground, and I find it a little bit sad that we see less of a contrast these days, especially in England, because of the uniform use of Ongar loam, a practice started in the 1990s when Harry Brind, who had completed a brilliant resus-citation of the square at Surrey, became the national pitch consultant.

His work might have improved some pitches, but I would love to go back full circle to the days when the natural soil from the local area is the soil you use to make up the square, and the pitches are taken on their face value. I know there was a later attempt a decade ago to make all first-class venues similar in terms of the pitches they produced, but this, I believe, is what you get when pompous idiots with money, but scant knowledge of what actually makes the game great, are left in charge.

Another thing ripe for a comeback is the 1970s cricket attire: the open school-style shirts, exposing a tuft of chest hair, with a huge gold medallion nestling somewhere between. Courtesy of video recordings and reruns on the BBC on wet-weather days during live Test transmissions, this was the earliest cricket I watched in any detail, and that was the image Dennis Lillee and Jeff Thomson completely rocked.

In the mid-1970s West Indies were not yet the force of the global game and so these two freakishly quick but ruggedly handsome Aussie blokes were the Hollywood stars of fast bowling. Lillee, with his massive 'tache, was an absolute style icon. And he knew it. He even had the posing down to a T. My old Nottinghamshire team-mate Paul Franks used to do a fine impression of him, walking back to his mark after bowling a ball, wiping the sweat off his brow with a flick of one finger and giving the camera a Blue Steel glance like Ben Stiller in *Zoolander*. Unfortunately, I can't see this kind of dress code and attitude infiltrating the current England dressing room any time soon.

Lillee was so flamin' cool in his headband, buttons missing due north of the belly. He was like the sheriff of international cricket fields, although his policing didn't always go so well. His on-field scuffle with Javed Miandad at Perth in 1981 was one of the funniest episodes you will ever see – Lillee's 'put-'em-up' Queensberry Rules demands followed by a cheap-shot kick at his opponent and Javed's sneaky swipe with the bat while the umpire's back is turned.

Later on in his career, Lillee dropped his pace to put greater emphasis on other skills of fast bowling, such as swing and seam. That's the sign of true greatness, isn't it? To take what everyone else is agreed is your greatest attribute – in his case natural speed through the air – and eschew it in favour of greater subtlety and variety. It was the same process that New Zealand's Richard Hadlee and the great West Indian Malcolm Marshall went through.

The impact of this reduced pace and increased quality would arguably be greater with someone sending down thunderbolts at the other end. Lillee was a wonderfully skilful fast bowler – metronomic, quick, getting the ball to dodge about while giving you nothing. So to have him operating at the other end to an out-and-out tearaway like Thomson must have been every batsman's nightmare. What an horrific combo to face up to when they shared the new ball. As a batsman, your relief bowler was the one bowling 100 miles per hour. Just digest what kind of a challenge they posed when working in unison, and then consider that they were sending down eight-ball overs under Australian playing regulations during that time, with no limitations on the number of bouncers.

They had the ability to do some serious damage, as one of English cricket's favourite sons, David 'Bumble' Lloyd, found out in famous circumstances during the carnage of the 1974–75 Ashes when the Lillee–Thomson axis was at its peak. Our Bumble actually came within a whisker of being English cricket's favourite eunuch after the blow he received from Thommo at the WACA.

Never, it was said, did Thommo bowl with greater pace and hostility than when, as a previously unknown quantity, he was a wildcard pick for that series. Australia won 4–1, and his 33 victims cost under 18 runs apiece. Stumps were splintered, as was the protective box worn by Bumble as a delivery reared up and struck him flush between the legs. These days you have full-on protection around the crown jewels, and dual thigh pads either side. In the 1970s, a pink Litesome, something Bumble unfavourably compared to the soap dishes you used to find in public toilets, was all that stood between you and castration.

'Because it was full of breath holes it splintered on impact and concertinaed my knackers,' he recalls, with a sentimental tear or two. 'Suddenly, everything that was supposed to be on the inside was now on the outside. If you want to get a tad more graphic, imagine a cactus growing the wrong way out of its pot.'

Yes, we get the picture. That really was an era when you put your body on the line. They used towels stuffed down their whites as extra protection, and there were still no helmets about. It was like the First World War, when the old-school tactic of charging over the top was met by that modern phenomenon: the machine gun. There was only going to be one winner in 1974–75, and the English ranks became so decimated through injuries that they had to turn to a 41-year-old Colin Cowdrey.

You can picture his answer to the SOS, can't you? Turning up in pinstripes, most probably putting aside a flute of champagne at some lunch at Lord's to take the call, with a big smile on his face, an increasingly rotund frame, doffing his cap, looking like your favourite uncle.

England had lost the first Test by 166 runs, and two front-line batsmen – Dennis Amiss and John Edrich – were ruled out of the second Test at Perth, so, with Geoff Boycott in self-imposed exile due to his uneasy relationship with then captain Mike Denness, England's selectors in Australia considered replacements and the consensus was that Cowdrey was the man. He had been playing social squash in the three months since the 1974 domestic season had finished but had not hit a cricket ball until he got to Western Australia 72 hours before the toss. Half a dozen hour-long practices to get used to the bright light and trampoline bounce and he was good to go.

During their second-wicket resistance, he wandered down the pitch mid-over and bewildered Bumble with the observation, 'This is fun'. He even offered his hand to Thomson during the onslaught, introducing himself: 'Good morning, my name's Cowdrey.' He took his fair share of blows, but he flummoxed the Aussies with a counter-attack of good humour and grace, making 22 and 41 on his comeback.

What a great chapter in the Ashes fable. Cowdrey versus Lillee and Thomson was like a contest from another era.

'How do you do? Jolly good game this, isn't it? My word, he's fantastically fast, isn't he?'

An English gent versus two unapologetically uncouth

fast-bowling rogues: the juxtaposition of the two makes the Ashes what it is. Cowdrey wasn't just your typical Englishman; he was your typical Englishman from another era. In the 1920s there were ten of these Cowdreys in every England squad. In contrast, there would be one chap with a colonial past in Australia's team, and the rest would be rednecks, growling and swearing at you, giving full range to the dozen words in their vocabulary.

Deep down, the Ashes still means a lot because historically it's the landed gentry against the people. It's the rich elite versus the proletariat. It's the human social struggle in a microcosm. The suited-and-booted against the cork-hatted bushmen. Of course, modern life is a very different thing altogether, with both England and Australia home to huge middle-class societies. But the series is a reminder of our shared past.

This was the most exciting age for Test cricket, I reckon. For one thing, it was branching out in terms of its development of equipment. There was Lillee's aluminium bat, of course – a fleeting experiment soon outlawed by the authorities. But the lasting legacy of 1974–75 was the manufacture of cricket-specific helmets. It changed the game for ever.

Ironically, the bouncer war that prompted it began when Tony Greig peppered Lillee during the first Test in Brisbane. After being caught, fending a ball off his face, Lillee walked off, muttering: 'Just remember who started this.' Despite a

flamboyant riposte from Greig when it was his turn to bat –
dropping to one knee to theatrically signal his own fours on
his way to a hundred – there was no doubt who finished it.

Thomson later revealed: 'I couldn't wait to have a crack at
'em. I thought: "Stuff that stiff-upper-lip crap. Let's see how
stiff it is when it's split."'

This beach bum, with high knees and a delivery-stride
trick of making the ball appear from behind his backside,
and his majestic sidekick Lillee made cricket front-page news,
and one of the reasons I believe it remains such a big deal
in Australia to this day is the fact that a generation of people
still remember 1974–75 and the impact it had on their
country.

Australia was not just taking on England; it was taking on
the world. This small island – in population terms, at least
– from a backwater of the globe was rallying against the
imperial elite and beating them. They were making a huge
global statement, demanding that other nations saw them as
top dogs.

Sport gave Australia an identity it was unable to aspire to
in other walks of life. Politically and economically they had
no chance of replicating this kind of success. It placed them
on the world map. Hair began to emerge on the chest of the
underdog country. Australia had produced tough cricketers
before but this was a line in the sand. From that point onwards
they would never take a backward step.

The success of the team influenced the generation that

grew up watching and arguably encouraged the development of the generation of saturated success in the 1990s – when people like the Waughs, Shane Warne and Glenn McGrath emerged. The first Ashes they would recall, I am sure, would have been the Lillee-Thomson series.

The rest of the 1970s included a couple of largely forgettable Ashes series because of the presence of World Series Cricket. In fact, at one stage England were effectively playing an Australian 3rd XI. However, the Kerry Packer revolution was yet to fully kick in when Geoff Boycott – returning for the 1977 series after three years away, and marking it by running out local hero Derek Randall in the third Test at Trent Bridge – produced one of those career-high moments that have punctuated the rich history of the Ashes.

To score your 100th first-class hundred in a Test match against Australia at your home ground of Headingley is a feat only someone with the most impeccable timing could achieve. As Geoffrey himself would only be too keen to tell you, he possessed impeccable timing. Watch the footage of the locals streaming onto the field in celebration, and you would be forgiven for thinking nothing of any great significance had ever happened in Yorkshire before.

It also meant a great deal to Boycott, who hosted a 40-year anniversary dinner party for 180 guests in August 2017 to commemorate it. No wonder, then, that he became so indignant during a modern-day classic *Test Match Special* wind-up on its eve when Jonathan Agnew convinced him that Leeds was no longer the venue recognised as the scene of his 100th hundred. During live commentary on the Test series between England and South Africa at The Oval, Aggers revealed, via the reading of a press release, a rethink by the International Cricket Council, world cricket's governing body, on the legitimacy of some of the matches Boycott had participated in during a 25-season career.

'Further to the recent request from the South African government,' Aggers read, 'the ICC has now considered the question of downgrading the status of all statistics, including runs and wickets, from the series played between England and the Rest of the World in 1970. The ICC agrees that the series was played against the spirit of the Gleneagles Agreement and, in the interests of keeping cricket free from political interference, all matches will be removed from first-class records. David Richardson, chief executive, says "Clearly, this will not prove popular with those cricketers whose records will now be amended, but we are looking at the bigger picture."'

Of course, Boycs fell for the bogus press release hook, line and sinker, dismissing as nonsense the suggestion that the hundred he scored during the fifth match at The Oval – which had been removed from Test statistics decades earlier – was now to be retrospectively erased from cricket's first-class database as well. It was a wonderful piece of radio, concluding with a rasp of 'you muppet, Agnew' as the prank was laid bare.

Boycott still viewed it as 'the greatest moment of his cricket career' when he reached three figures in that 1977 match via a classical on-drive for four off Greg Chappell. It wouldn't necessarily have been in his top 10 innings in technical terms but in terms of prestige there was nothing to compare.

'When the Yorkshire public came, they all just assumed and presumed that I'd do it. For me, that was the greatest compliment. They'd seen me get so many hundreds and play so many innings for Yorkshire, that they thought it was automatic. Seventeen guys had got 100 hundreds before me, but I was the first one to do it in a Test match.'

Date	Venue	Team	Scores	Team	Scores	Result
27/11/1970	Brisbane	Australia	433 & 214	England	464 & 39-1	Drawn
11/12/1970	Perth	England	397 & 287-6d	Australia	440 & 100-3	Drawn
31/12/1970	Melbourne					Match abandoned without a ball bowled
09/01/1971	Sydney	England	332 & 319-5d	Australia	236 & 116	England won by 299 runs
21/01/1971	Melbourne	Australia	493-9d & 169-4d	England	392 & 161-0	Drawn
29/01/1971	Adelaide	England	470 & 233-4d	Australia	235 & 328-3	Drawn
12/02/1971	Sydney	England	184 & 302	Australia	264 & 160	England won by 62 runs
08/06/1972	Manchester	England	249 & 234	Australia	142 & 252	England won by 89 runs
22/06/1972	Lord's	England	272 & 116	Australia	308 & 81-2	Australia won by 8 wickets
13/07/1972	Nottingham	Australia	315 & 324-4d	England	189 & 290-4	Drawn
27/07/1972	Leeds	Australia	146 & 136	England	263 & 21-1	England won by 9 wickets
10/08/1972	The Oval	England	284 & 356	Australia	399 & 242-5	Australia won by 5 wickets
29/11/1974	Brisbane	Australia	309 & 288-5d	England	265 & 166	Australia won by 166 runs
13/12/1974	Perth	England	208 & 293	Australia	481 & 23-1	Australia won by 9 wickets
26/12/1974	Melbourne	England	242 & 244	Australia	241 & 238-8	Drawn
04/01/1975	Sydney	Australia	405 & 289-4d	England	295 & 228	Australia won by 171 runs
25/01/1975	Adelaide	Australia	304 & 272-5d	England	172 & 241	Australia won by 163 runs
08/02/1975	Melbourne	Australia	152 & 373	England	529	England won by an innings and 4 runs
10/07/1975	Birmingham	Australia	359	England	101 & 173	Australia won by an innings and 85 runs
31/07/1975	Lord's	England	315 & 436-7d	Australia	268 & 329-3	Drawn
14/08/1975	Leeds	England	288 & 291	Australia	135 & 220-3	Drawn
28/08/1975	The Oval	Australia	532-9d & 40-2	England	191 & 538	Drawn
16/06/1977	Lord's	England	216 & 305	Australia	296 & 114-6	Drawn
07/07/1977	Manchester	Australia	297 & 218	England	437 & 82-1	England won by 9 wickets
28/07/1977	Nottingham	Australia	243 & 309	England	364 & 189-3	England won by 7 wickets
11/08/1977	Leeds	England	436	Australia	103 & 248	England won by an innings and 85 runs
25/08/1977	The Oval	England	214 & 57-2	Australia	385	Drawn
01/12/1978	Brisbane	Australia	116 & 339	England	286 & 170-3	England won by 7 wickets
15/12/1978	Perth	England	309 & 208	Australia	190 & 161	England won by 166 runs
29/12/1978	Melbourne	Australia	258 & 167	England	143 & 179	Australia won by 103 runs
06/01/1979	Sydney	England	152 & 346	Australia	294 & 111	England won by 93 runs
27/01/1979	Adelaide	England	169 & 360	Australia	164 & 160	England won by 205 runs
10/02/1979	Sydney	Australia	198 & 143	England	308 & 35-1	England won by 9 wickets

9

THE SOMERSET FARMHAND

HAS there been a more watched Ashes Test match than Headingley 1981? I doubt it and, thanks to the advent of the VHS recorder, we've all lived through the incredible experience with Ian Botham, haven't we?

Video recorders meant that every ball of international cricket in England could now be preserved for life. Your dad would have his own library in the front room and you would get the stickers on the spine of the cassette altered every time you recorded over the previous programme. Unless you accidentally taped *Gremlins* over something your parents hadn't seen and didn't want to own up, of course.

Not that you would ever dare to deface those sticker strips. Your handwriting was nowhere near neat enough for Dad's filing system on the wall – although this very fact at least rendered you blameless if a programme didn't tally up with its title. In a cricket-mad household like ours these tapes were there to be stored in the archives – and let's face it, no technology was ever going to usurp it.

Unlike these sleek, compact, easily storable tapes, though, the action has stood the test of time. England had a really good team. Botham and Bob Willis were in their pomp, the box-office attractions, but there were also some seriously good cricketers to complement them, some of the very best we have ever produced – players of the ilk of Geoff Boycott, David Gower and Graham Gooch.

The opposition featured a cast of Australians rightly viewed as some of the greatest to have donned the Baggy Green. They had the emerging Allan Border; Dennis Lillee and Rod Marsh were still around; then there was the English-conditions magician Terry Alderman. Every ball was on the BBC, and one of the things I loved about cricket at this time was its limitations. We only got to see the action from behind the stumps at one end, and subsequent generations have not had the chance to enjoy the action from that perspective. With only one set of cameras at the ground you would only watch from, say, the Kirkstall Lane End at Headingley or the Radcliffe Road End at Trent Bridge. And I liked that. It gave you, as a viewer, the sense of being in the ground, in amongst it. You watched the match sitting on your sofa, but the fact that the camera view was constant provided the illusion you were actually situated in row Z, seat 26. You were there, part of the whole experience.

From a visual perspective, the way you view the ball when

you are standing in the slips is quite different to how you see it from mid-on or mid-off, and the loss of that angle due to great advances in broadcasting has actually removed a crucial aspect. Nicks are a lot harder to spot front on, so you don't pick them up as easily in real time. But just recollect old dismissals of 1981 and the ball's deviation is discernible from third man. You can see certain clips in your mind's eye – Botham, open shoulders, humping the ball over the off side into open acreage.

Modern TV coverage means you tend to recognise edges behind the wicket from the noise that is made. More often than not you only see the deviation when you are shown a replay from behind. The same is true when you are actually on the field of play. On occasions the wicketkeeper and the slips will see the alteration in the ball's line even when the umpire and bowler have not done so. From your side the flight path has greater clarity, from theirs not always so, so they have to listen out for noises.

And so we have all been on that back row of the Ashes auditorium to enjoy the reruns of that rarity – Yorkshire's gift that keeps on giving. To really savour its greatness, though, you have to rewind a few weeks to the start of that 1981 series.

Having made the mistake of giving the captaincy to the best player rather than the man most qualified for the job, England were also lacking the power of their best player because he now had other things to think about. In both cases, that man was Botham, of course. In a dozen Tests as captain he had not won once; in a dozen matches as captain he did not register a hundred or bag a five-wicket haul. Throughout the series in the Caribbean against the best West Indies team ever, and arguably the best cricket team the world had ever seen, he held the captaincy on a match-by-match basis, and as the man himself acknowledged, that 'wasn't doing anyone any good'.

It was not the basis for establishing authority. Not that Beefy was an Establishment kind of figure. In fact, he was anything but, and it all came to a head in the second Test at Lord's when the blip in form culminated in the draw that put the Australians 1–0 ahead in the series. After completing a pair, he departed the famous turf, through the gate and up the steps to the Long Room. The footage of chaps turning the other cheek, looking away, is brutal. He resigned an hour after the second Test was over. Botham resolved to combat the silent treatment from the Lord's lords in his own way. He later wrote: 'Not a single MCC member looked me in the eye. From that day on I never raised a bat to acknowledge them.'

The enormity of this moment should not be underestimated. The disregard for the country's premier cricketer from the red-and-yellow blazers was quite outrageous. What followed was like a work of fiction. It was the reaction of the working-class hero to being put down by the moneyed

elite. Botham was the original man of the people; the equivalent of a farmhand from Somerset. So for him to go on and
have not just a good Ashes but the most stellar Ashes an
all-rounder could imagine speaks volumes for both his
immense skill and the robustness of his character.

His England team was getting hammered, and his personal
series was going nowhere. What Botham needed was a captain
that could bring out the best in him.

Give Beefy credit here. He might not be a general-
knowledge genius, but when it came to cricket he was as
streetwise as hell and he knew when someone was clued up.
He knew the people who could help him on the field. And
he recognised that Mike Brearley – who had given up the
England leadership to concentrate on establishing a career as
a psychoanalyst – was the man to help out, both for his sake
and for the sake of the country. Botham was a proud
Englishman; he wanted England to win and knew that
Brearley was the best man to make it happen. Yet not even
the greatest mind could have anticipated that he would
provide the motivation and guidance for the original
poorhouse-to-penthouse story.

Brearley was undoubtedly the brains in that changing room,
and despite being possibly the most effeminate man to have
featured in an Ashes series, when he spoke others listened. The
players were clearly keen to play for him. To meet this softly
spoken, deep-thinking man you might not think that he would
be the kind of character to draw out the extra, or the extra

special, from a West Country boy like Botham. But Brearley knew which buttons to press when it came to handling his alpha-male all-rounder and getting the best out of a once-in-a-generation talent. Whenever Beefy showed a reluctance to bowl in net practice ahead of Test matches, Brearley would chivvy him into it, although it often came with a caveat, as 'once or twice I had to be willing to fend off a few bouncers from him'.

As Brearley recalls in his revered book *The Art of Captaincy*: 'His idea of batting practice before an important innings or match is simply to get his arms moving and feel the ball on the bat. He will then amuse himself with some big hits. In my view, his apparently flippant attitude is not entirely unproductive. Certainly it is better than nothing. At times, whoever is his captain needs to make him turn his arm over and swing the bat.'

Getting your best players onside is a prerequisite for any successful captain or coach, and Rodney Hogg, the Australian fast bowler, once summed up Brearley's ability in this area by concluding: 'He had a degree in people.'

On a cricket field some people just click, people that you might not have anticipated doing so. I don't think that just because you have similar social backgrounds you are automatically going to connect. Some of the people I got on best with were wholly different to me. Andrew Strauss went to one of the best public schools in the country, and was a very intelligent human being. Equally, I got on very well with

Tim Bresnan, a lad who I am not sure went to school full stop. (Bres is actually a very street-smart cricketer; he's just not your first point of call to help you finish the crossword.)

In the build-up to this particular match in Leeds, the third Test of six and therefore the pivotal one, Brearley asked Botham if he was in the right frame of mind. Effectively – are you ready to play? Beefy's reply told him in no uncertain terms that he didn't want to miss matches of the magnitude of England versus Australia. 'Great,' was Brearley's response. 'I think you'll score a hundred and take 10 wickets.'

Six of those wickets for old Midas arm came in the first innings at Headingley, complemented by a half-century. Yet midway through the match it all seemed rather futile. England, dismissed for 174 in response to Australia's 401 declared, were asked to follow on. Only one team in Test history had won after being asked to follow on.

Famously, when England's second innings was disrupted by bad light, Headingley's electronic scoreboard screamed through the gloom like an electronic Ray Winstone. According to Ladbrokes, England were now a 500–1 shot to win the match. Remember to follow Ray and bet responsibly at this stage, folks.

The very fact that any of the Australians could ponder placing £50 on England at such outlandish odds was a funny after-dinner story until three Pakistani lads went to prison for spot-fixing in 2011. All of a sudden, no matter how innocent it was in 1981, that kind of thing began to look more sinister than it actually was. Lillee and Marsh got shouted down by their peers but still had a cheeky tenner and fiver respectively, employing the team's coach driver as their bookies' runner. For Ladbrokes it was an expensive publicity stunt, although any publicity's good publicity, so they say, right? Meanwhile, despite the high-prolife high-jinks punt being so controversial, the Aussie duo went unsanctioned.

In those days, Test cricket respected the Sabbath and so Sunday was a designated rest day. It also meant that on the Saturday night, both teams made good on their hangover passes with a boozy barbecue at Botham's gaff in Lincolnshire. England were in the mire, though, and as Bob Willis recalled: 'We all booked out of the hotel on the Monday morning, thinking that was the end of the game. Ian had other ideas.'

Botham's batting in the second innings represents sport at its very best. The most dangerous opponent you can ever face is the guy who doesn't give a damn any more. The one who's so down-and-out that the fear of failure disappears completely and the natural talent takes over. He had lost the captaincy, England were losing the game and he just said: 'No. Stuff this.'

'Why don't we have a bit of fun and see if we can take it back to them. That's what we did,' Botham recalls.

I cannot think of anything more dangerous for an opposition than coming up against a guy like him in that frame of mind. The fact that he smashed it everywhere with a smile on his face emphasised this sense of liberation.

'He was the only player in the world who would think he possibly could do it,' said Kim Hughes.

Allan Border says: 'I still have nightmares about it.'

When Graham Dilley joined him at the crease on the Monday morning, England were still 92 runs adrift, with only three wickets intact. With the game all but lost, the phrase 'Let's give it some humpty' was used.

Watching Botham was great but watching Graham Dilley, a man not really known for his batting, pull off some immaculate cover drives made it pure theatre. He wasn't just guiding the ball through the off side; he was throwing the kitchen sink at it.

Dilley has that kind of face, almost like Plug from the Bash Street Kids, and under that mop of blond hair he is trying to look deadly serious, as if to show he is up for the fight. Then Beefy catches his eye and he breaks into a boyish giggle. It's wonderful drama.

In that kind of situation positivity is rewarded by Mother Cricket and so even the mishits were sailing into gaps. Yet even after the most thrilling entertainment, England were only defending 130 when they went into the field a second time.

Enter Bob Willis, bowling at the speed of light. He had been listening to hypnotism tapes beforehand, and each wicket is celebrated as if he hasn't snapped out of it. He turns round and simply walks back to his mark. It's bizarre but clinical at the same time. Here is the archetypal man on a mission.

His place in the match had been in some doubt due to a knee problem and he also had to combat illness to win the nod over John Emburey. Pushing off the sightscreen, he was an unstoppable force from the Kirkstall Lane End, his figures of 8–43 sealing the most famous long-odds success – until some Italian bloke called Claudio turned up in the East Midlands.

Every wicket has left an indelible mark on my memory. There was Mike Gatting diving in to take the catch from mid-on, looking like a bloated salmon. Then Graham Dilley re-emerges on the boundary to take a steepler of a catch, checking his momentum to stop himself tumbling back over it, then hurling the ball skywards in ecstasy. Willis's eyes are still glazed over as he hurtles from the field, dodging the invaders keen to be part of the 18-run win celebrations.

The whole thing was just magical. As Gower reflected in his typically laconic style: 'It's almost incredible to look back and believe it actually happened.'

Brearley was three wickets out in his pre-match Beefy prediction, but the fact that England's premier cricketer was back indulging in his favourite pastime – Aussie-bashing – was to bode well for the remainder of the series. Talk about motivating your trump card.

In 2005, people kept asking: 'How will this drama get any better?' Somehow it did. In this regard, it rivalled the 1981 series, because in both series England came back from the dead two matches in a row to claim a 2–1 lead.

Leaving Headingley in 1981, you would have considered it to be the most breathless Test match there'd ever been. It surely could not be repeated, so for Botham to go out in the next Test at Edgbaston and take 5–1 in 28 balls, bowling fast and knocking out stumps, was incredible. From the vantage point behind wicketkeeper Bob Taylor you can see him sprinting in to bowl. That was the Beefy I loved. Despite his blacksmith-shouldered batting brilliance, it was more for ball in hand that I idolised him.

Australia were 105–5, needing only a further 46 runs for victory, when Brearley turned to Botham for a spell from the City End. Running in to the crease, blond mullet bobbing in the wind, he produced a second masterpiece in a fortnight. It was like *Star Wars* and *Return of the Jedi* being released in the same month.

When he takes that last wicket of Terry Alderman with one that swung back in to rock leg stump, he runs up to the timbers, grabs one and punches the air. Whenever I think of Botham's Ashes that's the image I see, not a helicopter whirl of the bat above his head. Maybe because I was a bowler, I don't know. Perhaps also there's something about the act of finality. When you're batting there's lots of boundaries that add up, but a wicket as the final act of defiance has an attraction all of its own. And we know which of the two breeds of cricketer are more important. As a kid there are rhymes designed for you to remember all sorts of things – 'Richard Of York Gave Battle In Vain' for the red, orange, yellow, green, blue, indigo and violet of a rainbow, for example. In cricket, there is a straightforward one: 'batters for show, bowlers for dough', as they say.

The Eric Hollies Stand can provide the most vociferous support, and when a home bowler's got the charge on, incessant noise is what you would associate with the ground. But at this stage of the match every time Beefy jumped into his delivery stride he was met with silence – it was the ultimate etiquette. It was almost like an orchestra with a conductor.

That five-wicket spell undoubtedly added to the patriotic mood sweeping the country. The royal wedding of Charles and Diana had taken place on 29 July, the day before that fourth Test began, and Brearley put the desire of his men to add to the sense of a national celebration as a reason for his side's initial troubles in Birmingham, where they were dismissed for 189 despite winning the toss.

'Half-consciously, we may have wanted to produce carnival cricket to match the flag-waving post-nuptial atmosphere of the day,' wrote Brearley in *Phoenix from the Ashes*.

After England had conceded a first-innings deficit once more, this time it was John Emburey – recalled in place of Headingley hero Graham Dilley – who supplied crucial lower-order runs in the second. England were effectively eight wickets down for 98 before Emburey and Bob Taylor put on an even 50 in the penultimate stand of their 219 all out.

But the pitch was flat, ridiculously so in comparison to Headingley, and Botham was not particularly confident.

Brearley cajoled him by asking him to keep things tight for Embers, who was wheeling away at the other end. He certainly bowled straight, as three batsmen bowled, one leg before and one caught behind would suggest. The last, Alderman castled, left the figures for the spell at 5–4–1–5.

'I had bowled well – fast and straight – but on that wicket it should not have been enough to make the Aussies crumble that way,' Botham argued. 'The only explanation I could find was that they had bottled out. The psychological edge that we – and I – had got over them at Headingley was proving an insuperable barrier for them.'

Given what had gone before, Botham's 118 off 102 balls, including six sixes, at Old Trafford in the fifth Test seemed positively run-of-the-mill. On the highlights reel, Richie Benaud implores repeatedly: 'They mustn't give this fellow room outside the off stump.' Dennis Lillee then gets 'they're just not learning at all' as another cut four brings up his rapid fifty.

Whether they were to heed Benaud's lesson or not, Botham appeared to have the wood over the Australians after the 3–1 series victory in 1981. Although he wasn't able to prevent an under-strength touring team – a rebel tour to South Africa had restricted England's selection options – slipping to a 2–1 defeat down under in the winter of 1982–83, the return of the Australians to British shores in 1985 provided inspiration once more.

Unlike four years earlier, when he picked his own team off the floor, this was a series when Botham kept booting the Aussies when they were down. Never more emphatically than when, in the fifth Test at Edgbaston, with the scoreboard reading 572–4, he walked to the crease and pummelled the first delivery sent down by Craig McDermott into the second tier at the Pavilion End, following up with a repeat dose from his third.

England were already well on their way to a telling second win of the series courtesy of David Gower's double hundred, and three-figure contributions from Tim Robinson and Mike Gatting. Kent swing bowler Richard Ellison did the majority of the damage with the ball, both there and in the sixth Test win at The Oval, although Botham claimed three wickets in each of the final three innings of the series, to finish with 31 all told. In fact, whenever there was an Aussie ready to be chucked on the barbecue, there was Botham ready with the skewer.

Even the mere thought of facing up to them in a Test match could inspire him. Such as in 1986–87 when, after a sorry sequence of warm-up matches, including defeat to Queensland, the *Independent*'s cricket correspondent Martin Johnson summed up the problems: 'There are only three things wrong with this England team,' Johnson wrote. 'They can't bat, they can't bowl and they can't field.'

Botham rallied Mike Gatting's bunch of *can'ts* by urging them to forget what had gone and to focus on the eleven-

Don Bradman batting against Worcestershire on the Invincibles tour. Between 1928 and 1948 he amassed 5,028 Ashes runs, a record unlikely to be challenged.

England would regain the Ashes under Len Hutton, left, in 1953, but at Trent Bridge in 1948, he and fellow opener Cyril Washbrook couldn't stop Bradman's team winning by eight wickets.

Bradman's Invincibles at Worcester before the first match of the 1948 series. Back: Ian Johnson, Arthur Morris, Ernie Toshack, Keith Miller, Don Tallon, Ray Lindwall, Neil Harvey. Front: Bill Brown, Lindsay Hassett, Don Bradman, Colin McCool, Sid Barnes.

Australian fast bowler Ray Lindwall, left and right, modelled his action on Larwood. He played in four Ashes-winning sides, but in 1954–55 it was his bouncers that shook up Frank Tyson and inspired him to bowl England to their first away win for 22 years.

Australia's Brylcreem Boy Keith Miller was a key part of the team that dominated the first three post-war Ashes series. An indestructible all-rounder, he formed a rapid new-ball partnership with Ray Lindwall and made three Ashes centuries.

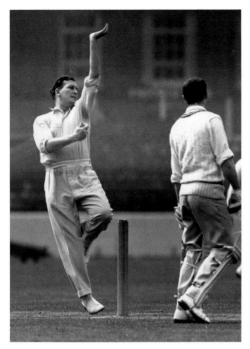

Jim Laker's 19 wickets at Old Trafford in 1956 is a record that may never be broken. But my mum got very emotional when I passed his Test wicket tally of 193 in 2012–13.

Ted Dexter shares a glass with Richie Benaud after England take a 1–0 series lead at Melbourne in 1962–63, inspired by eight wickets from Fred Trueman.

Richie Benaud, holding his Baggy Green, is clapped from the field at Old Trafford in 1961 after his six second-innings wickets won the Test and put Australia 2–1 up in the series.

Despite opening the second innings at Trent Bridge in 1964, captain Ted Dexter couldn't force a win and the Test was the first of four draws in a series England lost 1–0.

Geoff Boycott at Trent Bridge in 1977, where he returned to Test cricket after three years of self-imposed exile.

Fred Trueman, before he found true fame introducing arm-wrestling in *The Indoor League*, bowls in the 2nd Ashes Test at Lord's in 1961.

Fiery Fred, who didn't always agree with Ted Dexter's captaincy, takes the applause in the 5th Ashes Test at The Oval in 1961 after becoming the first bowler to take 300 Test wickets.

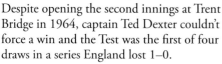

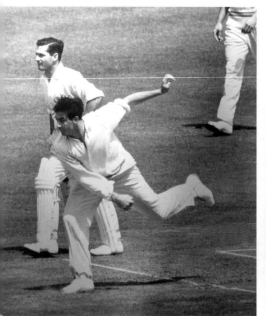

Bowling with pace and hostility, 1970s style icons Dennis Lillee, left, and Jeff Thomson, right, led the attack in one of the most exciting eras in Ashes history, one that would inspire generations of Australian cricketers.

Non-striker Tony Greig looks on as captain Mike Denness avoids a Thomson bouncer at Melbourne in 1974–75. Two of Australia's most famous 'tache-wearers, Ian Chappell at slip and wicketkeeper Rod Marsh, keep their eye on the ball.

When Kerry Packer – seen here arriving at Lord's with Richie Benaud – introduced World Series Cricket in 1977, a knock-on effect was a couple of largely forgettable Ashes series.

Colin Cowdrey, here batting for Old England in 1980, was flown in to face Lillee and Thomson in 1974–75, aged 41. He played in ten Ashes series, the first in 1954–55.

The Ashes was sparked into life again in 1981 by the heroics of Ian Botham, seen here being congratulated by Bob Taylor, captain Mike Brearley and Mike Gatting after taking the first-innings wicket of Graeme Wood in the 3rd Test at Headingley.

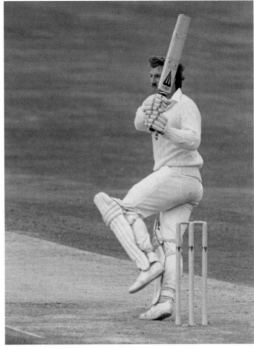

The other hero of the 1981 Headingley Test, Bob Willis, who took 8–43 in the second innings, bowling at the speed of light.

Beefy hooks a ball from Geoff Lawson during his game-changing innings of 149 not out.

The crowd takes the field to acclaim Botham as he faces the cameras after inspiring England to a memorable victory at Headingley in 1981, having been forced to follow on.

Dennis Lillee loses his cool in one of the funniest episodes you will ever see, squaring up to Javed Miandad at Perth in 1981, separated by umpire Tony Crafter.

David Gower on his way to 123 at Sydney in 1990–91. The series, which England lost 3–0, is better remembered for his antics in a biplane during a match against Queensland two weeks later.

versus-eleven battles ahead. Typically, he scored a hundred in the opening match.

Of course, he was always a man of actions rather than words, and of all his addictions it was beating Australia that proved the most powerful. Even the Aussies themselves didn't seem to mind losing if the result contained strong traces of Beef. Never was it stronger than in that joyous comeback of all comebacks in Leeds.

Date	Venue	Team	Scores	Team	Scores	Result
18/06/1981	Nottingham	England	185 & 125	Australia	179 & 132-6	Australia won by 4 wickets
02/07/1981	Lord's	England	311 & 265-8d	Australia	345 & 90-4	Drawn
16/07/1981	Leeds	Australia	401-9d & 111	England	174 & 356	England won by 18 runs
30/07/1981	Birmingham	England	189 & 219	Australia	258 & 121	England won by 29 runs
13/08/1981	Manchester	England	231 & 404	Australia	130 & 402	England won by 103 runs
27/08/1981	The Oval	Australia	352 & 344-9d	England	314 & 261-7	Drawn
12/11/1982	Perth	England	411 & 358	Australia	424-9d & 73-2	Drawn
26/11/1982	Brisbane	England	219 & 309	Australia	341 & 190-3	Australia won by 7 wickets
10/12/1982	Adelaide	Australia	438 & 83-2	England	216 & 304	Australia won by 8 wickets
26/12/1982	Melbourne	England	284 & 294	Australia	287 & 288	England won by 3 runs
02/01/1983	Sydney	Australia	314 & 382	England	237 & 314-7	Drawn
13/06/1985	Leeds	Australia	331 & 324	England	533 & 123-5	England won by 5 wickets
27/06/1985	Lord's	England	290 & 261	Australia	425 & 127-6	Australia won by 4 wickets
11/07/1985	Nottingham	England	456 & 196-2	Australia	539	Drawn
01/08/1985	Manchester	Australia	257 & 340-5	England	482-9d	Drawn
15/08/1985	Birmingham	Australia	335 & 142	England	595-5d	England won by an innings and 118 runs
29/08/1985	The Oval	England	464	Australia	241 & 129	England won by an innings and 94 runs
14/11/1986	Brisbane	England	456 & 77-3	Australia	248 & 282	England won by 7 wickets
28/11/1986	Perth	England	592-8d & 199-8d	Australia	401 & 197-4	Drawn
12/12/1986	Adelaide	Australia	514-5d & 201-3d	England	455 & 39-2	Drawn
26/12/1986	Melbourne	Australia	141 & 194	England	349	England won by an innings and 14 runs
10/01/1987	Sydney	Australia	343 & 251	England	275 & 264	Australia won by 55 runs

10

GOOCH'S MAGNETIC PADS

B Y 1989 I was hooked on England–Australia matches. That summer I was prepared, like everyone else, for another England win. England were going to walk the Ashes this time because this was clearly the weakest Australian team ever. Never had a worse one departed from their shores and the result was a formality. Or at least that is what the media, and the bookmakers for that matter, led us to believe.

Australia were rank outsiders at 11–4 to win the first Test, and these days you might have got even more generous odds. They had next to no chance. Everyone knew it. Only, it turned out everyone was wrong.

You see, there was this bloke called Steve Waugh. Not the Steve Waugh that had played in 1986–87, mind. Nah, this was an upgraded version who simply churned out runs for fun while masticating furiously. The image of the summer was Waugh, with chewing gum whirling around his mouth, propped up on his bat handle at the end of yet another fruitless over for an England bowler. Such was the ease with which he played that he wasn't actually dismissed until the third Test. It was a monumental moment when the 585th delivery he'd faced that series burst through him, to strike the stumps and give the debutant Angus Fraser a maiden Test wicket.

Fraser was one of 29 England players selected to face Australia across six matches, a tally second only to the 30 they used in the five-match campaign of 1921. Continuity of selection is always preferable if possible. That it wasn't in 1989, however, was partly the result of an horrendous injury record. Each of the six squads selected had to be altered on the eve of the respective matches due to one ailment or another. Then, at the end of the summer, the rebel South Africa tour limited the number of available players.

By the end of the campaign, the fast-bowling resources had been stretched to their limit. Having started in Leeds with one county stalwart, Phil Newport, in the XI, and gone through a list including Fraser, Phil DeFreitas and Greg Thomas, England finished at The Oval with another, in Alan Igglesden, who was summoned 24 hours before the start of the match. The England team manager Micky Stewart tried to put this hurried call-up into some sort of context by telling reporters Igglesden was their 17th-choice seamer. Just the kind of confidence-boost you need when facing an Australian team 4–0 up and baying for blood, eh?

Not that it was the only faux pas when it came to the pacemen. Good old Ted Dexter, the newly appointed chairman of selectors, was renowned for gaffes during his time in office. None compared to the one he made at Trent Bridge 1989, though, when attempting to sift through the wreckage of an innings defeat for some positives.

'Who can forget Malcolm Devon?'

You just couldn't make it up.

Mistakes littered the performances too. The first – in the first Test – was arguably excusable. Win the toss at Headingley? Bowl, right? A no-brainer, one would think. Surely no England captain could be blamed for inserting the opposition at such a bowler-friendly ground? Except that the groundsman, Keith Boyce, had recently relaid the pitch and recommended batting first to David Gower, returning as captain four years after defeating the Australians 3–1 on home soil.

But when one of the plethora of weird and wonderful coins Gower took with him to the middle for the toss – including a French franc and a threepenny bit – landed his way up following Allan Border's wrong call, he opted to bowl in the belief that the swinging ball would do for the Aussies just as it had done in the tour-match defeat versus Worcestershire at New Road. Only problem was it was too cold to swing. And it didn't seam, either.

In those days Headingley nibbled about all day, producing regular positive results, and Tests there tended to feature the selection of horses-for-courses seamers who were taking wickets in county cricket. Newport had taken 10 wickets in the loss that Worcestershire inflicted on the Australians, making the best possible use of the pronounced seam on the Readers ball. Gower's second wrong call then, in one of his most affable moments, was to acquiesce to Border's request to play with the more batsman-friendly Dukes.

Australia had a pretty poor record coming into this particular series, winning just five of their previous 30 Tests, with recent losses against Pakistan and West Indies. What might have been overlooked, however, was the fact that another team in world cricket had an inferior record: England. They had won just three of 34, and so if the Australians were going to turn things around, Mr Hindsight would tell you this was the perfect opportunity to do so.

With Newport neutered and aerial movement conspicuous by its absence, the Australians feasted on a one-dimensional attack. John Emburey, a team-mate of mine on my Northamptonshire debut, had been left out on reputation – that of Leeds, not his. Newport, debuting as the biggest swinger in town, was not seen again in the remaining five Tests of the series.

In contrast, Australia possessed the series' trump card. Of the 41 wickets Terry Alderman took, 19 of them were lbw. He used to tiptoe up to the crease, a bit like a kid trying to sneak past his mum and dad's bedroom first thing in the morning to get a sneak peak of *Going Live!*, then slip in close to the stumps, releasing the ball, seam proud, from in front of the umpire's eyes.

This wicket-to-wicket tactic allowed the umpires to watch the trajectory of the ball all the way down the pitch. They had the best seat in the house to see its journey from A to B. A being Alderman's right hand; B, Graham Gooch's front pad. The Stuart Surridge pads in question were a one-piece affair with an unusual all-in-one knee roll attached. Somewhere behind them there appeared to be a leather magnet, because whenever Gooch pulled them on, Alderman would locate them. England's best batsman lasted four Tests before being dispatched back to find county form with Essex, returning for the finale at The Oval.

Undoubtedly, Gooch's troubles were part of the problem for England, but nor could the selectors unearth anyone to score runs at the other end. Across the six Tests, England used six different opening batsmen and the constant search for fresh blood was exaggerated because of Mike Gatting's rebel South African tour, the players for which were selected at the back end of summer.

The lack of continuity could hardly be blamed for the overall result, because the series had already been conceded by the fifth Test of six. But all this gave an opportunity to David Capel, and as a Northamptonshire supporter I naturally viewed him as England's saviour – a theory enhanced when he walked in to bat for the first time. My reaction would have been the common one throughout Northampton when he hit Alderman for four first ball: 'See, that's how you do it.' Unfortunately, he was out to his third, to that epidemic – the Alderman leg-before.

These Australians were pretty cool in their baggy, cable-knit woollen jumpers with the big 'V' around the neckline. Not that they particularly needed them. It was one of the hottest, driest summers in memory, and proved to be a great one not only for Steve Waugh, but also for another of Australia's future captains, Mark Taylor.

For a few years, Allan Border's team had featured David Boon and Geoff Marsh as openers, but Bobby Simpson, the Australian coach, believed in Taylor's ability to bat long periods and was influential in pairing him with Marsh once the Texaco Trophy one-day series – which England claimed by losing fewer wickets in the tied middle match – was over, shifting Boon down a spot to number three.

Australia's new opening partnership was a dogged one and as time passed England increasingly struggled to separate them. The recall of Taylor following a couple of failed previous appearances also provided Australia with a left/right combination at the top of the order. They got better as the matches went on, peaking in the fifth Test at Trent Bridge, where they were inseparable throughout the entire first day. Their 329-run stand surpassed the previous record opening stand of 323 by Jack Hobbs and Wilfred Rhodes in Melbourne in 1911–12. Taylor, who contributed a half-century in every single match, amassed 839 runs in all, second only to the great Sir Donald Bradman's tally of 974 in 1930.

Even though it was a pretty hot summer, Australian spin was rarely seen, with all but 11 of the 103 wickets claimed going to the seamers; the Australians barely allowed the shine to go off the ball, keeping the sweets in their pocket the whole time. Trevor Hohns, Australia's leg-spinner, was not required to make much of an impact but was always tidy enough when he did get the chance, and he was occasionally given a helping hand by the English batsmen. Never more so than in the fourth Test at Old Trafford when Ian Botham, dressed like a *Star Wars* stormtrooper in his white helmet, ran down the pitch and aimed a huge swipe at a regulation leggie – he'd have been stumped by a mile if the ball hadn't cleaned up his off stump.

The statistics summed up the differences between the sides perfectly. While Alderman ran amok with 41 wickets, backed up by Lawson's contribution of 29, Neil Foster, England's leading bowler, managed just 12. Australia won the series 4–0, but it could so easily have been a whitewash, with rain reducing the Edgbaston Test by 10 hours and bad light intervening at The Oval.

Australia even produced impressive returns when it came to extracurricular activities. Even before a half-century on the field, David Boon had raised his metaphorical bat at 30,000 feet, after downing 52 cans of Castlemaine XXXX on the inbound flight, surpassing the previous high of 44 held by Rod Marsh (although I have heard it first hand from Rod that he carried on drinking cans that weren't counted on the stopovers). He was comatose for the next 48 hours and got a ticking-off from the tourists' management, but as statements of intent go it was pretty impressive.

This was the first series I sat through from start to finish. Although I had watched the 1986–87 series in Australia, that Ashes seemed like a lifetime ago when I switched on the TV to watch the matches live on the BBC in my living room. Because I was a bit older, I got it more, and I watched it all day long. Unfortunately, my devotion coincided with the start of complete Australian domination. For the next decade and a half we barely won a Test match, let alone fought for a series, and it took some bloke called Fred to come along and bowl the over of the century to change everything.

Through the second half of the 1980s the England captaincy had turned into a bit of a pass-the-parcel affair, with David Gower and Mike Gatting handing it off to each other. If one of them was not in possession, the other was, and Gower was brought back into the leadership role in 1989 to inspire memories of 1985, no doubt, following Gatting's vetoing for this particular summer. With misdemeanours involving Pakistani umpire Shakoor Rana and allegations (denied by Gatting) of a dalliance with a Nottingham barmaid appearing in the tabloids good old Gatt was not keeping up the desired image of the gentleman captain. Gower, on the other hand, had the perfect characteristics: privately educated, he still batted with the freedom of the public schoolboy and also enjoyed the right after-hours pursuits – annulling the post-play press conference at Lord's to hot-foot it across London to see the musical *Anything Goes* was the *pièce de résistance* for me.

It was Gower's actions away from the field of play that were the memorable feature of the 1990–91 tour of Australia, too. England were 2–0 down with two to play when, during a match against Queensland on the Gold Coast, he and fellow England batsman John Morris sneaked out to the nearby airfield and persuaded some pilots to fly a couple of Tiger Moth planes over the ground in celebration of a Robin Smith hundred.

It caused a furore, not least because they were playing in the match at the time, but I suppose you can guess my take on it. The jeopardy of leaving the ground, with even a minimal threat of not getting back in time for when you are fielding, brings a huge smile to my face. The positive effects such a stunt might have on morale far outweigh the magnitude of the crime. Quite frankly, if I had been in that England dressing room I would have found it flippin' hilarious.

Once again, England were not enjoying the best of series, the Ashes had eluded their grasp and the best they could hope for was a 2–2 draw. If anyone could get away with a prank, however, it was arguably Gower, whose superb personal form had seen him record hundreds in both the second and third Tests. Against Queensland, the tourists were also on their way to their only first-class victory of the trip when, shortly before lunch on the third day, Morris, whose opportunities had been limited, completed a hundred, then got out, not long after Gower's dismissal.

At the interval, Gower mentioned to Allan Lamb and Robin Smith that he fancied a flight in one of the planes that they had seen skirting the Carrara Oval throughout the preceding days, and Morris, who overheard, was keen to be in on any excursion. Gower knew Graham Gooch, who had been made England captain after Gower's resignation in 1989, would put the kibosh on the plans if he got word, and so this particular discussion remained a clandestine one.

The Tiger Moths were supposed to fly above 2,000 feet, but with some persuasion from Gower, the pilots dipped to nearer 200 feet moments after Smith completed his own hundred. Smith's partner Lamb, in the know, playfully pretended to shoot them down with his bat.

Not many others knew the identity of the passengers in these biplanes, but one of the pilots had tipped off the press (there were even a couple of publicity shots taken later), so that soon changed. By the time they returned to the ground, a reception committee had formed and Gooch asked them directly on their return to the dressing room whether they were the magnificent men in those flying machines.

'Who, me? Heavens, no,' came Gower's reply.

Perhaps it was a good thing that the original idea for them to drop water balloons and bomb the pitch did not come to fruition. Clearly, some of the other players were involved and were looking out for them getting near to the ground – it's very hard to distinguish someone's face when they are sitting in a Tiger Moth. It was 100 per cent the kind of prank to bring a team together when you are losing.

What made it even better was that Graham Gooch, a man without a particularly large sense of humour, was captain. He would not have enjoyed it at all. Nor would coach Micky Stewart, a stickler for the rules and regulations, or tour manager Peter Lush have seen the funny side of things. It was so English, so eccentrically stupid. The Tiger Two must have known they were heading for hot water.

It might be said that the team management had the last laugh, fining Gower £1,000. Lush issued a statement branding the episode 'immature, ill-judged and ill-timed'. It's an incident that stands out from that tour, but there was another one on the field to rival it – one that summed up David Gower's career in Test cricket. And it was just around the corner, in the penultimate match of the 1990–91 Ashes, the fourth Test at Adelaide.

At that time, Gooch and Gower represented the two very different directions English cricket could take. Gower was descended from the gentry, his distant relations being the Leveson-Gower family, the Dukes of Sutherland. He was the most laid-back, beautiful-looking batsman in the world, someone who played the game in a debonair manner and with a devil-may-care attitude. He had a laissez-faire outlook on preparation too, believing that training was very much an optional choice and not one he would generally plump for.

Gooch was the antithesis of this, someone who eschewed the opportunity to make strokes from the MCC coaching manual look beautiful, relying primarily on drilling his game and getting physically prepared for the gruelling demands of a five-day Test match. I am not sure that Ian Botham was on Team Gooch either when it came to this obsession with fitness. Beefy was very much sex-and-drugs-and-rock-'n'-roll in all aspects of life, and there were no separate rules for cricket.

The straw that broke the camel's back came with Gooch and Gower at the crease late on the third morning at Adelaide. Because they were on the verge of the lunch interval, the Australians set up an elaborate plan to get into Gower's mind, posting a deep square leg about 20 yards off the boundary rope. Craig McDermott persisted with a line outside leg stump and was taken for runs on a couple of occasions. So he probably couldn't believe his luck when, as casually as you like, Gower flicked the final ball of the session nonchalantly off his hip, straight into Merv Hughes's hands.

At the other end, Gooch's face was a picture. It said: 'Enough is enough.' Gower journeyed on to New Zealand later that winter, as planned, but was overlooked the following summer and bowed out of international cricket, following a fleeting comeback of three appearances against Pakistan, towards the end of the 1992 season.

For the next decade, you could argue that England lacked the unorthodox type of cricketer that Gower represented.

Until Andrew Flintoff arrived to buck the trend, and challenge the rules, everyone fell into line and did what they were instructed to do. There were no off-the-cuff cricketers coming through and prospering at international level, yet supporters like me were desperate for a maverick, a free spirit – someone they could relate to. Although Gower was not a man of the people, he was still very English, and he appealed to me because of his ambivalence towards authority. He spurned defensive play whenever possible, preferring to take on the attacking option whenever he could, and that was a sure way to get younger generations interested in the game.

Not that Gooch's methods were wholly wrong. For example, both he and Gower happened to do well in that 1990–91 series, with their contrasting individual styles. They were two of the three men to manage 400 runs in the series – David Boon, of Australia, the other. What that showed was that contrasting methods can work, and personal choice rather than autonomous instruction is the way to go. You can't force a uniform way of playing onto an entire team.

What that team was crying out for, in my opinion, was a top man-manager: a Mike Brearley, an Andrew Strauss or, perhaps the best of the lot, Michael Vaughan. Imagine David Gower playing under the leadership of Vaughan. He would have been prolific. Vaughan's great strength was to liberate his players from any concerns, from worrying about the consequences, and Gower's only instruction would have been to express himself. He would never have taken a leak in the garden at Downing Street, mind, because, with his connections, he would have been at Buckingham Palace, having a cup of tea with the Queen instead.

One of Australia's cricketing royalty was dethroned for that Adelaide Test in 1990–91: Steve Waugh was dropped after 42 consecutive matches, and to add insult it was his twin brother, Mark, who replaced him, scoring a hundred to boot. The fact they could do this just emphasised what rich resources Australia possessed at the start of the 1990s.

In contrast, just as in the 1989 series, England players dropped like proverbial flies. Some of the injuries were a bit weird too. Gooch suffered from a poisoned finger which kept him out of the first Test and so Allan Lamb captained the team. That would have been quite a contrast in styles, you would have thought. I can just imagine him starting his team talk with a 'Hey, hey, hey, boys.'

Other things were occupying my mind at this stage of life, particularly Louise Jenkins and Penny Anderson, my classmates in 1BJ at Sponne School. And there were distractions aplenty for a posse of England players who were easily distracted. Lamb, captain for the first Test, was asked along with Gower to go to the casino by Kerry Packer mid-match despite it being more than 50 miles away. Who were they to turn him down? I know I would have gone. But you can also imagine that kind of behaviour getting back to those in charge, who would be appalled.

This post-match behaviour was fairly typical when it came to county cricket, though. At that time, if you got in before midnight you were quite obviously ill or 99 not out overnight. Come on. If Kerry Packer asks you in his brusque Australian manner: 'Hey, boys, fancy a night at the casino?' of course you are going to go. That's just too much to resist. Although Lamb insisted he was in bed before the clock struck twelve, it was not enough to avoid a reprimand.

Rather like Gower, who top-scored in both innings of a low-scoring defeat in the first Test at Brisbane, Lamb was able to deliver high-class innings at the drop of a hat, and the 140 he made in three hours in a tour match at Ballarat was an example of this. His decision to run back to the hotel after play, however, was not so clever. He damaged his calf, a recurring injury he first suffered in similar circumstances on a tour of the Caribbean. It just shows that when you're doing well, scoring runs, trying to go the extra mile to impress the captain and coach is a game for mugs. That's a time to have a beer to toast your success, followed by a few more beers back at the team hotel.

I confess I tried this ridiculous practice once, on the 2008–09 tour of the Caribbean, before I was assured of my place in the England team. It was in Antigua in what turned out to be the lead-up week to my Test recall. Having been overlooked for the second Test at the Sir Vivian Richards Stadium – Andrew Strauss and Andy Flower, the interim captain and coach respectively, opted for Monty Panesar as the sole spinner – I was so hacked off that I ran back on the final practice day. All I can say is that I clearly wasn't thinking straight, as it is not something I would have done before, and certainly not something I did afterwards. When that match was abandoned after half an hour due to the poor quality of the run-ups, I came into the reckoning for the replacement match at St John's, took some wickets and didn't look back.

Phil Tufnell, one of my predecessors as an England spin bowler, and now a dear colleague on *Test Match Special*, was a member of the 1990–91 bowling attack, although this was the tour in which he became more famous for his fielding. It was so bad that the Australian supporters were all over him like a rash. Unfortunately, he had a tendency to draw attention to himself with his escapades. Never more so than when he missed a run-out in a one-day international at Sydney, the easiest run-out ever.

You would think the safest place he could be, given his lack of prowess in the outer, would be at the bowling crease. But he spectacularly disproved this theory when, with the Australians 88–4, Mark Waugh cut one of his deliveries to point. Cue brotherly misunderstanding as Steve Waugh hurtled down the pitch for a single. With Junior unmoved, the senior twin had given himself up more than halfway down when Tufnell fumbled the gentle lob to him at the bowler's end. The throw couldn't have had a better trajectory, passing as it did directly over the top of the bails. However, the Cat didn't just fluff the catch, he somehow produced a full knock-on that would have left Eddie Waring, the most sympathetic of commentators, speechless. Even then there was still time to recover. Yet in his panic, he retrieved the ball and hurled it past the now unguarded stumps, allowing Waugh to jog back into his ground.

Of course, Tuffers guaranteed himself a world of hell every time he crossed that white line in England–Australia matches thereafter, attracting plenty of abuse and some interesting sledges. In those days the Aussies liked their barbs to extend to the written word, holding up placards to make sure their messages hit home, with lines like 'Hey, Tufnell, lend me your brain. We're building an idiot.' According to his accounts, even the home umpires began sledging him. Bless the Cat, I absolutely adore him.

Date	Venue	Team	Scores	Team	Scores	Result
08/06/1989	Leeds	Australia	601-7d & 230-3d	England	430 & 191	Australia won by 210 runs
22/06/1989	Lord's	England	286 & 359	Australia	528 & 119-4	Australia won by 6 wickets
06/07/1989	Birmingham	Australia	424 & 158-2	England	242	Drawn
27/07/1989	Manchester	England	260 & 264	Australia	447 & 81-1	Australia won by 9 wickets
10/08/1989	Nottingham	Australia	602-6d	England	255 & 167	Australia won by an innings and 180 runs
24/08/1989	The Oval	Australia	468 & 219-4d	England	285 & 143-5	Drawn
23/11/1990	Brisbane	England	194 & 114	Australia	152 & 157-0	Australia won by 10 wickets
26/12/1990	Melbourne	England	352 & 150	Australia	306 & 197-2	Australia won by 8 wickets
04/01/1991	Sydney	Australia	518 & 205	England	469-8d & 113-4	Drawn
25/01/1991	Adelaide	Australia	386 & 314-6d	England	229 & 335-5	Drawn
01/02/1991	Perth	England	244 & 182	Australia	307 & 120-1	Australia won by 9 wickets

11

THAT DELIVERY

F EW Englishmen had seen him bowl previously but none
of us who witnessed Shane Warne's first ball in Ashes
cricket will ever forget it. It was one of the defining moments
not only of Ashes battles but of the sport of cricket itself.

Those who had been privileged enough to watch Warne
beforehand arguably had not necessarily seen the real deal in
action. Australia held him back at the start of the summer
of 1993 to the extent that, even in the warm-up games, the
touring captain Mark Taylor urged him not to bowl his big
leg-spinners as they didn't want to give the game away.

It was said that he bowled for rhythm and rolled out a
few gentle leggies but never gave it a real rip. Taylor knew
he had a miracle worker when it came to this peroxide-haired,
junk-food loving, spin-bowling genius. But at that stage Tubby
preferred him to draw attention for what was in his barnet,
not in his hand.

When bowlers make their first international appearances in England you generally know what to expect. But at this stage of his career Warne was not really rated back home. His 11 previous Test appearances had yielded a couple of decent performances, although there were grumblings after he started with a single wicket in his first two against India.

But the delivery to Mike Gatting in Manchester on 3 June 1993 was cricket's JFK moment. Everyone knows where they were. It was the school holidays and I was down the cricket club with my dad, watching the match with his Northampton Saints team-mates. I remember it not looking like a great day for spinners. It was a bit overcast, a bit miserable, cold and drizzly. A day for the seamers if ever there was one.

On his approach to the crease, the screwed-up face suggested he was walking into a strong wind. But then he unleashed this unbelievable, heat-seeking fizzer that pitched outside leg, gripped on the pitch and spun back and hit the top of off stump. As Martin Johnson, in the *Independent*, wrote: 'How anyone can spin the ball the width of Mike Gatting boggles the mind.'

Gatt was a fine player of spin and his look just said: 'I don't believe it.' It was like a meteor hitting the world. Warne had arrived.

Imagine if that ball had been dragged down, landing halfway down the track, and been pulled for four. Would Shane Warne have been the Shane Warne we came to know? Undoubtedly he would have, because he had such supreme talent, and it wouldn't have changed him or his attitude towards the game, I am convinced of that. But that first ball in Ashes cricket began his legend, creating some of the mystique he would live off for eight Ashes series. He produced *the* most unplayable ball to England's best player of spin. I was mesmerised by Shayne Warne from the get-go.

I cannot recall ever seeing him bowl badly, and I can only remember two people getting on top of him consistently. Brian Lara, of the West Indies, refused to be bowled at by him and really took him to town, to the extent that Warne always had to be on top of his game against him to get him out. The other one was V.V.S. Laxman, most memorably in the match in which India were asked to follow on at Kolkata in 2001. Laxman scored 281, one of the six Test hundreds he reserved for Australia. None of the other five could match the majesty of this one. He repeatedly hit Warne over extra cover for four via lofted drives, which were unbelievably ambitious and courageous shots in the circumstances.

Warne took 708 Test wickets across 15 years and in all that time he never bowled full tosses or long hops. Or at least if he did they were always sent down in isolation. Even one of the long hops that he did bowl, he reckoned he sent down on purpose. It turned out that he had set a trap for Alec Stewart during the 1994–95 Ashes, dragging one down for him to hit for four, just so he could bring out the flipper to full effect in the following over. With that pre-planning, he made one of England's most prolific players look like a mug.

Warne is quite simply the best bowler to have played international cricket, not just Ashes cricket. The Australian selectors obviously knew they had a diamond in their midst and their captain Mark Taylor would have known what a weapon his team possessed just from facing him in the nets. Keeping him under the radar couldn't happen these days, not with the saturated 24-hour media coverage that we have. Someone somewhere would have picked up on the fact that this guy was a freak when it came to the art of leg-spin. There would be footage all over social media.

A quarter of a century ago there was not, and how could the England batsmen be anything but cautious against him after his grand entrance at Old Trafford? Spin bowling is all about getting revolutions on the ball. Like hitting a table-tennis ball, or slicing a second serve, the more topspin or side-spin you put on the ball, the more it swerves in the air. In this instance, Warne spun the ball so bloody hard that it swerved and dipped below Gatting's eyeline to land outside leg stump before redirecting off the pitch. That's why kids like me were transfixed.

From a spin perspective, leg-spin is nigh-on impossible to teach. You can either get the rotations on the ball through the use of your wrist or you can't, and the control required to produce the Gatting dismissal is ridiculous. Don't ask me why it is harder to get more spin on the ball as a wrist-spinner than a finger-spinner. It just is. It's why leggies are such precious commodities. Scientists may come up with evidence to disregard this theory, arguing that technically it is not any different, but, speaking as a practitioner, to turn your hand the other way and release the ball backwards out of it is unnatural.

Yet Warne definitely had an effect on me. Although I couldn't bowl leg-spin, I wanted to rip the ball as hard as I could to emulate him. He was a breath of fresh air because the best spinners in the world at that time weren't massive turners of the ball. They might have got more wickets than their contemporaries, and in all probability that would have been because they turned the ball more, but they weren't bowlers who would go down in history for producing huge turning deliveries. Three times that series, Warne claimed wickets with ones that spun 18 inches, starting with his Gatting ball.

Tim May, the guy at the other end to Warne, was as much a hero to me primarily due to the fact he bowled off-spin, the same as me, but also because he didn't look like an international cricketer at all, and that held a special appeal. He looked like the guys that Dad played club cricket with at weekends, and he bowled with a permanent grimace on his face, as if he was taking part in the Southern Hemisphere Gurning Championships.

Subsequently, I found out that the facial expressions were nothing to do with this, or constipation, or a tic. He was pulling them because of the massive hole in his finger that bowling off-spin in England at that time created. The Dukes ball, when it got wet, caused serious damage to your hand if you were trying to grip it across the seam because of its coarse nature, and I was learning this concurrently, suffering bloody fingers whenever I bowled.

May proved influential in my career in this regard, because the 14-year-old me saw that if the best off-spinner in the world was suffering like me, that was all right, and I had to just get on with releasing the ball off my knuckles. Otherwise, I might have been convinced by the all-knowing coaches armed with their MCC manuals that it was because I held the ball wrong, and that I ought to try going back to the 'holding the doorknob' technique, whereby you turn the ball in a similar manner to opening a door.

So between them, Warne and May did more for me than just about anyone else through my adolescent cricket. Warne for his ability to spin the ball so far, and May for his will-ingness to keep ripping it as hard as he possibly could. They also worked together effectively in tandem, complementing each other perfectly, as spinners who turn the ball in opposing directions often do. It was similar to when I played alongside Monty Panesar for England. One of us spun it in to the bat, the other took it away, and so we were asking different ques-tions from each end.

As a teenager I couldn't have been more inspired by these two Australians, and if you had paused things there and then patriotism would have gone out of the window. At that stage I would rather have played for Australia than England. I had yet to learn the words of 'Land of Hope and Glory' off by heart, and knew little of The Dam Busters, so I simply favoured the team that had the best spinners.

Warne, this bleach-blond, redneck surfer kid straight off St Kilda Beach, could not have been more Australian if he tried. The hairstyle, the name, the sunblock smeared across his cheeks. But Australia also possessed the biggest on-field character of the age in Merv Hughes, who stepped up from support act to take the new ball and lead the attack when Craig McDermott, so often the scourge of England in the past, succumbed to a twisted bowel that ruled him out of the series. It was telling that the Australians were so confident in the understudies in their bowling attack that they didn't bother to call up a replacement despite the loss being inflicted early on tour.

Hughes was a huge unit, yet when he ran up to bowl he almost skipped across the turf, like a cartoon cat chasing a mouse. He was a walking juxtaposition: comical one moment, ferocious the next. The rage that usually consumed him immediately after he had hurtled down a delivery increased threefold when Graeme Hick walked in to bat. And the comical Wyatt Earp facial growth just added to his persona.

Around that time we got a family cat. Originally I wanted to call him 'Merv' in the big guy's honour, but when the cat was delivered, he was tiny and jet black, so I had to name him after one of my other global cricket heroes, Gus Logie. I told Merv this years later at an after-dinner speaking engagement and he just laughed: 'So what you're telling me is that you preferred Gus Logie to Merv Hughes? Good man.'

A pretty tame response in comparison to his on-field comebacks such as 'Turn the bat around, the instructions are on the back'. Or my personal favourite, delivered to Pakistan's Javed Miandad, who had said: 'You're too fat to be a bowler – you should be a bus driver.' When Javed nicked off soon afterwards, big Merv eschewed the team huddle, ran to the picket fence that circled the perimeter, held the gate open for Javed, put out his hand and said: 'Tickets please, mate'.

Merv has always been an affable bloke away from the field but on it this competitive beast came into his own. Iced up, and wrapped up in preparation to play – it looked like he was held together by bandages whenever he rolled up his trouser legs – he sent down an average of 60 overs a Test in 1993. Anti-inflammatories got him to the finish line, but he literally gave his all before his knee gave up, and the pounding his body took ended his international career.

Hughes also came close to ending the career of Hick, as the chief exponent of Australia's mental-disintegration policy. As the Aussies' sledger-in-chief, his moustache could be seen tickling the back of Hick's neck, laced with poisonous jibes, on several occasions as he ensured the verbals reached their intended target. The Australians chipped away at Hick's confidence, and he struggled to cope, experiencing the axe before a triumphant recall at The Oval, where he struck 80 in the first innings and England defeated Australia for the first time since December 1986.

Everyone around the country could feel the pressure on Graeme that year, because he remained the hot young thing of English cricket. Things had not begun well as an international batsman, in the face of a West Indies bombardment two years previously, although the maiden hundred off India in Mumbai earlier in 1993 suggested he was ready to return the dividends people anticipated.

This was the guy who had plundered batting records for Worcestershire during his seven years of qualification, including 405 in one innings versus Somerset in 1988. West Indies' tactic was to bomb the living daylights out of him in his debut series, and Australia, or more accurately Hughes, just carried on where they left off, targeting him as England's best player.

The expectation on Hick to do well was incredible and not something you could imagine these days. His reputation had gone before him from the moment he arrived in the UK from Zimbabwe as a teen. Here was someone who was dominating county cricket and who was expected to transfer that onto the international stage. He was going to change the game with the numbers he could produce. But delivering on that kind of potential is a different thing altogether.

Coping with this kind of situation brings its own challenges. When Hick qualified, it was anticipated that he wouldn't be the best player in England any longer; he would be the best player in the world. People truly believed that this would be the case. But just like another England batsman touted for greatness, Mark Ramprakash, Hick fell into the trap of believing Test cricket was a lot more difficult than it actually was. He really built up the challenge of facing the best bowlers in the world, questioning whether he was up to it. Half of the battle is accepting you are good enough – because if you weren't you wouldn't have been selected in the first place. It meant he never possessed the self-belief to score the number of runs his ability suggested.

Australia made sure he got extra attention, chiefly because they were scared of the damage he could inflict. Allan Border would signal for Hughes every time he came to the crease – 'Because Graeme had such fantastic ability, we would test him in other ways,' Hughes himself later said. Following three dismissals to the hirsute fast bowler came confirmation that the mental battle had been won: Hick was dropped after the second Test.

Hick ended up with a perfectly acceptable Test record for the age in which he played, but when you study how good he was, and I know this from bowling at him in county cricket, a mark of 31.32 was not his ceiling. He really should have averaged over 60; he was that good. Equally, I got him out a few times because, despite having such a solid all-round game, he wasn't the greatest player of spin bowling. Or at least he wasn't the greatest player of spin bowling when he was trying to bat properly. Whenever he wanted to smack a bowler around, regardless of their style, he could do it, hitting wherever he wanted, whenever he wanted. But when the ball started turning, he would consign the attacking shots to the locker, bat properly and treat the challenge like a Test match, transforming the balance of the contest comprehensively.

Speaking as a spinner, I always saw this regression into his shell as a chance to get him out. It is not that he had a particularly bad technique, far from it, but if you are good enough as a batsman you never allow the bowler to bowl at you. You try to smack them everywhere and push them onto the back foot. From a bowler's perspective, you always fancy getting players out if the ball's turning, and when the batsman starts giving you more respect than is due, that's when you're most likely to do so.

If only Hick had been able to replicate the general attitude he applied towards batting for Worcestershire. At times he would look impregnable with the Three Pears on his chest; shame the same was not said often enough when it was Three Lions. He touched genius at times but, like Ramprakash, could not transfer that performance to the top level.

Ramps was so intense, it did him few favours. He put Test cricket on a pedestal, when going the other way might have been a more successful approach for him. The biggest secret

I ever cracked was that Test cricket was a lot easier than any other level you played at. It was a lot easier than anyone ever publicly made out.

If you use the pressure and play with it, you can turn it to your advantage. Cricket is always a one-on-one contest between the best batsman and the best bowler on opposing teams. And I always liked the percentage of winning that challenge. The negative way of looking at this is that you are up against the toughest possible opponent.

I am sure if those two had their time again, using a decent psychologist, they would double the amount of runs that they scored. In a way, the fact they went on to become very good coaches emphasises the point. They were such good technicians, able to understand the art of batsmanship, but ultimately they could not reach the mental place required to succeed. As coaches they would be great because it is not them that has to go out and deliver, and that was what they couldn't always implement.

It has been a long-term Australian tactic to attempt to undermine the biggest threats amongst opponents, often targeting captains. The theory is that if the best are taken down, others will meekly follow. Phil Tufnell tells a good story about Ramps back in the 2001 series that shows how they like to get into a player's head space.

Bizarrely, during the 1998–99 tour of Australia, Ramps made four scores of 14 during the Test series, including the final three innings in Melbourne and Sydney. (This trio came immediately after an unbeaten 47 and three consecutive fifties, scores that showed he *could* succeed against them.) So when, upon his England recall in 2001, he made it four in a row, and then five out of six, with a pair of 14s in the first innings of Tests at Lord's and Trent Bridge, the Australians were reaching his ear from all parts. 'Let's make it six,' and 'Get your money on number 14,' the close fielders chorused. He got past the mark this time. But only just, and then he gave it away with an uncharacteristic heave at Warne.

This highlighted the kind of psychological hold Australians had on Englishmen during the 1990s, so it was so refreshing to witness the emergence of Darren Gough on the 1994–95 tour. Unfortunately, he broke his foot in the new year and had to come home, but with his up-and-at-'em attitude, and 20 wickets in three appearances, he showed others the way to go.

Goughie did not give a toss who he was up against, and cared little for the reputations of the Australians. Here was an example of someone who had the right attitude towards playing Ashes cricket, and he was one of the major signs that we might finally be constructing a team that could compete and take them on. Even the Australian crowds took to him. They always did respect the opposition player that stood out in a losing cause.

Unfortunately, though, it was offset by some of the other picks by Ray Illingworth, now chairman of selectors. The final act of his predecessor, Ted Dexter, towards the back end of the 1993 series was to appoint Mike Atherton as captain. England then won the final Test of 1993 at The Oval, their first against Australia since December 1986, and it was supposed to signal a new dawn.

Aside from Gough there were no other shining lights in 1994–95. We didn't have a charismatic spinner of our own to take on Shane Warne, who claimed eight-for in the second innings to wrap up victory in the first Test in Brisbane and a hat-trick in Melbourne, while in the batting we had two golden oldies. Graham Gooch was 41 and Mike Gatting 37.

Gatt was rather portly at this stage of his career but was still deemed to be amongst the best batsmen in the country, playing in his fifth Ashes series. He scored a hundred in the fourth Test at the Adelaide Oval, a real painstaking effort compared to the ones he used to score.

The 1994–95 series really belonged to Craig McDermott, who teamed up with a relatively fresh-faced Glenn McGrath for the final innings of the series as England were blown away at Perth for 123, and Australia wrapped up a 3–1 win. McDermott bowed out of Ashes affairs with 32 wickets at 21 runs apiece, yet his impact was small fry compared to what Warne and McGrath would go on to achieve together.

This was an Australian team that was moving on, consigning their predecessors well and truly to another era. In Michael Slater they possessed a batsman for the modern age too. One who played totally on instinct. Before him, David Boon and Geoff Marsh had been quite stoic at the top of the order, as had his captain, Mark Taylor. But he revolutionised the way an opening batsman looked in Test cricket. Players were emerging around the world who attacked more against the new ball, predominantly in one-day cricket. However, Slater adapted the attacking approach for the longest form of the game, most memorably by crunching the first ball of the series from Phil DeFreitas through the covers for four.

It set the tone. This Australian side were evolving into the first one to score at four runs per over regularly during sessions in Tests, and their overall rate was pushing 3.5 by the mid-90s, which was seen as absolutely electric. When you consider that going at faster than three runs an over was seen as being so different, so futuristic, it makes you wonder how anyone actually fell for the game in the way I did when I was growing up. But we were very different from the younger generation today, when everyone is after instant gratification. Everything has to be clipped, quick and short for modern attention spans. But during my childhood, we got to appreciate a slower pace to life. And this included the way cricket was played.

This was also an era in which a single England Test win over Australia was celebrated feverishly. Not surprising when you have waited 2,430 days for one to come along, I suppose, as was the case for the 1993 series finale success, the second match of Atherton's captaincy. Sure, it was a dead rubber, but England had not won rubbers of any sort in the previous three series. However, it also began a bit of a trend of England finishing the Ashes with a consolation win.

In 1994–95, they went one better: although the victory in the fourth Test at Adelaide – where injuries meant the XI that took the field in MCC sweaters were effectively the last men standing – came after the Ashes had been conceded, a share of the series was still on the line. England had even dominated the early stages of the preceding match at Sydney, where Gough took six-for to up the mood, and Athers declared with Hick on 98 to deflate it. Of course, normally if something looks too good to be true it's because it is, and so it proved here. On paper there was the chance for 2–2. Reality bit, however, as Australia rounded off with an emphatic win in Perth, this time by a whopping 329 runs.

What made the 1997 Ashes series so different was that it began with a win. England had a new-look team, with several younger batsmen providing a fresh impetus. In later years, the lack of mental scars against the Australians was cited as one of the reasons Michael Vaughan's 2005 team were able to finally beat the Australians, and this played a certain part in the way England started eight years earlier.

There was a real swagger about this 1997 England team, and it was on display during the one-day series that preceded the Tests. England didn't just win, they whitewashed the Aussies in the Texaco Trophy, and it was 19-year-old Ben Hollioake in particular who woke people up and showed what was possible when talent was paired with a no-fear attitude.

That Australian team came with big reputations, but he didn't care. He arrogantly hit Glenn McGrath over his head and then slog-swept Shane Warne into the Grand Stand at Lord's during a pulsating innings in the second Test. He showed that if you took these blokes on they were beatable. Unfortunately, as it turned out, the teenager was only presenting a teaser of the way life could be. At that point I am not sure we really had what it took to grab hold of the situation and make it happen on a more permanent basis, as Mike Atherton was not a caution-to-the-wind kind of captain. We were still laying the groundwork for future England teams, nudging closer towards having cricketers who believed they could beat anybody.

At Edgbaston – what a place to start an Ashes series – England showed they could by maintaining the momentum of the 50-over side. They bowled Australia out in fewer than 32 overs on day one, as Darren Gough and Andrew Caddick demonstrated what a lethal partnership they could be, supplemented by the raw pace of Devon Malcolm. Nasser Hussain followed up with a brilliant double hundred, and even though the out-of-form Mark Taylor scratched for a hundred in response, it was a minimal turnaround in fortunes and the final result was a hammering as England cantered home by nine wickets.

It was hard not to get carried away by it all. England were taking Australia on and being aggressive. For all the good that Nasser did for English cricket, and there was a catalogue of good stuff, I am not sure how, after that brilliant innings, he didn't realise that the way to take Australia on was always on the front foot. On that occasion, he instigated victory by pushing hard when Australia were down. Suddenly there was real hope and optimism that we might finally beat them over five matches. By this stage, there was a generation of cricket fans who had grown up forgetting, or not knowing, what it was like to win an Ashes. I was one of them. By then, 1986–87 felt like a completely different era. We'd watched that series in half-hour highlights on the BBC each night. So the 1997 series felt like something else altogether – and being in England and screened live on terrestrial TV made you feel a part of it.

Bloody hell, England were 1–0 up in the Ashes. This was brilliant. If you have grown up watching a particular team dominate your national side year after year, as I had, you can't help believing that they are better than they actually are. You start to fall for the invincibility tag. And the Australians put this to excellent use throughout Steve Waugh's captaincy period. You could play well against them but you felt they would inevitably win.

However, I later learned that one of the secrets the Australians kept to themselves was that they disliked opponents getting in their face. It is why they were so big on mental disintegration. They didn't want opponents coming back hard at them. They liked to be up against meek players who cowered under pressure; players who might not be any less talented but who couldn't cope with the mental side of the game when pushed. Australians like the reputation of always playing as hard as possible, and I think that got into the heads of cricket-watchers around the world. It was almost as though they had patented that way of playing and no one else was allowed to copy it. It's natural to be influenced by how your predecessors have played, I guess, but I found it was only when as a team you were prepared to stand toe to toe with them that you could see things for what they really were.

Darren Gough certainly had the aggressive attitude required, and in the Hollioakes, Adam and Ben, we had two cricketers with the fearlessness to put themselves out there – probably because they were both Australian themselves. The one-day series should have woken the whole team up, but unfortunately we couldn't get rid of the streak of Englishness that ran through the team, despite the victory in that first Test at Birmingham.

That was England's only live Test win over the Australians for 20 years. It was uncharted territory. How would the England players cope with it? The answer: they were terrified.

Our other wins had come towards the end of series, when players from the series-winning team naturally let their guard down and relaxed their intensity. Of course, players will say they always give 100 per cent and try their best, but when the job is done in a series, it definitely alters your attitude towards the latter matches. You just can't help it.

Yes, it was an awesome Australian team. But it was an Australian team that was beatable, as England had already proved in Birmingham. When you look at that England line-up, they had the potential to go down in history as some of the best cricketers this country has ever produced. They fell short of this, though, because they didn't seem to have true faith that they were some of the best cricketers this country has ever produced. They couldn't convince themselves that they deserved to be spoken about in the same bracket as their Australian adversaries.

We had enough to beat Australia when we truly believed, and there were moments in 1997 when the status quo was open for discussion, such as when Graham Thorpe dropped Matthew Elliott at slip off the debutant Mike Smith in the fourth Test at Headingley. Instead of walking off to leave the tourists five down cheaply, the left-hander went on to plunder 199.

'Don't worry, Thorpey, you've only cost us the Ashes,' Mike Atherton told him.

England did go on to win again that series, thanks to the brilliance of Phil Tufnell. Australia only needed 124 to win the sixth and final Test at The Oval, but on a dry and deteriorating pitch the Cat was world-class and his match-winning ability came to the fore. His seven first-innings wickets restricted the deficit to just 40 runs, and four more second time around, bowling with Andrew Caddick, completed the job. Let's face it, 3–2 was a much better scoreline than we had produced in previous years, and so despite it being another end-of-tour dead-rubber win, this felt more substantial – an occasion on which the believers had got their noses in front of the conservative naysayers in English cricket's general psyche.

On the evidence of 1997, Ashes series weren't yet quite as tight as the proverbial duck's derriere, but England wins were infiltrating the latter years of Australian domination. It was the same in Australia in 1998–99, as we triumphed in the fourth Test at Melbourne when the final session turned out to be four hours long. Dean Headley bowled like a dream and once again the chance arose of levelling things up in the final Test. It wasn't to be, but this was further evidence that we were working out ways to beat Australia. And if you can win individual matches, then there is always the potential to win a series.

When we lost Tests to Australia it was because we had let them get into positions where their superstars could win them the game with regularity. You don't want to allow Shane Warne the opportunity to defend 400 on the last day. In that scenario, he is going to influence outcomes.

Player for player, Australia and England matched up pretty well, but we didn't have the arrogance to compare. The kind that Mark Waugh displayed in walking to the crease on debut in 1991 and scoring a hundred, just as he'd anticipated doing. Australians play believing they are going to score a hundred every time they bat, and believing is half the battle at the highest level.

The obvious exceptions when you compared the players' qualities during this era were Shane Warne and Glenn McGrath, a partnership that contributed more than 1,000 Test scalps. Of course, we had no one to touch that level of class, but I won't have it that the other Australians on the teamsheet were all better individuals than their English counterparts. They just truly believed they were.

A case in point here was Stuart MacGill. When Warne missed the majority of the 1998–99 series through injury it allowed his understudy the chance to take centre stage. Now, Warne and MacGill were polar opposites as leg-spin bowlers. While Warne would never have a bad day, MacGill would bowl badly three times a day. His trick, though, was to follow his terrible spells with an unplayable one when he would turn deliveries square and clean up.

Leg-spinners were all the rage as we hurtled towards the millennium and I found it dispiriting to hear how England needed to unearth one for the good of our own cricket. I was playing in Northamptonshire's first team by this point, and being told that off-spin was dead was hardly what I wanted to hear. Arguably, the glorifying of leggies got into the minds of late 1990s batsmen. As negotiations about central contracts began, an obsession with developing wrist-spinners became a national topic.

But I reckon we were being hoodwinked into trying to copy others. There were answers on how to beat Australia staring us in the face. We had evidence of doing it sporadically and yet we weren't looking to, or able to, replicate it on more occasions. One of the most obvious weaknesses in the Australians' armoury, for example, was their inability to play swing bowling. Even when they were scoring plenty of runs, they would be vulnerable to nicking off if you could get the ball moving in the air. When it didn't get off the straight, you wouldn't have a chance of getting them out.

When it came to belief, I got first-hand experience of the difference between English players and those from Australia when I played against the 2001 Australians in a one-day game at Northampton. The match ended in a tie but they had no right to share the spoils. We had entered the final over needing three runs to win with three wickets intact, and then one off five balls, after Lesroy Weekes took two off Ian Harvey. Between them Weekes, Darren Cousins and Jason Brown couldn't score a run, ending with the last member of the trio being run out by miles off the final ball. Harvey was a highly skilled one-day bowler and he delivered a collection of perfect yorkers and off-pace deliveries when it mattered the most.

The 2001 Ashes was the series that showed what a poisoned chalice the England captaincy had become. When Nasser Hussain, who took the job when the only way was up as the ninth-placed side out of nine in the Test rankings in 1999, broke his finger in the first Test defeat at Edgbaston, there was a reluctance to take over the leadership shown by both Alec Stewart, the man Hussain had displaced, and Mark Butcher, who had not enjoyed his previous stand-in experience against New Zealand two years previously.

So it fell to Michael Atherton – arguably the England player to suffer most at the hands of Australia in Ashes history – to return to the job by default. If you are proposed as a future England captain these days, it is a prestigious award and one that provides you with an amnesty against being dropped. At that time, however, you knew that if you were appointed England captain you were going to suffer humiliations at the hands of the Aussies, take verbal abuse from supporters and be turned over by the press. In those circumstances, I don't blame Stewart and Butcher for backing off. Equally, Athers had developed a fairly strong jaw. Even moments of great personal triumph had taken unexpectedly intense turns for the worse. Never more so than at Lord's in 1993 when he had slipped scampering between the wickets and was run out for 99.

In 2001 the Australians barely paused for breath as they wrapped up the Ashes in 11 days of whirlwind cricket. Quite a turnaround from the start of the tour when they lost to an under-strength Middlesex and tied that match against Northants at Wantage Road. They were clinical and unwavering in their approach, and you couldn't begrudge wins to a bunch of cricketers who fully believed they could win from any situation against England. It was an attitude that they had cultivated over several years, and as the team evolved it became more evident that they were prepared to risk losing games sometimes in a bid to win them.

Never was that demonstrated more clearly than in the fourth Test at Headingley that summer when Adam Gilchrist, their acting captain with Steve Waugh injured, pursued the dream of a 5–0 whitewash with a creative declaration. At the time, a target of 315 did not appear overly generous, but it did give England a sniff and the one match in which positivity was displayed all round was the one that led to a home win, Mark Butcher carrying the team home with a splendid unbeaten 173.

Steve Waugh always said that the English cricketers he admired the most were the ones who took on the challenge, those that actually stood up to the Australians, treating these matches as full-on combat, a test of mental and physical strength. That is the way he played every time he pulled on his ragged Baggy Green cap, and he seemed to have made it his mission to ensure the Ashes were not relinquished in his lifetime. Having experienced defeat in 1986–87, it was as though he refused to believe losing was a viable option again while he was selectable.

Never did his character come through more strongly than in the final Test of the 2001 series at The Oval when, only a matter of weeks after being told he was out of the tour with a calf tear, he managed to get himself fit enough to feature in what was to be one last hurrah in Test cricket in England. Knowing it was to be his final tour, he did everything he could to get on that field, and even though it looked like he was doing a Long John Silver impression with the bat in his hand, he was still able to sign off with a hundred – the fact he managed it on one leg summing up the difference in attitude between him and others. Did we have anyone at that time who could have done something similar?

Afterwards, he developed a blood clot on his calf and got deep vein thrombosis on the plane back home to Australia, for goodness' sake. DVT is a potentially fatal condition, and although he played it down later, it was an innings that could have killed him. Perhaps by defying the medical prognosis to make it back onto the field quick-smart at the age of 36 he was also trying to prove a point to his own side that their standards should not slip – that they should aspire to keep up the determination to be the best, just as he had. There was no doubting that he was the toughest of Australians.

I loved him for what he had done during the 1989 Ashes. He was a pretty ugly batsman but one that got the job done. He was a bit of a scruff, but to me this was pretty cool and the fact he didn't care what he looked like added to his prestige. He just wanted to get the job done. He never smiled, a real no-nonsense cricketer who played in an uncompromising manner. Unfortunately, I never got to play against him. I would have loved that.

As it was, the off-spinner who got the chance to test himself against Waugh and co. in Australian conditions in 2002–03 was Richard Dawson, the hot young thing at the time in county cricket, a period in which just about anyone who bowled anything resembling off-spin got a go. If you had a gig on the county scene you were always going to play ahead of me at that stage in my career because Duncan Fletcher seemed to hate my guts. Not long after this, we saw the rise of Jamie Dalrymple and Alex Loudon to international cricket. Potentially, I could have been picked instead. I had played a single one-day international for England in South Africa three winters earlier before being cast aside, and if truth be told I couldn't have felt any further away from playing again.

What a scene in the fifth Test of the 2002–03 series at the SCG, the venue for what turned out to be Waugh's final involvement in Ashes cricket. This was his home ground and, as Tony Greig pointed out on commentary as he walked out to a roar with Australia 56–3, 'This guy is hero-worshipped in Sydney.'

He was under pressure for his place in the team and it felt like the entire nation was behind him to turn his form around. Even Englishmen could have been excused for getting a little sentimental as the landmarks fell and the cacophony increased, starting with a 61-ball fifty. Soon afterwards, he became only the third man in Test history to achieve 10,000 runs.

As Richie Benaud put it: 'One of the biggest ovations you will ever hear for someone who's made 69.' Oo, er.

But the *pièce de résistance* came when sixth-wicket partner Adam Gilchrist worked the single to put him back on strike for the final delivery of the day, sent down by Richard Dawson. Waugh, on 98, slapped a ball outside off stump through the covers in his trademark manner. Anywhere but there, Daws! But at least one of the nicest blokes to have played for England, and someone who has gone on to become a very fine coach with Gloucestershire, got to feature in one of the most celebrated Ashes moments – even if it was only a walk-on part.

From the moment my dad and I watched his first Ashes delivery together, in the 1st Test of the 1993 series at Old Trafford, I was mesmerised by Shane Warne, a spin-bowling genius.

Comical one moment, ferocious the next, Merv Hughes was an imposing on-field character in the early part of the 16 years of Australian Ashes dominance that began in 1989.

The perfect start – Mike Gatting can't quite believe it after Warne's heat-seeking fizzer pitched outside leg, gripped on the pitch, spun back and hit the top of off stump. Warne played in eight Ashes series, losing only one.

Australian crowds never let Phil Tufnell forget his botched run-out attempt during the 1990–91 tour. Here Tuffers desperately appeals for the wicket of Victoria captain Dean Jones in 1994–95.

Sharing a joke at Lord's in 1997, two captains who experienced very different fortunes in the Ashes. While Mark Taylor, left, won the three series when he was in charge, Mike Atherton, right, was on the losing side in all four in which he was captain.

Atherton acknowledges the crowd after being dismissed in his final Test, at The Oval in 2001, a match better remembered for opposing captain Steve Waugh's one-legged 157.

When he took over as captain from Atherton, Nasser Hussain, batting here in the 2nd Test at Adelaide in 2002–03, fared little better in Ashes series.

Sometimes it hurts. Winning the final Test at Sydney in 2002–03 was clearly no consolation for England's Ian Blackwell, Robert Key, Alex Tudor, Nasser Hussain and Steve Harmison – after losing the preceding four.

As they celebrate the wicket of Australia's Simon Katich in the 4th Test at Trent Bridge, Steve Harmison and Michael Vaughan display the passion that made the 2005 series the best Ashes tussle in living memory.

Andrew Flintoff is congratulated for taking the crucial wicket of Adam Gilchrist in the first innings of the 1st Test at Lord's in 2005, in which Australia were dismissed cheaply, setting the tone for the rest of the series.

Freddie shows his softer side as he famously consoles a distraught Brett Lee after Australia lose the 2nd 2005 Test at Edgbaston by just two runs.

The 3rd Test of the 2005 series at Old Trafford was drawn, but a fit-again Glenn McGrath returned to form with five second-innings wickets.

In the deciding 5th Test at The Oval, Matthew Hayden put together a potentially match-winning 138. A hard-as-nails character on the field, I loved playing with him at Northamptonshire.

Michael Vaughan hits out on his way to 166 in the 3rd Test at Old Trafford in 2005. Vaughany's captaincy, including his management of Kevin Pietersen, was crucial to England's memorable series victory.

Michael Vaughan's England celebrate winning back the Ashes after 16 years at the end of the 5th Test at The Oval in 2005.

As you were – normal service is resumed as England struggle in Australia in 2006–07 under the ill-conceived captaincy of Andrew Flintoff, here bowling to Matthew Hayden in the 3rd Test at Perth, which Australia won by 206 runs.

Mike Hussey, batting here in the 1st Test of the 2006–07 series at Brisbane, was right up there with anyone I ever played with as a technical batsman. In this series he averaged 91.6.

Andrew Strauss, passed over for the captaincy on far too many occasions, tosses up with Ricky Ponting on day one of the 2009 series – my first as a player – in Cardiff, of all places.

The 2nd Test at Lord's proved worthy of this royal visit. England secured their first Ashes victory there for 75 years, with Strauss and Alastair Cook, pictured, setting things up with an opening stand of 196.

The ball of the century? My drifting, dipping delivery to bowl Ricky Ponting in the 3rd Test at Edgbaston in 2009 was a dream dismissal.

'Come on, lads!' Flintoff, Strauss and an expectant Lord's Pavilion on the final day of the 2nd Test in 2009. Freddie defied considerable pain to put in one last superhuman bowling display, taking 5–92.

By the 5th Test at The Oval, knee problems had restricted his mobility, but once again it fell to Freddie to change the course of the match, running out Ricky Ponting with a direct hit from mid-on.

Date	Venue	Team	Scores	Team	Scores	Result
03/06/1993	Manchester	Australia	289 & 432-5d	England	210 & 332	Australia won by 179 runs
17/06/1993	Lord's	Australia	632-4d	England	205 & 365	Australia won by an innings and 62 runs
01/07/1993	Nottingham	England	321 & 422-6d	Australia	373 & 202-6	Drawn
22/07/1993	Leeds	Australia	653-4d	England	200 & 305	Australia won by an innings and 148 runs
05/08/1993	Birmingham	England	276 & 251	Australia	408 & 120-2	Australia won by 8 wickets
19/08/1993	The Oval	England	380 & 313	Australia	303 & 229	England won by 161 runs
25/11/1994	Brisbane	Australia	426 & 248-8d	England	167 & 323	Australia won by 184 runs
24/12/1994	Melbourne	Australia	279 & 320-7d	England	212 & 92	Australia won by 295 runs
01/01/1995	Sydney	England	309 & 255-2d	Australia	116 & 344-7	Drawn
26/01/1995	Adelaide	England	353 & 328	Australia	419 & 156	England won by 106 runs
03/02/1995	Perth	Australia	402 & 345-8d	England	295 & 123	Australia won by 329 runs
05/06/1997	Birmingham	Australia	118 & 477	England	478-9d & 119-1	England won by 9 wickets
19/06/1997	Lord's	England	77 & 266-4d	Australia	213-7d	Drawn
03/07/1997	Manchester	Australia	235 & 395-8d	England	162 & 200	Australia won by 268 runs
24/07/1997	Leeds	England	172 & 268	Australia	501-9d	Australia won by an innings and 61 runs
07/08/1997	Nottingham	Australia	427 & 336	England	313 & 186	Australia won by 264 runs
21/08/1997	The Oval	England	180 & 163	Australia	220 & 104	England won by 19 runs
20/11/1998	Brisbane	Australia	485 & 237-3d	England	375 & 179-6	Drawn
28/11/1998	Perth	England	112 & 191	Australia	240 & 64-3	Australia won by 7 wickets
11/12/1998	Adelaide	Australia	391 & 278-5d	England	227 & 237	Australia won by 205 runs
26/12/1998	Melbourne	England	270 & 244	Australia	340 & 162	England won by 12 runs
02/01/1999	Sydney	Australia	322 & 184	England	220 & 188	Australia won by 98 runs
05/07/2001	Birmingham	England	294 & 164	Australia	576	Australia won by an innings and 118 runs
19/07/2001	Lord's	England	187 & 227	Australia	401 & 14-2	Australia won by 8 wickets
02/08/2001	Nottingham	England	185 & 162	Australia	190 & 158-3	Australia won by 7 wickets
16/08/2001	Leeds	Australia	447 & 176-4d	England	309 & 315-4	England won by 6 wickets
23/08/2001	The Oval	Australia	641-4d	England	432 & 184	Australia won by an innings and 25 runs
07/11/2002	Brisbane	Australia	492 & 296-5d	England	325 & 79	Australia won by 384 runs
21/11/2002	Adelaide	England	342 & 159	Australia	552-9d	Australia won by an innings and 51 runs
29/11/2002	Perth	England	185 & 223	Australia	456	Australia won by an innings and 48 runs
26/12/2002	Melbourne	Australia	551-6d & 107-5	England	270 & 387	Australia won by 5 wickets
02/01/2003	Sydney	England	362 & 452-9d	Australia	363 & 226	England won by 225 runs

12

SOME BLOKE
CALLED FRED

MENTALITY plays a huge role in Ashes cricket and the contrast in the outlook of Australian and English cricketers was at the heart of such a one-sided stretch in its history. Australians truly believe it's their birthright to beat us. They are troubled by the thought of defeat. Call it a superiority complex, if you like.

Even when they go through relatively challenging times, they retain that belief; they keep fighting and pushing for a positive result. They have great resolve, to the point that it sometimes feels like there must have been a mass brainwashing experiment in the 1980s that persuaded them England could never defeat them again.

My predecessors did not want to win any less than I did, I am sure of that, but the problem as I see it is that they didn't have confidence they could do it. There were enough good players to create winning opportunities, but they simply lacked conviction. There always appeared to be a barrier in the way – one of their own creation.

Under Nasser Hussain, England had won Test series in Pakistan and in Sri Lanka, but the final frontier for an improving team proved too big to scale, and so the 2002–03 Ashes went the way of many before it, with pre-tour hopes dashed before a ball was bowled. Naturally, there was the usual phoney war in Australia's national press, with headlines demanding to know whether anyone in the UK could play cricket. And the tone for the drama was set when Hussain won the toss for the first Test at Brisbane and opted to bowl first.

To this day, he will say he thought there was a bit of moisture around the Gabba, that the pitch was not going to get any worse and a few early wickets would get England into the game. But in reality I think you could see in his eyes that he was overly wary about the quality of the Aussies. If you win the toss in a game you don't think you can win, you bowl first, don't you? It was a case of damage limitation from the word go.

To add insult, and to put the pitch's nature into context, Ricky Ponting launched Ashley Giles for consecutive sixes in the hour after lunch, and Matthew Hayden crunched more than 100 runs in boundaries on the opening day. Reaching the close on 364–2 was so dismissive, it really put England in their place. It also epitomised the way Australia prefer to play. They like to put the foot on the throat of opponents and apply more and more pressure.

Hayden was a fine exponent of this tactic – once on top he focused on minimising any chance of a fightback. That was certainly his modus operandi when I played alongside him at Northamptonshire. He loved to be dominant, asserting himself against bowlers from the off.

Without a doubt, the England team would have hated Haydos because he would be chirping away from gully, chest puffed out, big, brash and confident. He was physically imposing and it was like he was constantly reminding you that he was a bigger man than you in every sense.

Arguably, with his act of aggression in Brisbane in November 2002 he'd won Australia the Ashes by lunchtime on day one. 'This is what I think of you lot,' he said with the way he lined up the English bowling.

I confess that I loved playing cricket with Matthew Hayden. He was the most uncompromising human being I have ever met, and this hard-as-nails image he cultivated when he crossed the white line more often than not had its desired effect on opponents. And that makes the occasion it failed to do so even funnier.

We had played an early-season game in 1999 and lost, and this was his introduction to county-cricket captaincy. He really got annoyed about losing, whereas there was a bit of a culture of 'oh well, there's always tomorrow' at Northamptonshire and in the English domestic game in general at that time. He also hated the fact that myself, my older brother Alec and Richard Logan, three of our younger players, knew a lot of the blokes we were playing against. He told us we were too chummy with everyone; simply weren't hard enough. Not that we were having cosy chats on the field of play; we were not. We just weren't getting completely stuck into them, and that did not go down well with our overseas player.

We were playing Glamorgan next match, and he told us: 'We're going right at them – all right? Talk to them after the game, sure, but on the field you are their worst nightmare.'

Next day, Alun Evans was walking out to open the batting. Alun was a lovely lad from West Wales. For those that aren't familiar with him, he was also deaf as a post, and wore hearing aids.

As we entered the field, Haydos strode up behind him and let rip: 'You weak *****! You don't deserve to be on the field with us. We're going to grill you, mate; you're in for a tough time.'

As our captain peeled off into the slip cordon, I told him: 'I think you're wasting your time there, Haydos. The lad can't hear you.'

'**** off, Swann. You should be having a go at him too. ******* deaf, my a***.'

Cue comedy-gold moment as Evans takes guard. As he was lining up his bat, the umpire George Sharp shouts: 'That's two, Alun.'

A second later, Evans pipes up: 'Can I have two, please, George?'

I have no doubt that Hayden's early career experience shaped his behaviour. He endured a really tough time when he first played for Australia, missing out on Test selection in the 1993 Ashes when, after featuring in the one-dayers, Michael Slater, his rival to partner Mark Taylor at the top of the order, was chosen.

That was a first-wicket alliance that lasted for some time and there were seldom opportunities because of its success. In one-day cricket, he was dropped amid accusations of possessing hard hands and an angled bat. No more than a one-trick pony, or in cricket terms a flat-track bully, some said, and so when he did get his chance again in the winter of 1996–97, his technique was under scrutiny once more. Although he dominated bowling attacks in Brisbane and Perth, he did not repeat the dose when things got dusty in Sydney.

There was a debate about whether he deserved what represented not a second but a third chance as an international opener with Australia in early 2000 and so when, through sheer volume of Sheffield Shield runs, he got another he decided to grab it. Forced to reconsider his way of playing, he concluded that his previous method was not suitable and he chose to make significant alterations to aspects of his game. Perceived as being a weak player against spin bowling, his reaction tells you why he is one of the characters that I admire most in the global game.

Technically, he was not as good a player as Mike Hussey, another Australian batsman I played with during my time at Northamptonshire. But he was a more prolific run-scorer for a while because when he went out to bat he fed off this unrivalled self-belief. He taught himself to dominate and bully bowlers physically and mentally. Suddenly, a guy with a poor record against spinners went to India and dominated Harbhajan Singh in his pomp.

He would often win the psychological battle by choosing a delivery and hitting it for six, a calculated gamble sending out the message that he was in control, not the bowlers. Subsequently, they might bowl badly. I didn't see anyone to compare with Hayden in using this kind of tactic. His Test batting average on the subcontinent was 51.35, even higher than his outstanding career average of 50.73.

There was an army of cricketers who didn't like Haydos because he was so cutting on the field, turning it into the most hostile environment possible. He was perhaps the hardest sledger that I played with or against. He simply didn't take any nonsense. As an Australian cricketer he wanted to be as tough an opponent as he could; he despised the pursuit of fame and fortune, and couldn't give a hoot about appearing on *Top of the Pops*. It's one of the reasons he clashed with people like Kevin Pietersen. He epitomised everything that Kev was not. Off the field he was one of the nicest blokes going.

* * *

Hayden proved to be a massive influence on me, mostly through the way he went about things. In his head, he just didn't take no as an option. He was unwavering in his pursuit of success, and during a two-year period as Northants captain sometimes he would make us see things differently too.

During the 1999 season, we were involved in a televised NatWest Trophy third-round match against Essex at Wantage Road. At the halfway stage most of us thought we were dead and buried. Essex had posted 281 from their 50 overs, and at the time that was a phenomenal score. A winning score.

However, Hayden was having none of it: 'Nah, if they can get it, we can get it.'

Typically, he cracked a hundred, others batted around him and we got over the finish line with two full overs to spare. It was comfortably the highest successful chase between two first-class counties in the competition that year.

So I had a great admiration for the mental side of Hayden's game: both the willpower to achieve and the belief in your own ability to overcome those you are up against. He was always striving to be the dominant person in any situation, and that rubbed off on the rest of us. Seeing one of your team-mates dominate a two-way scrap always provides collective confidence in a dressing room. Cricket logic might be telling you one thing, but if you've got the body language of one of your team-mates telling you another thing entirely, that can be a greater influence.

Hayden's positivity made a connection with me because

when it comes to cricket my glass is always half full. For example, whenever records are flagged up on the TV, I always challenge the notion that history should be a guide to whether a team will be successful or not. What a load of tosh. Just because a team got bowled out for 100 in 1932, it doesn't mean the same result is going to occur on the same ground 80-odd years later.

Incidentally, while we are on the subject, why are cricketers so terrified by numbers? And why do English ones worry so much about getting ahead of themselves? I have been part of England dressing rooms where people have purposely set conservative estimates, as though thinking bigger is effectively placing a rock in your path to trip over.

Contrast that with a few of the Australians I have played with who were always more up front on the issue. David Hussey was a good example of this. While with Nottinghamshire, if he recognised we were on a good pitch, he would insist publicly: 'Four hundred and fifty is the absolute minimum here, boys.' He wouldn't accept any less than that, he didn't want others to either, and so he wasn't scared to say so.

Hayden was one of the best batsmen of his era through a combination of force of personality and brute strength. He was an intimidating presence, standing 6 foot 3 inches tall, and could crunch a ball like few others.

As a technical batsman Mike Hussey was right up there

with anyone I'd ever played with, in fact. He didn't get a chance to play Test cricket until his thirties but it didn't surprise me at all, once he had started playing for Australia, just how well he did. Not that he began the 2001 county season, as Hayden's replacement, so well. After a month or so he had barely scored a run, struggling in our white-ball matches and making scores of 18, 21 and 3 in the Championship. One game, after he got nicked off early doors, he turned to us in the changing room afterwards and said: 'Jeez, you guys must think I'm rubbish. The worst overseas player ever.'

We reassured him with replies like: 'Don't be silly, mate, you'll come good.'

Secretly, of course, we were thinking: 'Yeah, we do.'

But what a transformation from the moment he hit a fifty against Surrey in May: hundred followed hundred, and he passed 2,000 Division One runs for the season. Arguably, it had done him some good not playing that well when he first came to England, because it made him so determined once he did start churning out the runs. If he had come over and started with a couple of hundreds he might have taken his foot off the pedal a bit and relaxed, but he maintained his intensity because he wanted to show us that his start had been a false one. He was equally prolific the following year too, dwarfing my career-best 185 versus Gloucestershire with 330 at the other end. We shared a triple-century stand.

As fate would have it, I also got to play with his younger

brother at Nottinghamshire. Dave Hussey did not have a personal CV to match that of either his brother or Hayden, but he was phenomenal in first-class cricket during his nine seasons at Trent Bridge. Like them he scored hundred after hundred, but he was also quite unlike any other Australian I had come across during my cricket career. He was more your typical English mickey-taker.

One of the first things he did when he got to Trent Bridge was to superglue our coach Mick Newell's shoes to the floor. Mick could be stern at times and that made him a great target for wind-ups, and he was on the receiving end of a barrage. No one was safe, however, and another of Dave's tricks was to superglue two-pence pieces to the bottom of people's trainers. They would have no idea while they were walking about in the pavilion, but once outside there would be an awful racket from all the scraping along the Tarmac. Another of this very funny man's crackers was to place an advert in the local paper: '8 kittens for sale, need a good home call 07768 XXXXXX.' Mick is on the phone regularly as a county director of cricket and England selector but perhaps not as much as he was over one weekend in the Noughties.

Dave was almost a polar opposite to Mike as a player – quite loose, reliant on power and a fantastic eye. I remember Shane Warne getting stuck into him one year when we played in an away game at Hampshire. Huss had a go back and then instructed his Victorian team-mate to shut the hell up.

He hit him for four sixes in a row. They were massive blows, to win the game for us, and he didn't think anything of it. He just walked off, acting as if what he had just done – taking a bowler down that we all considered invincible – was perfectly normal.

Just as in previous generations, Australia had depth behind their national side in the first decade of the 21st century, and another of their nearly men, Adam Voges, also joined us at Notts. He is possibly the palest human being I have ever met. To the extent that whenever he took his top off, Mark Ealham used to make ghost noises: 'Woooaaah!'

'V' was always a target for me. Above his peg in the dressing room, I used to write 'token ginger', and when the dressing-room attendant painted over it, I simply got my Sharpie out to write it again. When he had a couple of lean games, we assured him that he would not be dropped as in England it was law that you had to have at least one ginge in every team. In some company this would be considered bullying, of course. But those who enjoy dressing-room jinks will hopefully recognise camaraderie. He certainly did. He was a great team man and you could see why he fitted in so well in the Australia dressing room at such a late stage of his career making his test debut in 2015, aged 35.

These Australian imports were not better cricketers than a number of English players in domestic cricket, but they'd had it drummed into them that they were the best cricketers in the world, vastly superior to Poms, and it was their destiny to come over to county cricket and cream it, because that's what Australians did. It was certainly what their predecessors had done.

During the 1980s and 1990s Australian cricketers would check in as overseas players and learn how to adapt to English conditions and combat lateral movement. The ball tends not to swing in Australia so when first confronted with it, some Aussie batsmen struggle, and a season in county cricket provides plenty of practice. It doesn't happen as much these days, though, certainly not for an entire season. This is partly due to the saturated international schedule and partly because Aussie players are much more likely to take a gig in the Indian Premier League than a county contract for the summer.

Dare I suggest that this shows in their lack of proficiency over here in recent years, most obviously in their captain and number-one-rated batsman, Steve Smith. He's an unbelievably talented player when the ball is not doing anything. He will drive you straight down the ground all day if the bowlers are unable to extract any movement, and his cross-batted strokes are great. But as we saw in the 2015 Ashes series, whenever the ball deviated he was in trouble, resulting in an average of less than 10 in the three Tests that were played in typically English conditions. Equally, it was no surprise that in the two Tests that encouraged the batsman and did little for the bowlers he scored two hundreds. In finishing as Australia's top run-scorer, some commentators suggested he'd had a good series. But I reckon he'd had a terrible one, because he scored next to nothing as soon as the ball swung, which was a big part of why his team lost those three matches.

At the same time, there is no longer as big a migration from this country down under in the winter. At the age of 18 and 19, English lads used to go over and learn the game the Australian way by playing a season of grade cricket. But that has now been scuppered to some degree by counties putting young players on 12-month contracts. Instead of allowing guys to spend a few months getting some sun on their backs in Australia, they have you running up and down Ilkley Moor, or facing throw-downs in an indoor centre somewhere as Christmas approaches. To me it would be much better for their development to be learning, hands on, in very different conditions.

The year of 2005 will always be special – it's the year I won my first County Championship title. However, most people with an interest in cricket were focused on the best Ashes tussle in living memory.

Because I was just a county cricketer my role was pretty much like the rest of the country – that of an ordinary spectator. There was a real fervour created before a ball had been bowled in the series, instigated by the one-off Twenty20 match at Southampton. It was only the second 20-over international ever and England hammered Australia to put down their marker. There was an atmosphere reminiscent of Euro '96 about the one-day series that followed. The fact that England were able to out-power Australia in 20-over cricket, then muscle them aside in the ODIs, had everyone asking the same question: Is it our time at last?

We have Michael Vaughan to thank for the fact that it was. Attitude is crucial in taking on Australia and he was facing arguably their finest team in history. If not the outright best, then as good as any that had gone before. But he undermined their policy for success by making sure that his England team's mindset was right. Australia's players wanted opponents to feel inferior and give up. They wanted to turn them into pushovers. The reason that they respect Vaughan so highly is that they recognise he instigated a prolonged stand against it.

There were lots of small acts of defiance during the series, such as Steve Harmison cutting Ricky Ponting's cheek at Lord's and England getting into Matthew Hayden's mind by placing fielders in unusual positions on the drive. Australia weren't allowed to play in the alpha-male manner to which they had become accustomed.

Part of the reason New Zealand are so successful at rugby, in my opinion, is their carrying out of the ceremonial haka before kick-off. It is a symbol of their physical superiority, their warlike spirit. Australian cricketers' aggressive body language had a similar effect under the captaincies of Steve Waugh and Ponting, but Vaughan's method of fighting fire with fire reduced the impact and the Australians didn't appear to have an answer to it.

Of course, skill is also required to succeed at the highest level, but it requires courage and conviction for it to flourish. So for me, Vaughan's most significant act of the summer arguably came during the finale, on the day the urn was returned to English hands at The Oval, because it was he who instructed Pietersen to go out and hook when the Australians sent down a barrage of bouncers. The Ashes were on the line and Pietersen was clearly caught in two minds at lunch.

'Just go and whack it,' Vaughan told him.

It was the fundamental reason that England won. In Vaughan, they had a leader really backing them up and allowing them to play expressively. It was such a refreshing change from what we had seen before.

I found on the 1998–99 England A tour to Zimbabwe that Vaughan was a brilliant man-manager as a captain. While Duncan Fletcher, the England coach, was in my mind the most miserable human being on the planet, Vaughan was hard to dislike when you played for him. He was the head-strong front man required to get the best out of some massive egos. Andrew Flintoff's respect for Vaughan was crucial and the fact there was a northern core to the team would also have put Fred at ease. Vaughan was even able to connect with KP, and get him to use his arrogance positively by going out and playing for the team.

England also possessed the perfect bowling attack in 2005. They had the genuine away swing of Matthew Hoggard, the pace and bounce of Harmison, the aggression and control of Flintoff and the wildcard in Simon Jones, the quickest of the four and the finest exponent of reverse swing. Of all of them, though, Fred stood out because he was the workhorse. When your workhorse is sending the old ball down at 90 miles per hour and ducking it this way and that, there is little respite for the opposition. When the fast men needed a rest, there was Ashley Giles – cruelly nicknamed 'Smash-me Miles' in some quarters, but for me a great bowler and a solid-as-oak character in the dressing room.

Having depth to your attack is crucial, because it is the bowlers that win you Ashes series, without a doubt. Batsmen will win you the odd game, but equally they almost lost the fourth Test at Trent Bridge when it was all but over, chasing 129.

The tone of the series was set when Australia were bowled out cheaply at Lord's in the first Test, something that had not happened in years. It was a ground where Australia normally set batting records. But this was an innings of major discomfort even before the psychological blow of Ponting, one of the best players of fast bowling in the world, getting smashed in the helmet grille by that Harmison bouncer.

During that period, Harmy was so fast, just thinking about the prospect of batting against him makes me shudder. In addition to his speed, he was able to extract exaggerated bounce and the ball always seemed to be following you. He had all the attributes to justify his number-one status in the world bowling rankings. Overall, he had a good international career, and the statistics backed that up – such as his return of 7–12 against West Indies in Jamaica in 2004. It's sad to think that if he is remembered for a single delivery, some people will recall the one at Brisbane, the first of the 2006–07 series that went straight to Andrew Flintoff at second slip. Come on, he was just giving his mate an early touch, to settle the nerves.

In the 2005 series, the planning for each of the Australian batsmen was pretty exemplary. I'm not sure that they foresaw Hayden being susceptible to driving on the up before a ball was bowled, but once they latched onto it they undoubtedly got into his mind by placing men in unusually close catching positions. It may only have led to one catch being taken, but it arguably contributed to him playing in a different way. Sometimes being wary of playing certain strokes contributes to lbws, and this was the case on a couple of occasions. England's bowlers totally shut down Adam Gilchrist by attacking him hard from around the wicket. The world game's great counter-attacker had become submissive to the point of being strokeless.

'Batting at Old Trafford, I felt under so much pressure I was exploding from it,' Gilchrist later said. 'Standing over the bat, hearing the crowd was unbearable. My eyes and mind were playing tricks on me. I wasn't seeing the ball, or the bowler: I was seeing the entire ground. I felt hyper-aware of every little thing – the crowd, the sightscreen, the pavilion, the trees outside, the clouds – as if my focus was on a thousand different things instead of just one.'

They became the best England team we have ever had not because they possessed the best individuals but because they worked so well as a unit. Man for man, others may have been superior, but the way they came together under an inspiring leader made them so special. They changed the way people thought about the abilities of the respective two teams, including some in the Australian dressing room.

Even though Australia administered a bit of a hammering in the first Test, it was clear that the pre-series prediction of a whitewash from Glenn McGrath – who bowled us out twice at Lord's in his customary manner, looking to hit the top of off stump and getting players caught behind or in the slips – was hogwash. Clearly, the public were feeling excitement at this series like none in living memory too. The opening-day crowd was the biggest at Lord's for 60 years.

When the series moved to Birmingham for the second Test I got involved as one of the twelfth men. Nottinghamshire did not have a County Championship game that week, so a couple of us were asked to head to Edgbaston to help out with dressing-room duties and be potential substitute fielders.

One of the first people to cross my path when I turned

up at the team hotel was Duncan Fletcher. It certainly didn't look like he'd been briefed that I was on twelfths that week. He looked like he needed to see a doctor. As it turned out, he holds a grudge. We had previous, including an incident on the tour of South Africa in 1999–2000 when I missed the team bus, an indiscretion that I had been reprimanded for. Not being considered for England selection in the aftermath was further punishment, and even five years later he didn't appear to be letting it go.

But I vowed to ignore Duncan's reaction, get on with the job I'd been asked to do and keep out of his way. This became difficult, however, when during the warm-up game of hand hockey on the first morning I pulled a muscle in my back. It meant that halfway through one of the most historic days in Ashes cricket, I had to seek out Kirk Russell, the England physio. I knew Kirk well – he was previously our physio at Northants.

'Mate, I'm in agony here, can you help me?'

He told me to hop on the bed, and he had not been working on the problem long when Fletcher walked around the corner and inquired: 'Which one of my boys needs work today, eh?'

Suffice to say there were numerous expletives when he found my ugly mug looking up at him. At the time I never believed that I would play for England again anyway, so it was all a massive joke, really. I wasn't going to let anything ruin being around the team for a week like that.

I have since met around 20,000 people who claim to have been at Edgbaston on the day when McGrath trod on that stray cricket ball. Of course, they also claim to have seen the event in question first-hand too, which is amazing, really, because it was a good hour before the start of play and the ground was relatively empty. I know this because although I didn't see the incident itself, I was on the outfield to witness the aftermath as he was carried away to the dressing room.

When you lose someone of the calibre of McGrath, the match-winner a fortnight earlier, it must be enough to scramble the brain. Suddenly, Australia did what English teams might have done in the past – they panicked. For some reason Ricky Ponting thought it would be a good idea to bowl, despite losing his attack spearhead and having the opportunity to put more daylight between themselves and England with a big first-innings score.

Marcus Trescothick played brilliantly to set the tone, not only for the match but for the way England were to play for the rest of the series, with his rapid 90. He deserved the personal accolade of a hundred.

He challenged the norm by attacking Shane Warne as soon as he came on to bowl. Usually, Warne would be brought into the attack and men would congregate around the bat, but this time England's batsmen were not prepared to sit and wait for their fate. They wanted to take the challenge head on. Warne floated one up in his third over and Trescothick smashed him straight back over his head for six. There was no emotion – there rarely was with Tres. He didn't sulk, smile or laugh; he just got on with things as if he'd merely patted the ball back down the pitch, marking his guard and waiting for the next delivery.

A switch had flicked. This England team sensed they were good for wins if they played as they could – as they would against any other opposition. The England supporters sensed it too.

By the time I departed from my odd-job duties late on day three, just after Steve Harmison bowled Michael Clarke with a dipping slower ball, the atmosphere inside the ground was electric. Australia were eight wickets down and on the verge of defeat. I don't think cricket had ever been like this before. The noise levels were like those of a football match between two local rivals. And the England fans were right behind the team's quest to challenge history.

There was a mood of optimism bathing the country that summer and in Andrew Flintoff they had a seemingly working-class hero to worship.

Flintoff was a brute of a man and in Birmingham he undoubtedly intimidated the Australians with his aggressive, genuinely hostile fast bowling. This was something new to this generation of English crowds and they were absolutely loving it. Of all the roars unleashed by the throng over those few days, the one for his dismissal of Ricky Ponting in the second innings was truly incredible.

There are those who reckon England would have folded

if Australia, requiring 107 with two wickets intact at the start of that Sunday morning, had completed a sensational heist. Who knows? Like every other England fan I was just glad Steve Harmison produced one last-effort ball and Michael Kasprowicz flapped unconvincingly. Never have I been so pleased to see Billy Bowden's crooked finger raised.

If that felt like the sort of game that England used not to win, there was another uncustomary sign in the third Test at Manchester when Australia held on for a draw, nine wickets down, in yet another exhilarating finish. A lot was made of Michael Vaughan making his team look at the Australians celebrating on the balcony afterwards. Previously, if England had celebrated a draw in that way, the Australians would have called them weak and publicly humiliated them. Psychologically, this revealed a shift in the balance of power. I wonder, if they had their time again, whether they would still celebrate.

To save a game like that was crucial to Australia's hopes of retaining the Ashes, of course, but while I could understand jubilation in the dressing room, to display those emotions in public seemed very un-Australian. Australian cricketers have habitually tried to keep their emotions under wraps when they are not on top. They are not keen on letting any sign of vulnerability show, a bit like bad gamblers who only ever talk about their winnings. It is actually an admirable quality to have when it comes to cricket, because you are always trying to reinforce the positive, and this was an example of them letting their guard slip.

The one player who stood out for me during this celebration was Justin Langer, who was on the balcony pumping his fists. Maybe this was because I'd had a couple of run-ins with him in county cricket. Langer would always try to get stuck into the younger players and intimidate them. Invariably, he would test your mettle by standing at point and staring at you. If you happened to catch his eye, he would snap back at you: 'What are you staring at, mate?' He would pick on you for absolutely no reason. One year, however, I made a point of getting back at him.

In a county game at Lord's, he said: 'You think you're the bee's knees. You just don't know how hard a higher standard is.'

Luckily, I remembered his Test debut when he got knocked out by the West Indies.

'You should know, mate. How's your head?'

He once even tried to pick a fight with David Ripley, my team-mate at Northamptonshire, who might qualify as the nicest man in the world. In contrast, Langer was anything but. Following retirement, however, I can now appreciate his behaviour for what it was. He was trying to get to players like me, to detract from their games, and to some extent his plan to unsettle had worked.

Reacting to provocation can show an opponent that you are under pressure, as was the case when Ricky Ponting exploded in the fourth Test, the penultimate of the series, at Trent Bridge – giving Duncan Fletcher, the England coach sitting on the home balcony, the spray as he returned to the dressing room after being run out by the substitute Gary Pratt. Although there had been no breaking of the rules with the use of Pratt as a substitute, Ponting believed England were pushing the realms of fair play with their constant interchanges for toilet breaks. To me, getting wrapped up in such stuff highlighted that the Australian captain was no longer just thinking about his own game.

I should have been thinking about my game on 28 August as England secured the 2–1 advantage in Nottingham. I was on my first return to Northampton with Nottinghamshire for a National League game, having moved counties the previous winter, but players on either side were transfixed by what was going on up the M1, particularly on the final evening when England sealed the game.

In those days, Wantage Road had an old-fashioned electronic scoreboard that used to flash up the latest scores from elsewhere, and every time England lost a wicket in their second innings, chasing a target of 129, it ran across the ticker – '32 for 1', '36 for 2', '57 for 3' and so on. Each one drew moans, groans and gasps, and the tension when it got to '116 for 7' was unbearable – you couldn't help flashing your eyes over in the direction of the scoreboard anticipating an update, and unsurprisingly even the umpires, Peter Willey and Neil Mallender, appeared distracted by the events elsewhere.

Then nothing actually changed for what seemed like about half an hour. Had whoever was running the board gone for a cup of tea? The tension as Ashley Giles and Matthew Hoggard negotiated the last leg of the chase could be felt all around the country, and when the final update came through there were cheers on the pitch and in the stands and I punched the air.

It was a similar kind of experience a fortnight later on the final day of the series. The coverage that week included *BBC Breakfast* being presented live from The Oval. Channel 4's audience was in excess of 12 million people. But I was listening to the radio commentary driving back and forth from the Park Hospital in Nottingham. My troublesome elbow was playing up and it meant I missed a County Championship match against Kent to see a specialist.

Alex Tudor, an old mate of mine, was summarising for 5 Live. Tuds and I first played against each other in the Under-11s and his voice provided a really calming influence. Lunch was approaching and there was plenty of time to go in the match, but he was steadily talking down the clock. There was no excess excitement in his voice. It had the soothing tone you would expect from a captain in that situation.

England's actual captain, Michael Vaughan, meanwhile, was persuading his star batsmen to seal the deal by taking Australia's potential fourth-innings target out of reach. Kevin Pietersen was unbelievable in that series, and one thing I could never deny is that Kevin has been a truly magnificent player. He could do things that other players could only dream of. That series, his first as a Test player, Pietersen was absolutely fearless in his approach and had a temperament that allowed him to play strokes that others only saw in their dreams. Vaughan tapped into this by encouraging him to counter Australia's bouncer barrage with hooks. It was hairy – he could have got out a couple of times on the boundary – but the fine margins went England's way, just as they had when he was dropped twice early in that innings of 158.

Looking at it again now, some of the shots he was playing show how loose he was in comparison to what he was like later in his England career. Yet, for me, he was an infinitely better player in that first series because some of the balls he hit for four made your jaw drop and he didn't treat any bowler with respect. Shane Warne still got 40 wickets in the series but he lost their one-on-one. Imagine what would have happened if Kev had just concentrated on being that brilliant batsman of 2005 . . .

I could never get my head around this supposed issue Kev developed against left-arm spinners. When I first played with him, he would have just hit them out of the ground and not thought about it. But because he read the papers and listened to the opinions of others too much he got it in his head that he had a weakness after being dismissed a couple of times. To me, this was a classic example of how thinking the wrong way can really affect how good a player you are.

He was arguably the best batsman the England team has ever had, but his record does not reflect that. The issue with left-arm spinners, plus other distractions – fame, fortune, sending text messages to South Africans about the England captain, whistling in team meetings – stopped it happening. He should have averaged over 60 and yet his mark was less than 50.

His series-high 473 runs was a magnificent achievement for a debutant, and his performances denied one of his team-mates exclusivity when it came to influence on that England team. While the 1981 series is rightly known as Botham's Ashes, for all its similarities to that series, 2005 is not known as Flintoff's Ashes. Well, not outside Fred's house, anyhow.

Fred did receive recognition for it, of course, but ultimately it ended in disaster. Twelve months later, England made the classic mistake, and one I fear they made again in 2017. Who is our best player? Who is the man of the moment? Andrew Flintoff. Right, let's make him captain.

Fred is not captaincy material. He has a larger-than-life public persona but is not necessarily the extrovert he portrays. He is someone who needs to be loved and man-managed. That was not going to happen when he was thrust into the job of captaining England in an Ashes series in Australia.

Undoubtedly, he was the fulcrum of the team as the all-rounder, but he was not a leader in the captaincy sense. For that you need someone who is more cerebral, who has time to reflect and calculate the decisions that are being made; someone with an understanding of different people from different backgrounds. That's not Fred. As a cricketer he was instinctive, someone who led with his actions, not necessarily his words; someone who never gave much consideration to things beyond his own game.

Andrew Strauss, his rival to deputise for the injured Michael Vaughan that winter, was born to be England captain – or South African captain, the choice was his – yet the ECB hierarchy ignored his claims on this occasion, and even turned to Kevin Pietersen before him in the long run. How had they not learned their lesson after the debacle of 2006–07?

In contrast to Pietersen, Strauss had the respect of everyone in the dressing room and was truly the cleverest man in the room. He would have won hands down on that front. On a subconscious level, if someone more intelligent than you is speaking about something, what they say instantly becomes more believable. A core principle of any good team is that everyone buys into the same thing. Strauss was a very good public speaker, someone who didn't stutter, um and ah, and was also a very approachable and naturally affable chap. You knew that you could be honest with him and you would get the same level of honesty back. That is not to say he wasn't stubborn. He was. But his skill was not to be overly forceful, so even if you weren't getting your own way, you still wanted to play for him.

I'm the first to admit that I was extremely petulant at times, but when I stamped my feet Strauss just treated me with disdain. One example was on the tour of South Africa in 2009–10 when I hit Mark Boucher on the pad and immediately knew it was out. When my lbw shout was turned down, I demanded we call for a review but Matt Prior, behind the stumps, was not convinced: 'Nah, it was sliding, mate.'

I urged Strauss to call for it, threatening to withdraw my labour if he did not. He fixed his eyes on me and said: 'Just get back and bowl, you baboon.' Of course, I dropped my head bashfully and did as I was told. I don't think I even made too much of a fuss when the replay on the big screen suggested I'd been right all along.

Being the figurehead of a losing Ashes team must be extremely tough. Fred himself has documented how he turned to alcohol during that 2006–07 tour. Well, I'm not sure what he'd been turning to for the previous dozen years when he was regularly blasted around the county scene. Those bottles of red Hooch he used to neck in Nottingham nightclubs were no mocktails.

It's true that there were injuries galore to contend with – some players began the series half-fit. And, of course, Australia's great players – Shane Warne, Glenn McGrath and Matthew Hayden – were intent on revenge for the blip on their CVs. But had Michael Vaughan been captain in 2006–07, I'm convinced things would have been different, because he had the skill of instilling self-belief. If you watched England during that series they were a very timid side, and he would not have allowed that to be the case.

During the infamous second Test in Adelaide when defeat was snatched from the jaws of victory, the same team that had declared six wickets down on 551 in the first innings was indulging in talk heading into the final day of 'batting until tea to make the game safe'. They didn't manage to make it safe, getting bowled out cheaply and leaving Australia a chase of just 168. In contrast, Vaughan would have been aping the attitude of the Australians themselves and urging his team to attack, to make sure they were way out of range well before the tea interval.

In future years I heard players who were involved in that series discuss how things could have been so different if Andrew Symonds had been given out lbw in the fourth Test at Melbourne: 'We were robbed there.' Good grief, England were 3–0 down going into that game, yet they were fixated with being denied a sixth wicket in Australia's first innings. Symonds, who at that stage averaged 18 with the bat in Tests, had walked to the crease at 84–5. Fair enough, having scored a modest 159 themselves, removing Symonds would have swung the balance towards England. Instead, a 279-run partnership for the sixth wicket, also featuring Matthew Hayden, dictated another survival expedition. But that was all small beer. The 2006–07 Ashes had slipped from England's grasp before Christmas and the summer of 2005 seemed like a distant memory.

It was as if the golden elixir they had picked up in 2005 had become too hot to handle all of a sudden. We had gone back to being old-fashioned, safe and very English. There was a sense that Australia had been waiting for their chance to restore order from the moment that the ticker tape was released in Trafalgar Square 15 months earlier – to restore the mental hold they had enjoyed for so long over England teams.

Date	Venue	Team	Scores	Team	Scores	Result
21/07/2005	Lord's	Australia	190 & 384	England	155 & 180	Australia won by 239 runs
04/08/2005	Birmingham	England	407 & 182	Australia	308 & 279	England won by 2 runs
11/08/2005	Manchester	England	444 & 280-6d	Australia	302 & 371-9	Drawn
25/08/2005	Nottingham	England	477 & 129-7	Australia	218 & 387	England won by 3 wickets
08/09/2005	The Oval	England	373 & 335	Australia	367 & 4-0	Drawn
23/11/2006	Brisbane	Australia	602-9d & 202-1d	England	157 & 370	Australia won by 277 runs
01/12/2006	Adelaide	England	551-6d & 129	Australia	513 & 168-4	Australia won by 6 wickets
14/12/2006	Perth	Australia	244 & 527-5d	England	215 & 350	Australia won by 206 runs
26/12/2006	Melbourne	England	159 & 161	Australia	419	Australia won by an innings and 99 runs
02/01/2007	Sydney	England	291 & 147	Australia	393 & 46-0	Australia won by 10 wickets

13

GETTING A TASTE FOR WINNING

TAKING the wicket to seal the 2009 Ashes was as close to pure ecstasy as I reckon it is possible to get in professional sport, a feeling made all the more special for two other reasons. Firstly, it came along when I was not especially striving for it, and secondly it fulfilled a pledge I had made to my victim on the eve of the series.

Mike Hussey became a good friend during our time together at Northamptonshire and during a phone conversation earlier that year, he told me that he'd had a vision about how the series would conclude.

'I've got a feeling that I'm going to hit you for four at The Oval to win the Ashes,' he told me.

Of course, that was not something I was prepared to accept, so I hit back with: 'Nah, I am going to get you, caught bat-pad, to win it for England.'

I could not have imagined how prophetic my words were to prove.

In that fifth Test at The Oval in 2009, a triple strike from Steve Harmison left us one wicket shy of completing the 2–1 victory and as I had bowled all day I felt I deserved to be the one that delivered the final act. However, as Hussey had a hundred to his name, I anticipated that my best chance of this was to hunt some rabbit pie by getting number 11 Ben Hilfenhaus on strike.

To that end, a deep point had been set to give Hussey the single, and so when I released the delivery in question, the second of the 103rd over of the innings, what followed was the most beautiful of surprises. The ball didn't spin much; it just bounced and Hussey prodded it straight to Alastair Cook at short leg. As it nestled in his hands, I experienced the most stomach-tingling sensation.

Believe me when I say that no matter how many times you've imagined it as a kid, it is not a moment you actually practise for, so what happened next was impromptu guff, albeit glorious impromptu guff. I veered off to my right and slid on my knees, not even waiting for umpire Asad Rauf's finger to go up. Next moment, Andrew Strauss hauled me back to my feet and it was just pandemonium out there on the edge of the pitch as the team embraced.

The whole ground was going absolutely mental. Sometimes you look forward to something so much that it's a bit of a let-down when it actually happens. Not so when the prize is the Ashes. To celebrate with your team-mates, and particularly those who are close mates, is one of the privileges of being an England cricketer.

The most cherished photograph from my playing career is of myself, Cook and Jimmy Anderson sitting in my favourite spot in the Oval dressing room, with our England caps on, arms around each other. We're all smiling, and Cookie has the urn aloft.

Beer also tastes pretty good at the end of a hard series. In Ashes of yesteryear the two teams used to share drinks together daily after play, but Australia captain Allan Border put a stop to that practice in the final series of the 1980s. He was still haunted by his previous trip when, in his own words, he was 'a nice guy who came last'.

Latterly, socialising is reserved for the final evening, which makes it quite special. It's nice to welcome opponents into your dressing room after such an intensely hard-fought series. We were all endeavouring to come out on top, we just had different badges on our chests.

A big thing is made of the hatred English sportsmen have for Australians, but that is a big misconception because we don't hate them in the truest sense of the word. As with all great rivalries, the essential ingredient in our relationship is a mutual respect. In fact, I have always been the sort of person who enjoys watching his mates on the opposition do well, as long as the result goes our way, so I was pleased for Mike Hussey in the Oval Test. He had been under immense pressure that tour, due to an uncharacteristically poor run of form, and his hundred made sure he retained his place for the following winter.

It was a wonderful end to a series that began slowly from my perspective. It wasn't until the Australians' second innings in the second Test at Lord's that I took a wicket. Partly this was down to a pre-match injury ahead of the first Test in Cardiff (who would ever have imagined England playing an Ashes Test in Wales?), which was erroneously being billed as home to some kind of spinners' snakepit in the build-up. From my experience, despite a hullabaloo being made about the ball ragging square following a couple of domestic one-day games, what turn there was at Sophia Gardens tended to be slow. So despite the fact that the selection of myself and Monty Panesar meant England fielded two spinners in a home Ashes Test for the first time since 1993, I remained cautious about such forecasts. Glamorgan had shelled out £3 million to get this match and it was in their financial interests for it to go all five days.

I had cut my hand in the nets and for some reason, instead of covering it with a plaster, it was decided to glue the wound. It seemed like a good idea at the time, I suppose. But the lack of feeling around my knuckle made the whole process of bowling feel quite alien, and I am not sure why I was experimenting ahead of the biggest match I'd ever played. What made me think sending a dozen balls down in the nets was suitable preparation I do not know. Unhappy at how it felt and how it restricted me, I opted to rip the resin off midway through the contest, and although there was discomfort and a bit of blood, it felt considerably better.

If any further evidence were needed of the true nature of the pitch, Jimmy Anderson and I shared a 68-run partnership in nine overs on the second morning. This led, in the second innings, to my first and only taste that I can recall of Ashes sledging. Doing the media rounds on the second evening, I had joked that, given that my unbeaten 47 had boosted my Test average to 76, I should clearly now be recognised as the best batsman on either side. Unfortunately, it appeared tongue-in-cheek humour was still an alien concept to some Australians in 2009.

From silly point, Ricky Ponting greeted me with the only words he said to me during the series: 'So you think you're the best player on either side, do you?'

In the plummiest English voice I could muster, I came back with: 'Oh, Richard. I didn't realise you could read.'

It might have diluted the impact the Australian captain was trying to make when Brad Haddin burst out laughing behind the stumps. Not that much actually affected Ponting on the field, mind. He had a reputation as the hardest silly point in the world, and for good reason.

Later in the series, at The Oval, Matt Prior was batting and Ponting stationed himself under the batsman's nose. Matt used to have a shot which was like an off-drive but played with more of a flat bat than a textbook straight one, and when he made contact the ball really flew off the bat, as it did on this particular occasion when facing Marcus North's off-spin. The ball bounced up and struck Ponting flush in the mush. Blood spurted from Ponting's mouth like something out of a zombie flick, prompting Prior to ask: 'Are you all right, mate?' Ponting, treating him with complete contempt, simply turned his head, spat out the blood, fixed him with a stare and in the most measured of ways replied: 'F*** off.'

I digress, so back to the first Test in Cardiff. There were 25 minutes remaining before tea on the final evening and Australia seemed intent on bouncing me out. Troubled by the lack of bounce, Peter Siddle pinned me three times in one over with short balls. I feared being lynched by my teammates more than being struck, so instead of hooking and pulling, I took a peppering – once on the arm, once on the head, once on the hand.

My contribution towards saving that first Test was 73 minutes, but my dismissal to Ben Hilfenhaus left work still to do, and the demise of Paul Collingwood seconds after 6 p.m. resulted in a deathly silence falling on our dressing room. He had played such a superb rearguard innings that no one expected him to get out.

The dramatic final-wicket stand between Jimmy and Monty that followed was like a tragicomedy. We were still behind when they came together but once in front the equation changed, and our management team worked out that we needed to bat until 6.40 p.m. to ensure that there was not enough time in the final hour for Australia to bat again.

Clearly, this message needed to be conveyed to our tenth-wicket pair, so our twelfth man, Bilal Shafayat, was dispatched to take new gloves to Jimmy. This also served to take a few more precious seconds out of the remaining time, lessening the chances of Australia – by now operating with two spinners to get through their overs quicker – sending down any more than the 15 scheduled.

Gamesmanship? Sure, but tell me a team that wouldn't have acted in the same manner. Everyone does it, although it was probably over-egging things when Jimmy signalled to the balcony again soon afterwards. This time, physio Steve McCaig was dispatched. By now Ponting was in no mood for games and he greeted the physio with quite a verbal volley. For McCaig this was a bitter blow, not least because, as an Australian himself, Ponting was his hero. Afterwards, though, as we reflected on things in the changing room, it brought smiles to our faces.

It is a tired old cliché to say that drawing matches like this actually feels like winning, and while we didn't want to be seen to be celebrating on the balcony like the Australians in Manchester in 2005, it was a pleasing show of spirit to stave off defeat from a position of five wickets down with five hours still remaining, and we were naturally very happy to be level heading to Lord's, a ground at which Australia had dominated Ashes matches since before the Second World War.

* * *

From an England perspective, the greatness of Lord's and its ability to inspire touring teams was an habitual problem and it became a focus of our discussions that week, as we tried to address how to turn around our fortunes there. If opponents were inspired by the grandeur of the surroundings, we needed to feed off it too, to feel that playing there was something out of the ordinary, something to be cherished.

'Look around this place,' I said, as we chatted on the outfield a couple of days before the match. 'Soak all this up. This is Lord's, the best ground in the world, we are playing against Australia, and this is as good as it gets, so let's love every single minute of this week. The architecture, the paintings in the Long Room, the whole history of the game is here. Let's not take it for granted. We will be playing at Headingley soon, and let's face it, that's a dump.' (It's not a dump, of course, but the chance to wind up some Yorkshiremen? I'll always take that.)

I cannot claim all the credit for what was to follow but I reckon my contribution was around the 95 per cent mark.

In truth, there were other factors involved in our first Lord's win over Australia for 75 years. One of them was Andrew Flintoff who, between the first and second matches, announced that this series was to be his final one in Test cricket, and he was intent on re-enacting some of his 2005 magic. Once your body starts giving up on you it's hard work, and that was particularly true for Fred at that point. He required jabs in the knee operated on earlier that year to extend his last hurrah.

'For the next four matches I'll do everything I need to do to get on a cricket field and I'm desperate to make my mark,' he said, adding: 'An Ashes series is bigger than any one player. The focus will be on England trying to win a special series.'

I am not sure he truly meant the latter. When you have enjoyed the adulation that comes with being the golden boy of a team that spectacularly and unexpectedly defeats Australia, as he did in 2005, how could you not want more? In July 2009, the pre-match cortisone injections were enough to get him through that week, and what a week it proved to be.

At the time I considered the potential loss of Kevin Pietersen to an Achilles injury as more of a threat to our plans – because of what he had done to Australia in the past and the way he could take a game away from any opposition. He did play at Lord's, but we were not to see him again in the series after that week, and we managed to cope better than I anticipated.

As it was, Strauss took up the mantle, punishing the Australians' inability to adjust to the Lord's slope by taking them for 161 runs on the opening day, and ensuring we scored in excess of 400 once again. In Australia's first innings, so well did our pace attack bowl that I was restricted to just one over. Not that you mind at a ground like Lord's, where it's fill-yer-boots time every lunch and tea interval. You don't want to be overdoing things on a stomach full of sponge pudding. The 200-plus lead also presented Strauss with the dilemma of whether to ask Ponting's team to follow on. Of course, the bowlers' union generally want a rest at times like this and so it was happy days all round when we batted again.

Set a world-record 522 runs to win, Australia suffered the controversial early dismissals of Simon Katich and Phillip Hughes – to a low catch referred to the third umpire and a no-ball not spotted by the officials – although neither could compare to the third, which provided my maiden Ashes wicket. I assumed Mike Hussey had nicked in regulation fashion when the ball arrived in Paul Collingwood's hands at slip. Astonishingly, however, video later showed that the ball touched nothing on its way through, landing in the footholes to fizz past the outside edge. Sorry, Huss.

As we were to experience in later years, Brad Haddin was a difficult opponent to shift at times and so when, alongside Michael Clarke, he snipped the target to 209 with five wickets intact it set up an intriguing final day.

Typically, Fred demanded centre stage. The atmosphere had been terrific throughout but the noise as we made our way through the Long Room on the fifth morning was something else, and he was responsible.

As we strode down the stairs, he turned round to the rest of us and said: 'Watch this.' Waving his arms in the air, he shouted, at the top of his voice: 'Come on, lads!'

The roared response by the egg-and-bacon brigade really lightened the mood.

Clarke was a good player of spin, so you can imagine everyone's surprise, not least mine, when he advanced down the track at me, attempting to hit through the off side, and simply missed a full toss, to be bowled. Crucially, his mistake exposed the Australian tail and Fred was able to embark on his final crusade.

With a brand-new ball in hand, you wouldn't have backed any lower-order batsmen in the world to survive, and Nathan Hauritz and Peter Siddle were simply blown away by searing deliveries that nipped back down the hill. The way he charged in, it was not apparent how much pain Flintoff was in that morning, and it was almost as if he had convinced himself that, once in battle with Australia, he became superhuman. The messiah pose in response to Siddle's rearranged furniture, though? Not so sure about that one.

Neither, in hindsight, am I convinced that he should have played for England again after that, as his knee problems meant that he did not contribute as much as he would have liked. His Lord's performance was magnificent, though, a fitting farewell for one of England's great modern players. He was just so fast that day, always at the batsmen. It was arguably his finest ever performance for England, and what a way that would have been to go.

When Mitchell Johnson missed a heave to leg 18 minutes before lunch, it gave me the honour of claiming the match-sealing wicket, and the knowledge that I had bowled much better than in the first Test in Cardiff.

Had Australia lost their aura? That was a subject of debate as we headed to Birmingham, 1–0 up in the series. Having not played against an Australian team before, I had not really considered whether or not they possessed an aura in the first place. To me they were just the latest ones in the way of us getting our hands on the urn. But people like Andrew Strauss, who had been whitewashed in 2006–07, were pretty well placed to judge. Take names like Shane Warne, Adam Gilchrist, Matthew Hayden, Justin Langer and Glenn McGrath out of the equation and answer the question for yourself. It was hardly controversial to suggest that this Australian team was not as good as their predecessors but in doing so, on the eve of the third Test at Edgbaston, in answer to a direct question at a press conference, Strauss stirred things up a bit.

Rain meant there was not much else to talk about during that third Test, other than the finest piece of bowling I had yet produced in an England shirt – surely the ball of the century, or at least the 21st century – dismissing Ricky Ponting on the fourth evening as we pushed for an unlikely victory. Two balls after having a stone-dead lbw turned down, I went wider on the crease and ripped the most perfect delivery. The ball drifted, dipped and then turned square to bowl him through the gate. For an off-spinner that is the dream dismissal. It was always nice to claim that emphatic kind of wicket, particularly against a batsman of Ponting's class.

Arguably producing a delivery like that heaped pressure on me to follow up with fifth-day wickets. Unfortunately, I was not able to do so. Quite frankly, I bowled like a novice, and Australia comfortably averted the threat of going 2–0 down.

Behaviour between the teams always comes under the microscope in Ashes series, as we have seen well enough through incidents chronicled in these pages. It didn't do much for the image of snarling warfare some like to maintain between the teams when a diplomatic incident arose on the first morning of the third Test at Edgbaston.

When Brad Haddin broke a finger in the warm-ups, Australia had already named their team. By the laws of the game, the final XI is final, and Andrew Strauss could have upheld those laws. Equally, by its spirit, and tradition, he could assent to a late change in personnel, which is what he did. When it comes to it, in that kind of situation you do unto others what you would wish for yourself, and Graham Manou was allowed to come in as replacement. Although we were all desperate to win, you also want to win the right way and against the strongest possible opposition. If Australia owed us one, it didn't take us long to cash in the chip.

After a draw at Edgbaston, we moved on to Headingley for the fourth Test. One way and another, the first day began in total chaos. At 4.30 a.m., we found ourselves semi-naked in the street, outside the Radisson hotel in central Leeds, following a fire alarm, set off when one of the guests left wet underwear to dry on a bedroom lamp. Spending an hour in the freezing cold and wet was not ideal preparation. Upon arrival at the ground, it was confirmed that Andrew Flintoff had been left out following concerns about him playing back-to-back Tests, and to cap it all, Matt Prior suffered a back spasm in the warm-ups.

With credit in the bank, Strauss managed to negotiate a delayed toss while our medical staff got to work. The half-hour grace period allowed Matt to prove his fitness. It was just about the only positive thing to happen for us that day. After winning the toss, we were dismissed for 102 shortly after lunch – Australia profiting from bowling a full Leeds length. In contrast, Australia came out and smashed it every-where.

One game up with two to play, we'd headed to Yorkshire in the knowledge that victory would seal the Ashes with a game to go. Instead, we were humiliated, to be honest. Not even sharing in the second-fastest three-figure stand in Test history with Stuart Broad – 108 runs in 12.3 overs, behind only New Zealand's Nathan Astle and Chris Cairns in simi-larly futile circumstances against England in 2001–02 – could improve my mood.

After the match Andy Flower, the England coach, called a team meeting to discuss the failings and the fixes required ahead of the series finale at The Oval. Normally, this kind of debrief would happen between matches, once the dust has settled, but in the circumstances it was felt necessary, and so during what should have been the third evening session, we raked through what had occurred and tried to put the traumatic downturn in fortunes into perspective. Between them, Flower and Strauss reinforced one simple fact: if we won at The Oval the following week, the Ashes were ours.

During those talks, the prospect of playing County Championship cricket was raised, something I was reluctant to consider. Putting myself forward to impress the management was not something I was keen on, and if I was going to play for Nottinghamshire it had to be because I felt the match practice would be beneficial to me. I did not. The match against Warwickshire was just two days away, so I said I was knackered and wanted a week off.

However, driving back to Nottingham that evening, my wife, Sarah, asked me whether I was sure about sitting out. On reflection, I felt that getting some bowling under my belt wouldn't do me any harm, so during that journey I phoned Andy to ask if he minded if I did play after all.

It was a takeaway curry that kiboshed that plan and so nearly terminated my Test summer prematurely. Next morning I was on the phone to Nick Peirce, the England doctor, informing him I suspected food poisoning, and therefore in the lead-up to the most important match of the 2009 season I endured the inglorious procedure of producing stool samples.

So rather than fretting about how I was going to get some wickets at The Oval, or over-exerting myself with another four-day match, I lay there being fed soup by Sarah that I could barely keep down. I am quite dramatic when I get ill and that week I was convinced I was dying. I was calling for the priest and reaching for the rosary beads.

Even when I arrived in London I did not feel right, and I thought I was going to collapse in the changing room from exhaustion after the first practice session. Yet there were signs that I was going to enjoy myself once the match started, given the way the practice pitches played.

'Good Lord, Graeme. You're going to have a field day,' Strauss said to me, after one spun sharply past the outside edge of his bat. A look across at the pitch suggested it was going to be very similar, so it came as a surprise to us when we heard that Australia were sticking with the same team that had defeated us at Headingley. Nathan Hauritz was not in their XI and Marcus North, no more than a part-timer, was their main spinner.

It was an unusual situation to head into a final Test of an Ashes with all three results possible. We had been on the canvas at times during that series, but so had Australia. It was markedly different from other tight series because there just weren't any close games. It ebbed and flowed over the five matches, but once a team got on top in an individual match they stayed on top for its duration.

Having won the toss for a fourth time, we were genuinely disappointed with our 332 all out in the first innings of the fifth Test, and it wasn't looking too clever for us when Australia meandered to 73 without loss in reply.

Then came one of Stuart Broad's hot streaks. There had been speculation about his place in the side earlier in the series, but within our dressing room we knew what a bowler of his class brought to the side. From nowhere, he had the ability to produce brilliant, wicket-laden spells. His most famous was to come in Nottingham in 2015, of course, and like that 8–15 performance, he made everyone feel that something was going to happen every ball.

One thud into Shane Watson's front pad totally transformed the atmosphere around The Oval. Even though few balls had misbehaved previously, the crowd now roared him in and suddenly the pitch resembled a minefield. Ponting chopped on, Mike Hussey was leg-before to one that shaped back in and Michael Clarke jabbed to short cover – Australia's four leading batsmen had been dismissed in a phenomenal sequence of 21 balls.

There is no doubt that in my career I profited from the Decision Review System, which came in later that year, and I reckon I used it pretty well, but I made the most of this particular pre-DRS occasion with some cheap wickets on the back of Broad's burst. Two of the four wickets I took were so bad I felt like giving them back, and might have done but for the fact it was Australians on the wrong end.

Throughout the series I looked to exploit Marcus North's high backlift, bowling from around the wicket, but the arm ball that did for him here was one of those optical illusions thrown up from time to time. Halfway through its journey,

I thought: 'Lbw', and therefore when it made impact I got excitable. So did the close fielders. Only after North, a lovely bloke who I'd played against since we were kids, walked off shaking his head in response to Asad Rauf's decision did it occur to me that he had got an inside edge – and a huge chunk of one at that.

Then Stuart Clark, who had slogged me all over Leeds, was taken at short leg for what appeared to be a regulation bat-pad. To be fair, he only missed it by about a foot and a half. Before DRS that's the way it went, and you had to take the good with the bad.

Once again, Broad and I had worked together a treat in tandem, just as we had with the bat a fortnight earlier, and we had preserved the trend of one side opening up a dominant match position. This one was built upon by Jonathan Trott's brilliant debut hundred in the second innings.

He had given us a glimpse of his ability, and indeed temperament, on day one with an innings of 41, but this was confirmation that he was made for constructing big scores at the highest level. His introverted, idiosyncratic mannerisms at the crease meant he paid little attention to the external stuff going on around him, giving him an unflappable air. Impervious to any pressure, he batted Australia out of the game.

Having set Australia another huge target, this time 546 in six and a half sessions, we were in need of one final act of inspiration. And in Flintoff we possessed someone who was drawn to the limelight like a moth to a flame.

By the very end, he wasn't bowling as quickly and wasn't moving that fast in the outfield either. Limping to the finish line was a pretty weak way for a player like him to head into retirement, to be honest, and because he was no longer the aggressor of just a month earlier, when he hurtled in from the Pavilion End at Lord's in one of the greatest physical efforts by an England fast bowler, his telling intervention came from the long grass.

Not able to field at slip due to this recurring knee problem, he swooped on his chance with Australia 217–2 when Mike Hussey turned the ball to mid-on and called for a single. Because I was at gully, I got into line with the projection of Fred's throw to back it up, and witnessed this swinging sidearm sling arc perfectly towards its target and dismantle the stumps.

Direct hits always get fielding sides excited, and as the crowd roared in anticipation Ponting wore the expression of a man at Tyburn. He knew his fate.

It was a truly great moment, the defining moment of that last day, and Fred milked it, of course. We were always going to win, I am convinced of that, but we did need something out of nothing to alter the momentum of the innings. Who better to provide it than Fred? His entire career was defined by match-winning performances in Ashes games.

Ponting's dismissal brought in Michael Clarke, and because he had proved so effective against me using his feet throughout the series, we countered with a plan, encouraged by the bowling coach Mushtaq Ahmed, for me to bowl around the wicket to him. Sometimes altering the angle you're bowling from changes what the batsman thinks, Mushy argued. And when a batsman in form changes his thinking, it can alter his approach at the crease.

It didn't, as it happened, but just five balls after we had terminated Australia's healthy third-wicket partnership, Clarke skipped down the track and turned to leg, only for the ball to ricochet off short leg Alastair Cook's boot into the hands of Strauss at leg slip. A flip onto the stumps barely raised a murmur from the other close fielders initially, as it was presumed Clarke had stretched to make his ground. But as Billy Bowden walked in from square leg, Matt Prior said: 'Surely that's worth a look upstairs?'

It was. Clarke had not made his ground. He had been Australia's best batsman by a country mile over the course of the series, and we got lucky with that dismissal, even though it came about because of the reflex actions of our close fielders.

Those two run-outs completely changed the atmosphere, and when Marcus North was out 20 minutes later, stumped, trying to sweep me, the noise from the stands was deafening. Yet it was not until the demise of Brad Haddin – the one player remaining with the ability to hit a quick hundred – that I knew beyond doubt the game was ours.

Because Haddin liked advancing out of his crease, and going aerial, we set the midwicket trap for a mishit by placing the fielder three-quarters of the way back to the boundary.

Strauss did not have to move a muscle. And if evidence was required that none of us had been practising our celebrations, you need only watch our captain's awkward jig of delight.

If you look at video footage of *the* moment, though, you will notice that everyone followed me and dived into a big huddle when Hussey succumbed, all apart from Cook who, having caught the ball, was running in the opposite direction with it wedged in his pocket. He had been told by his old Bedford School coach, Derek Randall, who claimed the decisive catch in the 1977 Ashes win – Rod Marsh off Mike Hendrick at Headingley – that his biggest regret was throwing the ball into the crowd. So Cook's idea was to keep this one for posterity. I reckoned there was a better place for it than his mantelpiece, though, and after a year of hounding him he agreed to donate it to the Lord's museum, alongside other memorabilia like Florence Morphy's original urn.

I only took 14 wickets in my maiden Ashes series, and contributed a few runs here and there, but there was something about the way the team was developing that I felt as much a part of its fabric by the end of it as I did at any time afterwards. It is a remarkable admission when I consider it, because my returns were not great and I definitely wasn't the finished article in international cricket.

That finishing process took place in South Africa in 2009–10 when I finally convinced myself that I was as good a bowler as I could be. I responded to being asked to be part of a four-man attack by starting at Centurion with a first-innings five-for, and with confidence soaring I made my highest Test score of 85. Nine wickets in the second Test, a victory at Durban, sealed a second man-of-the-match award in a row and the man-of-the-series award followed. That was my million-dollar feeling – not quite the same as Ben Stokes's after the 2017 IPL auction, I grant you, but the same sentiments. I knew I was wanted, and knew I belonged. For pure glory, though, nothing felt better than sitting in those beer-stained whites reflecting on victory over the Australians at The Oval. Waking up with a hangover yet feeling euphoric. This was my favourite of the three I achieved. Sure, the away win that followed was more of an achievement for the team, but there was just something about doing it at home that appealed to me.

Date	Venue	Team	Scores	Team	Scores	Result
08/07/2009	Cardiff	England	435 & 252-9	Australia	674-6d	Drawn
16/07/2009	Lord's	England	425 & 311-6d	Australia	215 & 406	England won by 115 runs
30/07/2009	Birmingham	Australia	263 & 375-5	England	376	Drawn
07/08/2009	Leeds	England	102 & 263	Australia	445	Australia won by an innings and 80 runs
20/08/2009	The Oval	England	332 & 373-9d	Australia	160 & 348	England won by 197 runs

14

THE ROAD TO SYDNEY

W HEN it came to preparation for the 2010–11 Ashes there really was no stone left unturned, starting as soon as the international summer had concluded against Pakistan in late September. Those of us who had anticipated an interim period to wind down and enjoy ourselves, following a long summer, received a rude awakening.

In fact, several of us had made travel plans following the one-day series against Pakistan, which finished on 22 September 2010. I had arranged to go to Las Vegas with a few of my mates to get away from cricket completely, whilst Stuart Broad was also due to be over in Vegas that week, on Luke Wright's stag do. So when we found out that our meticulous coach Andy Flower was already putting pre-Ashes dates into his diary, we feared the worst. And those fears were realised.

Andy believed that winning in Australia required a team

to be tight, and he wanted to work on our togetherness with a bonding trip abroad. So within 48 hours of the international summer's conclusion, instead of heading to the States, Stuart and I had passports in hand, joining the rest of the Ashes squad on a trip to a mystery location.

All we were told was that we would be travelling from Gatwick airport in the early hours of Friday, 24 September and we were given a list of essentials to pack. It was all outside wear, stuff like thermals, sleeping bags and strong boots. The need for that kind of get-up suggested this was not going to be some jolly on the beach and was hardly going to replicate the fun we might have had in the gambling capital of the world.

As departure came immediately after the Professional Cricketers' Association dinner at the Hurlingham Club in London, it also meant dashing back to our hotels to change attire at around 5 a.m. We found out upon arrival at Gatwick that our destination was Munich and in our shabby states of mind inevitably we decided that we'd been booked in to bond over strong ale at Oktoberfest. No such luck, however.

When we landed, we were met by two Australian blokes who struggled to conceal they had Special Forces backgrounds. They were a fairly stern duo, evading both eye contact and conversation equally efficiently as they shepherded us onto our transport – a couple of minibuses that took us on a two-hour drive to a field in the middle of nowhere. What turned out to be a four-day boot camp – designed to push us to the limit, physically and mentally, challenging us to work within a team environment and also to discover how far we were prepared to go as individuals – had been arranged by our security expert, Reg Dickason.

Over the next 72 hours we put up tents, hiked, shifted and lifted, and went through a series of army exercise drills. Bad language was outlawed and every time one of us swore it resulted in 50 press-ups on the spot. There was also a strict code of formality to the way we had to address each other. A similar forfeit to that of swearing was applied if we did not address each other as if we were back in 1905. The use of Christian names was banned, and so I became Mr Swann.

Our mobile phones were confiscated for the week, our meals came from ration packs and we dossed in tents rather badly constructed by our own hands. If Andy Flower had wanted to put us through the most exhaustive of weeks, he had got his wish. I hated every minute of it. Others would later say that they thought it useful for our development as a side, but I never was one for doing that kind of forced bonding. Authority and me never did see eye to eye, so being instructed to do this and that 24/7 didn't go down well with me.

Back home, Sarah was pregnant with our first child, Wilfred, and I knew I was going to see a limited amount of her over the next four months while we attempted to repeat the feat of Mike Gatting's England team in 1986–87 and retain the Ashes on Australian soil. Jonathan Trott was forced to pull out of this bonding jaunt because his wife, Abi, was due to give birth. For some reason he felt guilty about not being with the lads but, believe me, I would have swapped places with him in a heartbeat.

At nightfall we would gather around a big bonfire and hold group discussions or engage in role-play games created by our Australian hosts. What sleep we got each night was then broken by these two maniacs who woke us before dawn to trudge up the road in some kind of fitness drill. The one person who could have taken it all in his stride, Alastair Cook, turned up halfway through, having attended his brother's wedding. He's the kind of guy that loves the challenges we were being set and outdoor pursuits such as abseiling and rock-climbing.

Generally, the trip was viewed as a success, but it did leave us fearful that the exhaustion might cost us when it came to facing Australia a few weeks later. There was one particular moment of concern during a boxing session. We were all put into pairs and naturally no one fancied pulling Chris Tremlett's name out of the hat for their bout; we just had no one to match this giant of a man. Jimmy Anderson drew the short straw. One infamous punch to his body led to much fretting over the next six weeks, but thankfully Jimmy's cracked rib had just enough time to heal, and we went into our first tour match against Western Australia with a fully-fit squad from which to select.

* * *

Jimmy was to play a crucial role with the ball throughout the five Test matches in 2010–11, sustaining pressure on the Australian batsmen not only with the new ball but also later on in innings when it became soft. I think this surprised a few people, not least Shane Warne, who claimed before the series that if England were to have any chance of winning on Australian soil it required yours truly to claim 40 wickets, the same number he had managed during the 2005 series.

By this point, I had two years of success behind me and I was confident about bowling in a four-man attack against any batsman in the world and succeeding. There were those wickets against Pakistan (subsequently three of their players went to prison for spot-fixing, but I'll take it), plus a man-of-the-series award against South Africa. I took 50 wickets in the calendar year of 2009.

Naturally, I was confident in my ability to get batsmen out, but I also knew how important it would be to continue my holding role in our preferred four-man unit. The retirement of Andrew Flintoff had not only removed some of our X-factor with the ball, it had also reduced options with it generally, and that placed greater onus on those of us remaining.

My main objective within the new set-up was to tie up one end for Andrew Strauss while the fast bowlers rested and rotated. It did not prevent me enjoying success, and my first Test five-wicket haul came in the first innings against South Africa. But the team needed me to fulfil my obligation in a different dynamic, and I enjoyed the challenge of being the bowler who took 2–60. I knew if I did that, or better, I would be good for five or six wickets in a match.

Jimmy Anderson and Stuart Broad had established themselves as the new-ball pairing in the previous 18 months and were well supported by the likes of Tim Bresnan, Steven Finn and Chris Tremlett. As a team, we also had a good knowledge of the Australian batsmen we were going to be faced with, as most had played during 2009. Personally, as a spinner, the idea of playing on the Australian grounds, which tend to have big boundaries, also excited me. I knew if anyone was going to take me down, they would have to do so with the cleanest of hits.

We were also confident as a team that our bowlers would have sizeable totals to defend. Throughout our successful period between 2009 and 2013 we won matches by regularly putting 400 runs on the board. As it transpired, some of our batsmen were in the form of their lives in this period and the totals were even greater. Alastair Cook was a run machine, piling up 766 in all, with Jonathan Trott not too far behind him. Ian Bell and Kevin Pietersen also contributed big scores, and in Australian conditions imposing totals tend to be integral to success.

While Jimmy's rib healed perfectly, reducing fears that we would not be fielding our strongest XI in the first Test at Brisbane, I was temporarily concerned about my own place when I got struck on the thumb by a Tim Bresnan delivery while batting in net practice. Thankfully, the injury was not a fracture, merely heavy bruising, and my only discomfort came from the protective covering I had to wear over the thumb when I was in the field during the opening fortnight.

On tours like this it is always nice to get a few wins under your belt against the state sides, or at least have the better of the matches. So our performance against Western Australia in Perth at the beginning of November was pleasing. Having bowled them out twice to set up a run chance of 243, we showed intent by cantering home inside 50 overs. Unsurprisingly, perhaps, the Australian media soon attempted to pour scorn on our achievement, claiming that our opponents were the worst rabble selected by their particular state for 30 years.

Such nonsense did not infiltrate our thinking, however. One of Andy Flower's pre-tour challenges to us had been to win all three of our warm-up games, quite an unusual approach for your standard modern tour. Most of us had come into international cricket at a time when such matches ahead of Test series were little more than glorified practice, full of manufactured scenarios, and some even resulted in the removal of first-class status via the fielding of up to 13 players.

We were also up against history. On previous tours, state sides loved nothing better than upsetting England by producing victories of their own, thus undermining them ahead of the international matches. However, we were on course to complete the three-match clean sweep when heavy rain in Adelaide scuppered the push for victory against South Australia.

Even some clever thinking by the management team failed to derail the authoritative performances we were stringing together against the state sides. In an unprecedented move, it was arranged for our four-man bowling unit to travel to Queensland and acclimatise ahead of the first Test, while the remaining bowlers were selected in the match against Australia A at Hobart.

Our bowling coach, David Saker, an Australian who previously played for Tasmania, suggested the unusual splintering of our tour party when we first arrived in the country. He recognised that the conditions we would potentially face down south contrasted heavily with the sultry ones we would find just days later in the first Test. Allowing the four of us to become accustomed to this difference was to prove crucial. With hindsight, it also allowed the back-up bowlers we would use later in the Ashes to have not only match practice but also the confidence boost that came from securing victory without us.

Tim Bresnan, Ajmal Shahzad, Chris Tremlett and Monty Panesar scythed through Australia A's batting in the very English climate of Tasmania while we set out to get used to the extra humidity that Brisbane provides. Unfortunately, some wet weather restricted our net practice, but we were at least well rested ahead of the six weeks of grind.

My 47 not out in the 1st Test at Cardiff in 2009, left, took my Test average to an unlikely 76. After a cheeky joke in the press conference went over the head of the Australian skipper, I was treated to my one and only piece of Ashes sledging from the great Ricky Ponting.

I take the wicket of my old friend Mike Hussey, caught at short leg by Alastair Cook, to win the 5th Test at The Oval, and with it the 2009 Ashes. What a post-match celebration we had!

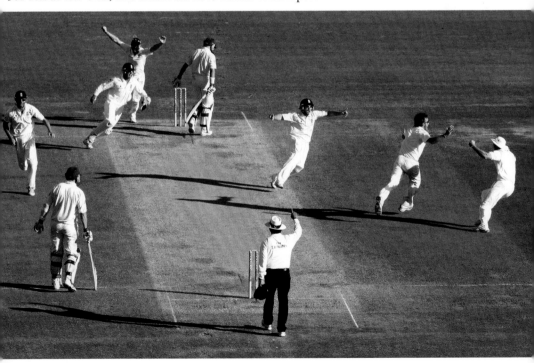

At the presentation at The Oval, a champagne-drenched Andrew Strauss holds aloft the replica urn bought at the Lord's shop, complete with £9.99 price tag.

Lord's witnesses the arrival of a new Ashes hero, as Joe Root – none the worse for wear after his pre-series encounter with David Warner – hits a six during his magnificent second-innings 180 in the 2nd Test of the 2013 series.

Left-arm spinner Ashton Agar reaches 50 in the 1st Test at Trent Bridge in 2013. He was eventually dismissed for 98, the highest score by a No. 11, having put on a record-breaking last-wicket partnership of 163 – all on his Test debut.

It was Phillip Hughes who shared the partnership with Agar, ending up with 81 not out. England went on to win a nerve-wracking game by 14 runs.

Future captain Joe Root, here being congratulated by Ben Stokes, was in fine form with the bat at Cardiff in the 1st Test of the 2015 series, top-scoring in both innings. He also picked up two useful wickets as England won by 169 runs.

Coming in with England at 3–43 in the first innings at Cardiff in 2015, not for the last time Joe Root steadied the ship, eventually being dismissed for 134.

For once, Jimmy Anderson went wicketless at Lord's in 2015, as Chris Rogers and Steve Smith piled on the runs and Australia cruised to a comfortable victory.

David Warner hits another boundary at Brisbane during an innings of 124 in the 1st Test in 2013–14, a series that, in hindsight, I should not have played in.

Mitchell Johnson, who had terrorised England in 2013–14, experienced one of his less successful matches at Trent Bridge in the 4th Test of the 2015 series.

At Lord's in 2015 Ben Stokes's first-innings 87 wasn't enough to save the 2nd Test for England, which Australia dominated with the bat.

Ben Stokes avoids a Mitchell Johnson bouncer in the 4th Test at Trent Bridge in 2015. This time it was the all-rounder's six second-innings wickets that contributed to an England win.

Australia's Michael Clarke, here at practice at Lord's in 2013, was one of the best batsmen I ever bowled at.

One of the great streak bowlers, Stuart Broad celebrates the dismissal of Michael Clarke at Trent Bridge in the 4th Test in 2015, the fifth of his eight first-innings wickets.

Broady can hardly believe it himself as he takes another wicket at Trent Bridge in 2015. Australia's 60 all out was their lowest total in an Ashes Test since 1936.

Alastair Cook's composed 85 at The Oval in 2015 as England followed on wasn't enough to save the final Test, but the series had already been won at Trent Bridge.

The 2015 Ashes-winning team celebrate at Trent Bridge. Back: Mark Wood, Jimmy Anderson, Stuart Broad, Moeen Ali, Jos Buttler, Steve Finn, Ben Stokes. Front: Adam Lyth, Joe Root, Alastair Cook, Ian Bell, Jonny Bairstow.

At this point, Ricky Ponting was under considerable pressure as Australian captain even before a ball was bowled, following defeat in India. The fact that the Australian media were getting stuck into their own team was taken as a positive sign in our camp. Even the prospect of playing Australia at their stronghold of the Gabba – a ground nicknamed 'the Gabbattoir' for the vicious defeats inflicted on tourists over the years – did not daunt us.

Not that we started particularly well. Being dismissed for 260 on the first day was a bit of a jolt, to be honest, not least because of the momentum we had taken into the match. Suddenly, most notably when Peter Siddle took a hat-trick, the Australian crowd resumed their traditionally supportive stance towards their own team. The roar that engulfed me as I walked to the crease immediately after Stuart Broad became Siddle's third victim was as loud as any I have ever heard on a cricket field.

Although Australia opened up a significant lead on first innings, courtesy of a triple-century stand from Mike Hussey, who had only secured his place in the side with a Sheffield Shield hundred the week before, and Brad Haddin, we didn't actually bowl too badly. My own performance was not quite up to scratch, and I wish we had been given the chance to practise at the Gabba itself in the build-up, but I could not fault the efforts of the seamers. It was a terrific Brisbane batting surface. Just how good was put into context when we batted again.

Despite a 221-run deficit to overcome, and scoreboard pressure playing its part, Alastair Cook and Andrew Strauss displayed outstanding dedication to crease occupation and with every passing half-hour our dressing room became a more convivial place. Cook, in particular, highlighted his ability to bat for huge periods of time during that match. In all, his double hundred spanned ten and a half hours and a score of 517–1 undoubtedly deflated the Australians. All the positivity they had developed over the opening couple of days had dissipated as they laboured for 152 overs in the field.

Things even got a bit nasty on the field for the only time in the series. Ricky Ponting went mad at Alastair Cook after he would not take his word on a catch claimed at midwicket. I don't know if it bounced or not – it was one of those that looked pretty tough to call on the TV replays – but Ricky went mental. Cookie came straight back with: 'Hang on, you don't walk when you nick it. You can't have it both ways.'

Our top three batsmen all scored hundreds and after negotiating a challenging position, Andrew Strauss could have opted to grind Australia into the dirt by batting on and on during the final day, but his declaration had dual purpose. Firstly, it was a sign of intent to take some wickets. Secondly, it delivered a psychological blow. It told Australia that not only had they failed spectacularly to develop their advantage, they had also been dictated to by opponents previously behind the eight ball. To pull out of the innings on our own terms showed the fight and intent in this particular England team.

It also provided some momentum heading to Adelaide. During my 60-Test career, I don't think an England team ever started as well as we did in the second Test. Having lost the toss, we were given the perfect start when Jonathan Trott ran out Simon Katich with a direct hit before the Australian opener had faced a ball, and when Jimmy Anderson nicked off Ponting and Michael Clarke in quick succession, Australia were 2–3.

Normally, teams dictate terms at the Adelaide Oval by piling up big first-innings scores. However, given the chance to exploit any early-morning movement on offer, Anderson's skill found a different way to get us ahead. Australia's first-innings score of 245 was put into context when Alastair Cook and Kevin Pietersen made use of the pitch – Cook hitting another hundred and Pietersen doubling up as we declared five wickets down for 620.

The selection of the left-armer Doug Bollinger in Australia's team was good from my perspective as it created a decent amount of rough outside off stump for me to aim into when we got a second go with the ball. A number of deliveries turned appreciably during my marathon 34-over spell on the fourth day, yet ironically it was one that didn't spin much that resulted in the prize wicket of Ponting, caught behind the wicket.

Try as I might, though, I couldn't separate Michael Clarke and Mike Hussey during the evening session. Instead, that honour went to Pietersen's off-spin. I had been toiling away for hours and yet Kev managed to dismiss Clarke with just his eighth delivery, an inside edge ballooning off his thigh pad to short leg. With his departure we knew Test victory was ours.

Only just, as it transpired. An early-morning burst on the fifth day allowed me the opportunity to claim the decisive wicket in another win over the Aussies, just as I had done at Lord's and The Oval in the previous series, bowling Peter Siddle, and complete my first five-wicket haul against Australia in Test cricket.

Collectively, by claiming the final six Australian batsmen inside 20 overs before lunch, we had also beaten another potential adversary. We knew that rain was forecast, but the velocity with which it fell from around 2.30 p.m. onwards told us that we had got the job done in the nick of time. Had a couple of their lower-order players stuck around, we might not have been celebrating going 1–0 up with a few beers in the visiting dressing room, but sat darning our luck instead.

The rain that afternoon was pelting off the buildings at the ground and by late afternoon the outfield was underwater. Victory came at a price, however, as Stuart Broad pulled a muscle while bowling and was ruled out of the rest of the tour. On the other hand, we knew there was able back-up in the fast-bowling ranks from the 10-wicket win over the Aussie second string at the Bellerive Oval.

From a leading position, however, we were brought back down to earth with a huge bump as one of the world's most inconsistent bowling talents struck hot in the third Test at Perth. In general, Mitchell Johnson endured a poor series, but as we knew from previous experience, and would find out more spectacularly on the following Ashes tour down under, when Mitch got things right he was absolutely deadly. His ability to push the ball across the right-handers then unpick them with one swinging back from nowhere had us in all kinds of trouble in Perth and sent us spiralling from 78–0 to 187 all out.

The WACA is a ground that has always encouraged the fast bowlers, being home to Australia's paciest pitch, and if there were to be any positives from that week at all they came in Tremlett making the most of the conditions. Having already lost Broad to injury, and with Steven Finn struggling for rhythm, the team needed at least one more of the pace bowlers to contribute if we were going to achieve our objectives on the remainder of the trip. Thankfully, from his very first spell Tremlett proved himself a real handful, getting the ball to climb sharply off a full length and leaving the home batsmen vulnerable to nicking off.

As well as being a great lad, Steven Finn is a hugely talented individual, but his career has not been allowed to develop as it should partly because he doesn't give himself the chance to be the bowler he could be. He has all the natural ingre-dients to be a phenomenal fast bowler: the height, the long levers, the raw pace. But he is just too hard on himself.

He gets so down on his performances that even after taking six wickets in Brisbane he was focused on the negative aspects of his bowling. He always seemed to be fighting demons. I constantly found myself telling him not to be so hard on himself. That some days he would bowl brilliantly and not be rewarded, while on others the opposite would apply. I am not sure, though, that he has ever snapped out of this cycle of self-analysis.

Away from the field, he is a lovely bloke, and as such became a butt of one of my jokes when I produced my award-winning Ashes video diaries. What better way to pass the time, and cure my inherent shyness, than being handed a camcorder by the ECB and told to connect with the fans back home? It allowed me to add 'documentary maker' to a CV already containing 'lead singer' and 'worldwide trend leader in hairstyles for men who look fifteen years younger than they actually are'. Here was a chance to provide an insight into what some of the England squad were like away from the day job. Yet when in one episode I revealed Steven Finn to be the most boring man in the world of cricket, he demanded an apology. Of course, in a subsequent episode it was a request I was only too happy to comply with: 'Steven Finn, I am sorry that you are the most boring man in international cricket.'

* * *

By the time we got to Melbourne for the Boxing Day test, the fourth of the series, our bowling attack was 50 per cent different from the one that had begun in Brisbane. All the talk before the MCG match was that the pitch would be similar to the one we had struggled on in Perth, and that bounce would be the undoing of us. However, the research conducted by our bowling coach, David Saker, a former Victoria player, suggested it would be lower and slower by some margin and that the large square would promote reverse swing.

If the series was in the balance, with the score 1–1, we also knew that the current position favoured us over the Australians. After all, two draws and the Ashes would be retained.

Christmas was an unusual experience for me as Sarah's departure earlier in the month – pregnant women are not allowed to fly any later than 32 weeks into a term – meant I hooked up with the singletons at our official dinner. Anyone who says Christmas Day in 30-degree heat is a wonderful experience has got no idea what they are talking about. Give me blankets of snow outside any day. The fact that the country had been turned white thousands of miles away and that I was clock-watching until Boxing Day didn't make me feel any better.

But my first experience of Melbourne's Boxing Day Test was quite frankly awesome. The noise generated by an 85,000 crowd was deafening. It was an absolutely insane experience. The only thing that sounded better, in fact, was our seamers completely silencing it. In just over three hours, overcoming a couple of early missed opportunities, Jimmy Anderson, Chris Tremlett and Tim Bresnan had rushed Australia out for 98. At the close of play on that first day, with the scoreboard showing England 157–0, there was only going to be one result. We entered the second morning with a lead of 59 and the pitch was as good as our overnight score suggested.

Our three-pronged seam attack had kept the ball in what some Australians liked to call the Avenue of Apprehension, and they profited in doing so as all 10 first-innings dismissals came via edges behind the wicket. It was one of those days when the good balls aren't too good and the ball flies to the fielders, who generally backed up their efforts with good catching. So to hear Australian former players slagging off the Australian batsmen for poor performances that evening seemed to be a bit of an injustice to me. Each one of Anderson, Bresnan and Tremlett had bowled with great skill, and a couple of those Australians had been in very good form during previous matches, most notably Clarke and Hussey.

Jonathan Trott ensured the one-sided nature of the Test continued with a brilliant unbeaten hundred that was almost exclusively made up of strokes through the leg side. To counter him, the Australian bowlers got wider and wider, yet he just kept wandering across to flip them off his pads. Backed up by Matt Prior, it meant that we secured a 415-run lead on first innings and had the best part of half the match to bowl Australia out again. Doing so would mean the Ashes remained in our possession.

As it was, we completed our task in three sessions, and although the ball was not turning lavishly, I really enjoyed playing a part in finishing the job. In contrast to previous matches on the tour, there were few bad balls from me, if any. At one stage I bowled five maidens in a row to Michael Clarke, and doing so undoubtedly caused him to lose focus when I altered the angle of attack to round the wicket. I also shifted Andrew Strauss from short midwicket to second slip – and would you believe that just four balls into the change, Clarke nicked it straight to him?

To be honest, although pleased with my efforts in tying the Australian batsmen down, it was the ability of Anderson, Bresnan and perhaps surprisingly Tremlett to get the ball to reverse-swing that proved crucial. The pitch was rock-hard, meaning that chunks were taken out of the leather on a regular basis, and working on one side's shine while the other was getting wrecked only accentuated the movement on offer.

If anyone was in any doubt about the team's motivation to complete a 3–1 scoreline, it dissipated pretty swiftly in Sydney.

'You will be a team that goes home having retained the Ashes,' Andrew Strauss told us before the fifth and final Test.

'But we can go back and forever be remembered as winners. Going home with a draw will take some of the gloss off. It is not how *I* want us to be remembered.'

We had got into that position by being pretty consistent as a team. In contrast, Australia had resorted to drafting in new blood. Having started the series with Xavier Doherty as their spin bowler, Australia played two Tests without selecting one at all, but conditions in Sydney demand at least one. The player selected was Michael Beer, a slow left-armer who had played only seven games in first-class cricket for Western Australia. Fundamentally, he was picked because he had got four wickets in a tour match against us at Perth. But to emphasise his impact, or lack of it, when his name was announced it caused consternation in our dressing room. None of us could remember him taking four wickets with any clarity, and so we actually checked the scorecard during a team meeting. It showed that although, yes, he did take four wickets, his victims were caught in the deep or playing poor shots, trying to up the run rate before a declaration.

With such bizarre selections, it felt like a turning of the tables was taking place and that Australia were making mistakes characteristic of England in the 1980s and 1990s. They also brought in Steve Smith halfway through the series, and I took it as a compliment that his role, according to the Aussies themselves, was to ape what I did for England. Can you believe that a man who would go on to become the world's number one-ranked Test batsman was first picked to stand at second slip, boost the mood of the team by telling a few jokes, score some runs from number seven and bowl a few overs of barely passable leg-spin?

The fact that the Australians went public with his credentials for selection left him wide open to banter on the field. Jimmy Anderson wasted no time in getting stuck into the new recruit when he first walked onto the field at Perth, demanding: 'Come on then, Smudger, tell us a joke. Thought you were some sort of comedian.' Cue wisecracks from slips like, 'His batting sure makes you laugh'. Smith wasn't the player he is now back then, and you would have struggled to predict his rise given his unorthodox technique.

Another of Jimmy's favourites used to be to greet every Mike Hussey boundary with, 'Shot, Dave', It wasn't until the third time they played against each other that Mike lost it and snapped back, 'I'm not Dave. I'm Mike Hussey.'

'Sorry about that, Dave,' Jimmy replied.

Just as at Melbourne, however, Australia failed to make the most of an absolutely belting batting pitch at the SCG and their 280 was 200 runs under par. They enjoyed the best of the batting conditions but the true nature of the surface was only revealed when we replied with 644, the highest England total in an Ashes Test in Australia. The intensity of our batting was matched when we fielded for a second time.

Tremlett completed the victory by bowling Michael Beer but it would have been fitting for Jimmy to have wrapped things up. He had been the one bowler on either side to sustain his authority over the opposition throughout the five matches, and Mike Hussey later confessed, over post-series drinks, that during a reverse-swing spell in Sydney he had no idea which way the ball was going to dart once it left his hand. With his 766 runs, Alastair Cook was in rarefied company. Of England batsmen only Wally Hammond had scored more in an Ashes series on Australian soil. Cook had spent more than 35 hours at the crease, and the adjudicators recognised his devotion to batting with the man-of-the-series award. For his flexibility with new ball and old, and consistency, I would have given it to Jimmy.

The support we had from the Barmy Army throughout the series was quite incredible. When there are 25,000 Englishmen roaring you on it is truly inspiring, and it drew a chuckle or two when they taunted the Aussies with 'Are you Bangladesh in disguise?' However, despite our brilliant relationship with them as a team, and our celebratory post-match Sprinkler Dance in front of them getting so much good publicity, I reckoned their treatment of Mitchell Johnson at the after-match award presentation was unnecessary.

Sure, it was fine to get stuck into him with their usual refrain, 'He bowls to the left, he bowls to the right, that Mitchell Johnson, his bowling is *****', when he was on the field. But to do it once the action was over didn't sit so well with me. I always had a great relationship with the Barmy Army guys, but I also believe in being humble in victory, and that wasn't our supporters' greatest hour.

It was also unusual, in my experience, for the post-series root-and-branch inquest to be carried out by Cricket Australia in the immediate aftermath of this match. I had always been led to believe it was an English preserve to call an inquiry into a team's failings. But the fact was we did the simple things well while the Australian side buckled under the pressure. Despite a great start to the series, in which they dismissed us inside a day, they struggled to bowl us out on a regular basis thereafter. If one side is taking 20 wickets and the other fewer than 10, it suggests a bit of a gulf between the two.

As an England team we had left an indelible mark on the Ashes and we made similar ones in the SCG changing room to toast our achievement. Everything inside is wooden, including the lockers, and there is a tradition of players signing them, so I took the opportunity to do so, scribbling 'Swanny Ashes 2010–11, winners 3–1' on mine. There was one other way I decided to remember one of my greatest moments as an England cricketer – the naming of my son, Wilfred Richard Sydney Swann.

Date	Venue	Team	Score	Team	Score	Result
25/11/2010	Brisbane	England	260 & 517-1d	Australia	481 & 107-1	Drawn
03/12/2010	Adelaide	Australia	245 & 304	England	620-5d	England won by an innings and 71 runs
16/12/2010	Perth	Australia	268 & 309	England	187 & 123	Australia won by 267 runs
26/12/2010	Melbourne	Australia	98 & 258	England	513	England won by an innings and 157 runs
03/01/2011	Sydney	Australia	280 & 281	England	644	England won by an innings and 83 runs

15

GOING FOR THE TREBLE

PLAYING in a Test match against Australia is as special as it gets for an England cricketer, and I am sure those in the Kangaroo Crew would say the same in reverse. So while organising back-to-back Ashes series in 2013 and 2013–14, spanning just six months from start to finish, was great for the administrators, for the players and public alike it was overkill. Less is more sometimes, and Ashes caps shouldn't be chucked about like confetti.

The reason behind such scheduling was partly down to a theory that had done the rounds for several years, and one that former coach Duncan Fletcher for one had convinced himself about – that England had never won a World Cup because it always came immediately after an Ashes tour, and the players were fatigued from their exertions down under.

Come on, talk about hiding from the truth. The real reason we didn't win a one-day World Cup was because we were so arrogant towards 50-over cricket and insisted we were playing the right game when we patently were not. That's just burying your head in the sand. Even then, why on earth would you take the crown jewels of world cricket and move them to accommodate a World Cup that in the eyes of most Englishmen has nowhere near as much prestige?

So it didn't sit well with me to play two series so close together. Of course, as it turned out, it was as if there were years between the two anyway because of the contrast in fortunes we were to experience.

We entered the year with a very settled team. We had reached number one in the world in Test cricket since the last Ashes and showed versatility in winning home and away. As a team we ticked most boxes: Jimmy swung the new ball, and was just as good an exponent with reverse swing; Stuart Broad had already proved himself to be an equally adept and versatile pace bowler; I bowled our spin; and whoever came in as the fourth member of the attack – Tim Bresnan, Chris Tremlett, Steven Finn or Graham Onions – more often than not did a great job. We had a really well-balanced bowling attack.

With the bat we had consistency and patience. There was not a hurried look to our cricket. What we did tended to be measured. Sure, there were exciting periods of our innings between 2009 and 2012 when people like Ian Bell, Kevin Pietersen and Matt Prior counter-attacked, but as a unit we were founded on some old-fashioned English cricket. We were patient, looked to bat a long time and didn't worry about whether it was a brand the crowd would pay to watch. Aesthetically pleasing we were not, with a top three of Andrew Strauss, Alastair Cook and Jonathan Trott. Sometimes they were about as easy on the eye as turps on your tonsils. But what we found was that people were excited about winning and we managed to achieve this regularly. I feel proud to have won 50 per cent of the 60 Test matches I played in. Personally, I would always back an exciting brand of cricket and I always tried to be aggressive on the field, yet quite truthfully if we were winning I couldn't give a monkey's.

For the England team, a few things had come together in India in the last two months of 2012. To start with, it was when Kevin Pietersen was seemingly trying to build bridges with his team-mates, post-text messaging opponents about our then captain Andrew Strauss and his quite bizarre YouTube denials, and losing faith in all his colleagues. During that period he was just being a good team-mate and concentrating on his batting. He was simply brilliant in that series: he scored a great hundred in Mumbai. I bowled well; Monty Panesar, a player whose form ebbed and flowed at times, happened to be in very much a flow stage when he was called into the team; and we had belief. We realised that if we could take wickets in India we could beat them, and our best chance of taking wickets would be through our spinners.

The best thing about the team was our resilience. We got

properly hammered in Ahmedabad and we could easily have lost the series 4–0 if we had not had the right attitude. Bouncing back to win the next two matches in Mumbai and Kolkata was possibly our greatest achievement during my time with the Three Lions on the chest.

It was the only series in my memory, before or since, that showed that as a collective we had cracked how to play spinners in the subcontinent. The way to do so is to attack them, never let them settle, and play them off the back foot whenever possible, which is what Kevin and indeed Alastair Cook did so successfully. What a disappointment then that the next generation of batsmen did not heed any of the lessons, reverting to type and being absolutely useless during the winter of 2016–17 in Bangladesh and India.

We were also in form immediately ahead of the Australians' arrival in 2013. Stuart Broad's priceless ability to look anodyne one day and, with his dander up, like a world-beater the next was to the fore when he had one of *those* spells against the New Zealanders at Lord's in the early-summer series. We had found them dogged opponents in a 0–0 draw on their soil earlier in the year, but on this occasion Broad went straight through them with 7–44 in a second-innings score of 68 all out – although you had to factor in that half of their team hadn't seen a red ball for two and a half months while they were participating in the Indian Premier League, and they were still shaking off the jetlag.

Of course, we didn't care a jot. In fact, following elbow surgery in March 2013 that caused me to miss the entire New Zealand away series, I was just pleased to be back out there on the field. My only concern was the state of my right elbow. I'll be honest, that elbow was a concern throughout my career. But I was used to managing it, particularly since my previous operation on it at the start of the 2009 summer, by missing one-day series to rest from time to time, as I had done in India before Christmas.

The fact I was able to take 10 wickets in the second Test win over the New Zealanders at Headingley suggested that the repeat operation by the Minnesota-based surgeon Shawn O'Driscoll would be good for another few years. To be back and contributing to another England win allayed fears that I might miss the start of a massive year.

Those wickets made the torture of being attached to a CPM machine – CPM standing for 'continuous passive motion' – worthwhile. I spent a fortnight with my right arm strapped into this contraption designed to extend the range of movement and reduce inflammation. Every hour was 50 minutes on, 10 minutes off, and in these 50-minute slots lay the opportunity for sleep. It was better than the alternative: not being ready for the first Ashes Test on 10 July.

My participation was placed in jeopardy again when I was struck on the arm by Essex's Tymal Mills while batting in England's warm-up match at Chelmsford. I was in shock for the first few seconds after I was hit. I couldn't feel my bat,

I couldn't move my hand and immediately the worst-case scenario flew through my brain. I had a sickening feeling of dread that I had done something serious, but I carried on batting, and to find out later in the day that it was only badly bruised was a massive relief.

My predicament was nothing compared to the problems experienced by Australia. Lurching from one crisis to the next, they had internally banned four players for not doing their homework during a whitewashing in India, and had Shane Watson threatening to follow Ricky Ponting and Mike Hussey into retirement as a result. They didn't appear to know what their first-choice XI was, either.

As a result, there were some new faces in the 2013 Australian touring party and so Gemma Broad, our analyst, provided us with footage of their batsmen – a selection of deliveries they'd faced over previous months. I didn't pay too much attention to mine because such montages tend to show lots of action but little context. It's all very well seeing someone get out 10 times to different bowlers, but I've always believed it is important to show the build-up to the dismissal, and assess the match situation.

My analysis of players was usually carried out on the pitch. All I was ever interested in establishing as a bowler was whether or not a batsman was aggressive in the first place. You get a hunch for this when they walk to the middle. Do they look confident? Are they up for the challenge? Are they just happy to survive? Body language always played a part for me when I came up against a newbie.

Ultimately, though, I judged an opponent on what they did the ball immediately after they first came down the wicket at me. I worked out during my time as an England player that most batsmen, believe it or not, would come down to the very first ball of an over. I am not sure whether they felt that was the safest ball of an over to do so, but they did. I backed myself to see it coming, and if I anticipated it I would bowl slightly slower and slightly shorter so that it would be a big turning delivery. That way, if they did come down I had the chance of beating them on either edge. If they were successful and hit a four or six, I would then want to know what they would do next. Would they try the English classic of waiting on the back foot for a slightly shorter delivery? Would they come again? Or look to sweep?

This helped me build a picture in my mind of how they wanted to construct an over. Then, my focus would purely be on how I could disrupt their plans – by trying to make them play six shots they didn't want to. Once happy with what a guy was doing, my photographic memory meant I knew where his feet would generally be going, and that helped. It was also an aid that although the Australian team was in flux, several of their players, such as Chris Rogers and Ed Cowan, were familiar through county cricket.

The instability in the Australian set-up extended to the management. Darren Lehmann was unexpectedly made coach at the start of the tour in a bizarre switch in Bristol. Mickey Arthur had travelled over in that position, but after the Australia A team responded well to Lehmann's methods, Cricket Australia announced the switch. At a press conference in Bristol, Arthur spoke about his disappointment regarding his departure, and then Lehmann was wheeled in to discuss his plans for the way forward. Talk about rubbing salt in the wound. It would only have carried a greater sting had the boot been delivered in Leicester. I have to say this as I was born in Northampton, whose wonderful Saints rugby team hate the Leicester Tigers, and now I live in Nottingham, whose famous Forest team are rivals of Leicester City. Truth be told, I actually quite like Leicester after scoring my maiden County Championship hundred there back in the day, but please keep this to yourself.

The first Test of the 2013 Ashes series was one of the favourites of my career. Hosted at Trent Bridge, my home ground, it made for a memorable week. The Red Arrows flew over on the opening morning, and the usual pre-series anthems provided the necessary pomp and circumstance.

We won the toss and batted first but managed just 215. With the ball swinging round corners, though, there is no one better to have on your side than Jimmy Anderson, and that score was put into context when we had Australia four wickets down for 53 runs on that first evening – including an unplayable delivery from Jimmy that beat Michael Clarke's outside edge and hit the top of off stump.

Next day the procession continued – until Australia's debutant number 11 walked out to bat. The selection of Ashton
Agar ahead of Nathan Lyon as their frontline spinner was
apparently something to do with Kevin Pietersen's ongoing
mental block against left-arm spin. Pound for pound, Lyon
was an infinitely better bowler, but the 19-year-old Agar
could also bat and was totally miscast coming in last, as he
was to show on that second day when from a position of
117–9 he helped open up a 65-run lead in partnership with
Phil Hughes. It was one of the most incredible innings of all
time, and the highest score in Tests by a number 11, but it
should never have reached anywhere near the levels it did.

Why not? Because, when the partnership was worth 14
runs, Agar was stumped off my bowling. Matt Prior whipped
off the bails and Aleem Dar sent the decision upstairs for
review. Replays shown on the big screen revealed he had
nothing behind the line. Aleem even said: 'OK, out, yes, no
problem.' Yet as we began to walk off, Marais Erasmus, the
third umpire, indicated 'not out' to the crowd. We couldn't
believe it. Matt Prior kept the still of the incident as his
mobile-phone screensaver for ages afterwards, and you could
clearly see the whole line behind Ashton Agar's shoe.

It was an incident that made a huge difference to the
context of the match. Although I was the one to catch him
out 92 runs later, I wish he had scored a hundred. It would
have been a great story. As it was, he had to settle for 98 and
an all-time high for a jack.

Bowling to number 11s was our Achilles heel for about 12 months. The previous summer Tino Best, of West Indies, had made 95, knocking us around Edgbaston to a full personal commentary. To whoever was bowling, he would say things like: 'You're not scaring Tino! You hear that? You're not scaring Tino, man!' Then, after proving his point by crunching cover drives, he would shout: 'Shot, boy! Keep con-centrating. You've got the bowlers at your mer-cy!'

We found it hilarious. He didn't mean it to be funny, of course, but it was like a comedy sketch all the way through. He'd not played for West Indies for three years and seemed intent on making up for lost time. As though this was payback for Andrew Flintoff's infamous 'mind the windows' goading that had preceded his dismissal in a Lord's Test years earlier. Perhaps that's why he was so full of chirp.

Again, it was a shame he was to be denied five runs shy of a hundred.

As the ball soared into the stratosphere from a heave at a Graham Onions delivery, Tino was shouting, 'C'mon, Straussy, man. Drop the ball! Please, drop the ball!' The most enjoyable innings I have ever been on the wrong end of concluded with a cry of 'Oh, for f**** sake!'

Tino's innings came on the fourth day of a match so badly affected by the rain that the first innings was not yet complete. It was already a dead rubber, whereas in 2013 Agar's was different because we thought we'd wrapped up the innings, and he counter-attacked to catch us cold.

The biggest 'incident' at Trent Bridge also involved Agar. It came during our second innings when Stuart Broad edged Agar's bowling, a pretty thin nick, and the ball was redirected to slip off wicketkeeper Brad Haddin's gloves as a result. Those people with limited knowledge of cricket would have seen it go into Michael Clarke's hands and considered it to be a massive edge. However, it was thin enough for Aleem Dar not to spot it and Stuart stood his ground.

I am all for walking, but I can understand other people will feel the pressure to stand their ground and use the argument that umpires are there to make decisions. It's wrong, but they will do it. The Australians, having burned their reviews, stood in disbelief, and the fact that it occurred at a crucial juncture in the contest seemingly added petrol to the flames. Broad and Ian Bell went on to share 138 runs for the seventh wicket.

DRS technology was still in its infancy, and most players were in favour of it because it was supposed to improve the percentage of correct decisions. But there had been some controversy in its application in the Champions Trophy in June that year and there were mistakes on either side in this particular match. Admittedly this one was a pretty poor decision, but despite the media furore – the *Courier Mail* in Brisbane led the inquest, calling Stuart a cheat and demanding that he should be punished, while even Michael Holding, commentating on Sky Sports, proposed a ban for acting against the spirit of cricket – not a single Australia player had a go at Broad. They were obviously peeved about it, but there was no war between the two teams.

Trent Bridge was not a great Test haunt for me in terms of wickets, even though it was my home ground. In fact, some of my worst returns came there, and on occasions I didn't get to bowl much at all. Like when Jimmy got 11 wickets in the win over Pakistan in 2010 and I sent down two overs all match. I didn't get a wicket there until my third Test appearance, against West Indies in 2012.

Yet I had been entrusted with trying to get that final Australian wicket on the final morning of the first Test, bowling in tandem with Jimmy. Australia were chasing a target of 311 runs and we had them nine wickets down, with 80 runs still required. Yet they kept chipping away at the target just as Shane Warne, Brett Lee and Michael Kasprowicz had done at Edgbaston in the 2005 series. So successfully that after claiming the extra half-hour available to force a result at the end of the morning session, we had to take a delayed lunch.

During that interval on the final day the dressing room had been as nervous as I had known in my life. The only people who could affect the game for us were the bowlers at either end, Jimmy and myself, and from my perspective I would rather have stayed outside in the middle until the game was over. It was horrible pacing up and down. I felt like an expectant father, only breaking the monotonous striding by diving under a cold shower. I just wanted to know either way what was going to happen. I've never been someone with patience when it comes to sport. For instance, I can't watch *Match of the Day* without knowing the results. I've always been that way.

There was hushed anticipation around the stands too, until Lisa Pursehouse, the Nottinghamshire chief executive, decided the crowd needed to be more involved. With 20 runs required on one side and one wicket on the other, there was going to be half an hour's cricket either way and so she dispatched Sean Ruane, the opera singer who had been hired to belt out the national anthems, onto the outfield to perform an impromptu medley of patriotic tunes like 'Land of Hope and Glory', 'Rule, Britannia' and 'Jerusalem' to whip up the home crowd. The wind was cracking the flags, a full house was well lubricated, and by the time we returned to the field, they were singing their hearts out.

It made for a great finale, and once again brought into focus the club's decision to ban Billy Cooper, the Barmy Army trumpeter. I went public in support of him, but Lisa just wouldn't budge, arguing that Trent Bridge had an ambience all of its own, a nicer atmosphere than any other ground in the country. Although I wouldn't disagree with that, for my part, I thought I owed Billy an attempt to get him in. The Barmy Army lads spend an arm and a leg to follow us to parts of the world you wouldn't ordinarily want to pay to go to. They're always there, doing their dawn patrols, staying up all night. Yes, they're all borderline alcoholics, but even so, to be a borderline alcoholic and start drinking at 6 a.m. in Bangladesh is a pretty stunning effort.

Alastair Cook spoke really well and told us we'd win because another chance would come our way. It might be a run-out, a difficult catch or another DRS verdict. We just had to make sure we grabbed the chance and maintained our composure. Jimmy created it for his fourth of the day, and tenth of the match. Not bad considering the lack of response in the pitch.

We have learned to accept technology, but in those early days there was a little less confidence in it, and there was no better example of this than the very end of the game, when Jimmy Anderson – who had bowled a 13-over spell either side of lunch – sent down a delivery to Brad Haddin. Aleem Dar gave it not out but everyone behind the wicket knew he'd hit it, because we'd heard the noise. Only Jimmy himself hadn't. With just 15 runs required for them to win, it was a tense moment as we debated what Hot Spot would show. I asked Brad whether he had hit it. 'Think so, yeah. Hope I get away with it.'

Did you know Trent Bridge is home to the biggest big screen in the country? It's actually the largest free-standing TV screen in Europe, and so you can see everything in minute detail. It displayed the tiniest white Hot Spot mark. With eyes like hawks we could see it. But even then we didn't want to tempt fate, only doing so when we heard Marais say through the third ump's microphone: 'You can reverse your decision.' The roar of relief when the final wicket was confirmed is something I'll never forget. It was quite a way to end what – despite its toing and froing – had turned out to be a nip-and-tuck Test match.

In contrast, the following week Lord's was witness to the worst Australian performance I have known. They just rolled over, like England teams of yesteryear used to at the same ground. We won the second Test by 347 runs, I finished with five wickets in the first innings, and nine in the match, including yet another result-clinching one, yet it was nowhere near the level of my top performances for England. I had at least three wickets handed to me on a plate.

This series was the best I ever saw Ian Bell bat. He was calmness personified – as though he finally believed how good he was after a decade around the national team. He'd always walked the line between knowing he was one of the best players in the world and worrying that he was not good enough to play for England. Most of the battle for him was in his head, not out in the middle, and quite frankly, he was the best technical player I've ever seen. Yet he had a habit of getting into bad trots.

Two scores of 109, his second and third hundreds versus Australia and 18th and 19th of his Test career, were the cornerstones of our wins in the first two Tests. His form throughout the series, wow. Once a batsman has received his first few balls, I have never known anyone give team-mates in a dressing room 90 yards away such a relaxed feeling. The only one to compare was Jonathan Trott. And I tell you what, with those two in their pomp I would have loved to have bowled spin for Warwickshire for a couple of seasons. It would have felt like you were never going to pad up.

What made Bell's efforts more impressive was that we were three wickets down early in nearly every game of the series, and we came back on each occasion. So it was a bone of contention for me when people suggested that rain at Old Trafford saved us from defeat in the third Test. The assumption was that because we were 37–3, having been set 332, that would have been that. Had no one been watching what went on previously? We wouldn't have lost. At Lord's we had been 28–3 and 30–3, yet we had condemned Australia to their second-largest defeat in Ashes history.

The forecast for Manchester was horrific, and to make things worse I was suffering man flu in the build-up, to the extent that I had the team doctor in my room all night on its eve. I was boiling up but felt freezing cold. I wanted to wrap myself in the duvet, and he had to keep pulling it off and sponging me down. Early the following morning, he forced me into a cold shower, and I have never felt worse arriving at a cricket ground. The sight of the Point, the new conference centre, does that to you, I guess.

In all seriousness, I hadn't shaved for a couple of days, I was shivering and I just knew we would end up losing the toss. So when Cookie walked back into the dressing room, he came straight up to me to apologise. I always wanted to bat first, and we used to joke about that fact, but he knew this was serious. I riddled myself with pills, to the extent that my recall of this particular match is minimal. I just floated on a co-codamol high.

Compared to Lord's, we found wickets a lot harder to come by in Manchester and the ones we did manage in the first innings were the result of a concoction of errors.

First, Usman Khawaja was wrongly given out caught behind off my bowling. He went for a big off-drive, and a noise sounded like he'd got a massive edge. He was given out by umpire Tony Hill but referred it. Replays showed he missed it by a foot, and any noise was from his bat clipping his pad, yet after several minutes of deliberation by the TV official, Kumar Dharmasena, Khawaja was still given out. Apparently, Dharmasena had not seen enough evidence to overturn Hill's call. But we all accepted later that it was another howler, like one that Jonathan Trott received in the first Test in Nottingham.

Then, Chris Rogers got out to me lbw 16 runs shy of a maiden Test hundred, having had his concentration broken the previous delivery when one of his mates emerged from an executive box and walked behind the bowler's arm. Next ball, he played round a straight one.

To top it all, David Warner came out at number six and nicked one straight to slip but remained adamant: 'Nah, I was nowhere near that.'

What a waste of a review that was. We already had a very dim view of him after he had punched Joe Root in a

Birmingham bar before the series, and so I almost cried with laughter at how stupid this was. He had waited for three Tests to get his chance, following his Cricket Australia-imposed ban, and he really humiliated himself at the first opportunity.

Another five-wicket haul, considering I felt like dirt all week, was not too shabby a return, but Michael Clarke, with a daddy hundred, and Steve Smith, 11 shy of three figures but contributing his first innings of substance against England, kept us out in the field for the best part of two days. Nevertheless, we would have taken the end result, a draw – the Ashes had been retained in just under a fortnight of cricket, a feat not achieved by an England team since 1928–29.

Generally there was a decent camaraderie between the two teams. At the start of the 2013 summer, well before the rest of the Australians arrived, Stuart Broad and I had had some fun with Eddie Cowan, who was over playing for Notts. We wound him up and convinced him that we'd been told by the England management we couldn't bowl to him in the nets, to deny him a good look at us.

A county stalwart like Chris Rogers, however, knew us only too well. I ended up getting him out a lot because of our two opposing attitudes aligning somewhere on our respective journeys. He was not the sort of guy to try to knock you off your length. He would happily block all day and wait for the bad one. I translated that as 'block all day, and wait for the good one', and so we were both happy with his policy.

It was always a good battle. He refused to throw his wicket away and a lot of guys on our side really liked Buck because of the amount of time he'd spent in our domestic cricket. There was a respect there from all our bowlers for the graft he'd put in before he faced a ball on his return to international cricket following a five-year hiatus, whereas a young kid of 20 coming into the Australian side wouldn't have got anything like that.

There were loads of reasons why he was the perfect fit for Australia. Primarily, Australia were after a new Justin Langer. He was left-handed and a tough little bastard, so Buck ticked the boxes there. He also had a very good record in English conditions, and was as good a bet as they had until another opener, such as Matthew Renshaw, stepped forward.

But he was not a natural player of spin: the way he played, his front foot went down the pitch, his leg splayed and any time he didn't get it quite right you were hitting his pad. Or if it turned, you would be finding his edge. He was a really good player, don't get me wrong, but I knew he didn't like facing me. Partly because he didn't like to sweep, and when a player doesn't have all the shots against spin you do feel you can get on top of them. So when he pulled that shot out of the locker to get his hundred at Chester-le-Street in the fourth Test, it was a relief for him that he made a good connection.

He later went into the press conference and said that we were all getting stuck into him, and that I especially had a few words. I don't remember saying a single word to him. As a bowler I didn't really chirp because it's not the kind of thing you want to do, in my opinion, especially a spin bowler. But him suggesting it maybe told you where he was at with his game against me.

Mentally, I knew I was going to get him out at some point if I just kept plugging away. He never put me under pressure, whereas someone like David Warner would always do something which involved a risk – a policy that was sometimes good for him and sometimes good for me.

Warner's style of play was what gave me confidence that we would defend 299 in the fourth innings at Chester-le-Street. Typically, Warner came out and played very aggressively. Australia were 109 without loss, then 147–1, yet at no point did I feel we would not win. I guess I felt what Australian players of a previous era must have felt – that we were the better side and would triumph in the end.

One of the reasons for this optimism was that nearly all of the Australian run-scoring was being done by Warner. Another was that the north-east skyline, which had dumped a load of rain at lunchtime to delay the afternoon session, was getting moody again.

At tea, we had just one wicket, but the bowlers' union got together and pledged to sort out our lengths. Stuart Broad reckoned we needed to bowl over the top of off stump more, fed up that we had been getting back-foot-punched. The three-line whip worked. Broad produced one of those Broad spells, the final of his six wickets at 7.40 that evening swelling his match haul to 11 and securing a third series win over Australia – the first such sequence since the 1950s. When he is hot, nobody can touch him. You always know there is a game-changing spell in him every now and again, and he bowled out of his skin in that last session just when we needed a bit of magic – I'm so glad he was wearing the Three Lions rather than a Baggy Green.

We stayed on the dressing-room balcony until the small hours, and there is no greater feeling in cricket than relaxing with your team-mates, enjoying the afterglow of an epic win. We soaked up the emotion, drank a few beers and had a good old sing-song. Winning the series in such a dramatic session of play – we took Australia's final eight wickets for just 56 runs – made it even more special. Let's be honest, retaining the Ashes in Manchester because it rained had been something of a damp squib. This was the right way to toast the retention of the urn. As things turned out, this was my last international victory.

To the Oval then, scene of plenty of consolation wins at the end of an English summer, only this time it was Michael Clarke trying to mind the gap, teeing up a fairly small chase on the final day of a rain-ruined match. It was a move which drew high praise from all quarters. It was good for cricket, apparently.

He had done it through his sheer love for the game, apparently. I am not convinced. It was a win-win situation for him and he was boxing very cleverly.

If he set up a low target and we chased it down, it didn't really matter because the Ashes were already gone, and he would remain unblemished by defeat when trying to engineer a consolation win. If they had won, it would have been, 'Good old Clarkey, he's the right man to lead us forward after all'. If we had lost a couple of wickets and played the match out, he would have occupied the moral high ground. What could possibly go wrong, from his perspective?

The declaration conspired to set up a great Test match finish. We were so close to the finish line, 206–5, needing 21 off four overs, and we would have won it as well had we been allowed to continue, when the umpires decreed we should not play in the dark and took everyone off.

To be honest, a 4–0 scoreline would have flattered us. But we certainly deserved the wins at Trent Bridge, Lord's and Chester-le-Street. Once you get into the habit of winning, some games just take care of themselves. That's what we discovered over a lengthy period of time. We got to number one in the world in the one-day rankings in 2013 because at one stage we went undefeated in 12 completed home games in a row. About half a dozen were rain-affected, including three against India, where we were really up against it. There would be a stoppage at the most advantageous point possible and then Duckworth-Lewis worked in our favour. Eoin

Morgan would then walk out and smash it around. When you're winning, things tend to go your way.

Even when we were winning, criticism coursed through some platforms of the media. Some people pointed out that Australia gained a first-innings lead in four of the five Tests and that we never posted a total of 400. That, I believed, reflected great credit on our ability to seize the big moments. Others became so blasé with our dominance over the Australians that they expected us to win. In a way I was just happy that I had got through the series without anyone focusing on the actual quality of my bowling.

Date	Venue	Team	Scores	Team	Scores	Result
10/07/2013	Nottingham	England	215 & 375	Australia	280 & 296	England won by 14 runs
18/07/2013	Lord's	England	361 & 349-7d	Australia	128 & 235	England won by 347 runs
01/08/2013	Manchester	Australia	527-7d & 172-7d	England	368 & 37-3	Drawn
09/08/2013	Chester-le-Street	England	238 & 330	Australia	270 & 224	England won by 74 runs
21/08/2013	The Oval	Australia	492-9d & 111-6d	England	377 & 206-5	Drawn

16

TOO MUCH OF A GOOD THING

WINNING three Ashes series represented obvious career highs for me. There is truly no better feeling as an England cricketer. The only thing that compares is being crowned a world champion with the Twenty20 team in 2010. However, it is a career regret that I didn't thank my lucky stars for what I'd experienced and call it quits at a perfect 3–0. I simply should not have gone on the 2013–14 tour.

Of course, I had to deal with all the brickbats about abandoning a sinking ship when I called time on my career in December 2013, and I will put the record straight on this in subsequent pages. But let me reveal that I already possessed grave doubts about whether my wonky elbow would get me through another gruelling five-match series months earlier. Possibly the worst thing for me, in fact, was finishing top wicket-taker in the 2013 series, because it convinced me I could squeeze one more tour out of it.

Statistically everything looked tickety-boo. The player-of-the-series award for 26 wickets at 29 runs apiece. Who wouldn't take that? Physically, however, I should have seen the warning signs. Had I been bowling on the same pitches a couple of years earlier, when in full control of my faculties, I reckon I could have taken 50 per cent more wickets. Honestly, it is not unreasonable to think that at my best I could have pushed 40 wickets at 20. The pitches we were presented with were really dry and they promoted spin. Occasionally, you live in denial as a competitor, and looking back I can pick apart some of my performances in the summer of 2013 and cringe.

Take Trent Bridge, where Australia's number 11, James Pattinson, batted for over an hour in their second innings when the ball should have been ragging, and yet I could barely turn it. Pattinson has some ability with the bat, but he was Australia's last man, a left-hander, and therefore a slice of rabbit pie for an off-spinner. Australia needed 80 runs to win the Test match, and they got to within 15.

In previous summers, I could hear the *f-f-f-r-r-r-r-r-h-h-h* of the ball as it made its way on the 22-yard journey from my hand to Matt Prior's gloves, and that's a thrilling sound when you bowl spin. The thing that made me successful at the highest level was that I was able to rip it harder, and get a greater number of revolutions on it, than my contemporaries. Peter Such, the ECB's spin-bowling coach, once asked me to Loughborough so that I could be tested for the exact number I could manage. It was for a research paper the ECB were doing. As it got me out of fitness work, I naturally agreed. I never asked for the results from it, because I knew that I was getting enough to get the ball to drift and then spin sharply.

Suddenly, though, after my operation in March 2013, this gorgeous-sounding whirl of the seam was a rare tune indeed, even when I was putting everything into orchestrating it. This was a fact. But not a fact I was about to shout from the rooftops. I was still able to get through, and do a passable job, and I considered the task ahead in Australia pretty straightforward: Jimmy Anderson would get a bundle of wickets, just as in 2010–11. Others would chip in too and all I had to do was bowl underarm from the other end. England would retain the Ashes. Job done. Thanks for the memories. See you later.

One of the problems I experienced, and skilfully skirted past during the summer of 2013, was the occasional loss of all feeling in my fingers in my bowling hand, which meant I could no longer guarantee where the ball was going to land. My muscle memory was still good, so I knew it would be roughly in the right area, but even the ball with which I dismissed Chris Rogers at Lord's – the most horrid of my 255 Test wickets, a wavy full toss that he missed, took in the box and neglected to review, despite replays showing it would have missed leg by the length of my chin – felt completely normal out of my hand. That should have been a warning sign. Some bowlers occasionally send down a long hop or waist-high full toss, but I was not one of them. I had kept high standards for a long time and such deliveries had been extremely rare. I ignored it by giggling and rubbing my hand in the dust.

The elbow problem had flared up again in New Zealand at the beginning of March, four years and almost 50 Test caps since my previous operation in 2009. It was agony from the start, and as we stood in the slips in the final warm-up match before the Test series, a defeat to a New Zealand XI in Queenstown, I told Alastair: 'I'm cooked here.'

I went off the ground and told the doc there and then I wouldn't be able to play in the Test matches. Ten minutes later, though, England coach Andy Flower came into the changing room and told me that he needed me to get out there and bowl at the other end. I don't think he thought there was anything wrong. I did what he asked but felt like crying, bowling with little accuracy and a great deal of pain.

The elbow felt exactly as it had done before my first operation and the words of my surgeon, Shawn O'Driscoll, came back to me. He'd told me in 2009 that the surgery might last me five years. It had lasted four of pretty intense international cricket, and so I knew I couldn't stick around. It had to be sorted again.

Back at the Mayo Clinic, Minnesota, I anticipated a similar procedure to the first one: the surgeon would simply take out the excess fragments of bone and I'd be good for another four years. Not so, unfortunately. As before, the surgery involved intrusion into my arm with a little drill and the removal of the rogue elements causing aggravation around the joint. However, Mr O'Driscoll explained that as I now had bits embedded in a nerve, there were some he couldn't risk touching. Had he attempted to do so, and made contact with the nerve as well, it would have led to loss of all feeling in my hand. On balance, I didn't think it worth the risk, so he removed what he could, and I began my recuperation watching Steven Finn block a Test match fifty on ESPN8. It was perfect viewing for someone in need of a good night's sleep.

I didn't lose any sleep over Darren Lehmann's comments in between the Ashes series that we had played boring cricket in our 3–0 home win. Pure mind games: symptomatic of a coach trying to deflect attention from his own side's fallibility. I am sure he would have been praising the England team to the skies had the scoreline been the other way around.

And there was more. Alastair Cook was a boring captain, according to Shane Warne, who retained the mantle of the Australians' chief sledger six years after retirement. Yes, what a bore. A tedious dullard, whose Test record since his loss on debut as permanent captain in Ahmedabad read played 13, won 7, lost 0, with a come-from-behind away win over the Indians and a clean sheet against the Aussies sandwiching a journey to number one in the ODI rankings.

We knew what such claims were intended to do – upset preparation, distract us from our game plan and get under our skins. Sure, we weren't at our best during that 2013 summer, but regardless of any fashionista's critique of our artistic merits, or Warne's observations on our captain's tactical nous, I believed we would be good enough to create history. No England team had won four consecutive Ashes series since the 1890s.

With the application of hindsight, however, the signs of a shift in the balance of power were there at the end of the 2013 summer. During the one-day series that followed the Tests in September, Australia recalled Mitchell Johnson, and he bowled like a cricketer reborn.

I wasn't playing because my arm had gone after the Oval Test and it was obvious that I needed some time away. In my heart of hearts, I knew I would never play another one-day international. But the lads that were involved were confronted by the supreme version of one of cricket's most enigmatic bowlers. We'd played against Mitch loads over the years but he'd never really got it together for any sustained period of time. There'd been the odd stunning spell here and there, but enough bad stuff thrown in to earn him the Mr Inconsistent nickname. However, this wasn't the Mitchell Johnson England were confronted with that September. He bowled at the speed of light, and either at the body of the England batsmen or at the stumps. He was in stunning form.

Jonathan Trott was dismissed from the first ball he faced

from Johnson, got peppered in the next match, and was dismissed by Clint McKay first ball again in the fourth ODI, his last of the series. I think Johnson got to him.

When Trott quit the 2013–14 Ashes tour one Test in, due to a stress-related illness, people suggested they hadn't seen it coming, but that was slightly disingenuous because there is no doubt that we in the England dressing room did spot that he was struggling. In truth, he should not have travelled to Australia in the first place. He'd visibly struggled during the one-day series that September, and some of the guys felt that he wasn't all right mentally.

He'd left the fourth ODI in Cardiff early, after registering a second golden duck in three innings, and it was an issue that we spoke about amongst ourselves privately. There were whispers between us that he shouldn't be going because he wasn't well. But when it became clear he was putting everything into overcoming his troubles – which included not sleeping – we as team-mates were only too willing to back his efforts. He was totally stressed but he was trying to fight through it.

Trott was a very popular member of the squad and when you travel around the world together, and become a tight team, you don't want to see any of your colleagues suffer. Everyone felt for him, and he was supported by Mark Bawden, the ECB psychologist, in the initial weeks of the tour. How stupid then that once the main event began, when the pressure was really on and Trotty was suffering most, Bawden was back in England.

Mental health is all too often given scant regard, but professional cricketers touring the world are prone to issues of this kind. You spend a lot of time away from home and mental-health problems hit in a way that you cannot always see. If someone gets physically ill the symptoms are often glaringly obvious. But when your illness is stress-related, the issue can hide itself away. It is why I believe a psychologist is more important for a cricket team than even a head coach or a director of cricket – 11 good cricketers, including a decent captain, plus a shrink in the corner can be the perfect formula. Stress-related illness was a taboo subject not so long ago but, thankfully, people in authority have recognised that it does not discriminate. It doesn't consider your walk of life, your wealth or how loving your family is when it strikes. However, teams will never have psychologists with them permanently while we still have the culture that sees rolling your sleeves up and getting on with things as the solution.

During the first Test of the 2013–14 Ashes in Brisbane in November he played a really poor shot – a shot Jonathan Trott would never usually play. Then, in the second innings he produced the most frenetic innings we'd seen in 49 Test appearances. Normally coolness personified, he was all at sea. Afterwards, he seemed a broken man in the changing room.

Losing a player of that quality was a blow, but rather than worry about that, our task was to concentrate on how we would respond to our 381-run defeat at the Gabba. We knew we were a very resilient team. We'd lost heavily in Ahmedabad

12 months earlier and roared back and won that series. As it turned out, however, things unravelled pretty quickly from that point.

After the first Test we were genuinely blown away by how well Mitchell Johnson had bowled, chiefly because he'd never displayed such control against us before. Previously, you might receive two balls an over wide of the off stump, and although he could get some reverse swing you knew you could score easily. Now, he was on the money and bowling rapidly. In the dressing-room post-mortem, some of the lads put it all down to the wicket. The Gabba was home to a fast pitch, it was argued, and it would all be different in Adelaide the following week.

But when we proceeded to lose the second Test on a slower, almost English-type Adelaide pitch we went through a player-by-player assessment of what we considered to be going wrong. Alastair Cook, as captain, went first and, although he is a great mate of mine, he got it completely wrong when he came out with, 'I think they want it more than we do'. That's the easiest cliché to spout in such a situation and is nearly always absolute nonsense. The 11 players out there with England shirts on were desperate to win. It was nothing to do with desire. Had Australia not wanted it as much as us just four months earlier? Of course they had.

When it got to Ian Bell, he said the batsmen had good game plans but were not executing them properly. Again, another weak cliché. Yet, around the room, guys nodded in unison. So, when it got to me, I changed tack: 'Hang on a minute. When is someone going to say: "We can't play this left-arm bloke called Mitch who's sending down lightning bolts"? Because that's what's been happening, what has been crucial to the outcome of these first two matches, and we don't have any theories on how to stop him, from what I can see. If we don't face that fact, we are going to get beat 5–0.'

It didn't go down well. Graham Gooch, the batting coach, turned round and accused me and Stuart Broad of not scoring enough runs down the bottom of the order. It was our fault, he argued, as we used to chip in with scores all the time when we were doing well; now we were considered to be soft wickets. Stuart's retort was that it would be helpful if we were walking in when their premier fast bowler had bowled more than half a dozen overs in the match, as seemed to be the case in the first couple of Tests, and he pointed out that the reason we were at eight and nine was that we were tail-enders, not top-order batsmen. It's always easier to chip in if your team is 300–6, rather than 87–6 and 117–6, as we had been in first innings so far.

From my vantage point, the honesty had disappeared out of the dressing-room window. People now seemed to be looking after themselves and their own agendas. The batting coach was refusing to admit the batters were batting terribly and blamed the bowlers, our coach Andy Flower was becoming angrier and angrier with both the media criticism and the players.

The cracks that were widening led to an inevitable falling apart. Over the years, every bad team I played in has done so when honesty has got up and left. A guy bowls badly, then walks off and blames his boots, the practice facilities or what he had for lunch. A batsman nicks off and it's not his fault, it's someone else's. It would have been more helpful if some of the top six had said: 'Do you know what, I've never faced a bloke bowling 95-mile-per-hour bouncers before. I'm not really sure what I'm doing. I need to work on that.'

Egos were kicking in. The very fact that the problem was being caused by a fast bowler meant none of them wanted to say: 'He's too quick for me.' While Johnson was not the quickest I had ever faced – nowhere near, in fact, when compared to Shoaib Akhtar – I think he might have been for a few others.

When I first started playing professional cricket, I reckon there were three I faced who were menacingly fast. Shoaib was not only considerably quicker, he also possessed a rather unique action that meant he hid the ball from you for rather a long time, as his bowling hand trailed behind his backside. When it appeared, you had a nanosecond to react.

The other two were both England bowlers, believe it or not. Yorkshire's Craig White, during my first year of county cricket, was ridiculously fast, and I later faced Andrew Flintoff in a televised Twenty20 game between Lancashire and

Nottinghamshire at Old Trafford when he was coming back from injury in 2006, trying to prove he was fit. He was bowling downwind on a quick wicket, with a brand-new white ball, which should have been quite easy to see. Red balls can be a bit of a blur when a seriously quick bowler is releasing them at his upper limit, but this white ball was passing through at such speed that it had a comet's tail. I went to hook – or should I say I went to parry one – the ball struck my arm guard and possibly flicked my glove. I simply wasn't waiting around to find out. It was good enough for me.

From an Australian perspective Brett Lee was also up there, although when I faced him he was no longer out-and-out rapid. Let's just say Johnson was bloody sharp. A lot was made of his improved fitness levels and ability to sustain his hostility throughout the whole series, to claim 37 wickets, but if you look at the number of overs he bowled (188.4), it shows how relatively fresh he remained. We weren't able to push him into those fourth and fifth spells when fatigue takes its toll on the body.

My own body had been an issue for me from the start of the trip. More accurately, a part of my body had been an issue. I was very anxious to test my elbow out and so, shortly after landing on Australian soil in late October, I asked to play in the first warm-up match against a Western Australia Chairman's XI at Perth, explaining that the last time we were there, in 2010–11, I had failed to get into any rhythm. I wanted to get a bit more used to the WACA ground. I thought it would be prudent for the team if I could get used to its bounce and the right length for an off-spinner to bowl. I also wanted to prove to myself that the elbow was good enough to get through competitive action. Such an opportunity was denied me, though, when Alastair Cook explained that this match had been pre-planned as a bowl-off between the fast bowlers Chris Tremlett, Steven Finn and Boyd Rankin to establish a pecking order behind the first-choice XI.

During that week I bowled a couple of double bouncers to Cookie in the nets. He thought I was messing around; we both giggled. But in my mind I was thinking: 'Oh no, for f***'s sake. This is horrific.' Even that early in the tour, I knew I was in trouble and so was my international career. So the last thing I needed was the rain that washed out the middle two days of the next match, versus Australia A in Hobart. It meant I was still a little concerned going into the final warm-up against the Cricket Australia Invitation XI that I'd bowled only six overs with a wet ball on the tour.

There had been talk of how the Australian batsmen would come hard at me when the series began, but I didn't mind that. Sometimes that helps to create chances and I was always a bowler who was happy to see batsmen taking risks. When you play against Australia you tend to go for more runs an over than you do against other teams and that's because of their general approach to the game. Chris Rogers was still there blocking the living daylights out of it, but around him were an array of attacking stroke-makers. Whether they had decided to come at me more aggressively than in previous meetings simply had no bearing on how things turned out, in my mind. I'd been more economical in previous series because I knew where the ball was going and had the control to prevent them being more successful against me. In this particular series, they wouldn't have had to be in ultra-attack mode to tick along at four an over off me because I was bowling an absolute shower.

My figures weren't great in the first Test in Brisbane. As a spinner, you know your role in the game changes with the situation, and in the first innings I had to do a holding role, which I did well. But we were completely on the defensive in the second Test at the Adelaide Oval after Australia built a substantial lead. The pitch was quite a big turner, especially in the second innings, but I couldn't get it off the straight. Meanwhile, at the other end Monty Panesar was ragging it.

Throughout my career I'd always enjoyed coming up against Brad Haddin because he was such a tough competitor, and someone who always liked to take me on with his lap-slog. He'd have his good days and score a few. Equally, I'd have mine and get him out. However, when I bowled at him in this match on a surface that should have guaranteed me the last laugh I felt completely powerless. He was hitting me wherever he wanted and, to add to the frustration, there was nothing I could come back with in response.

It was a horrible position to be in. All of a sudden, I felt like a 13-year-old fast bowler making his debut in a man's match. It was not something I had experienced with England before. In fact, it was not something I had experienced at any level of cricket before, and if I had, I would have given the game up immediately. What was coming out of my hand was embarrassing.

When you analyse things there are two types of bowler, I guess. One focuses on getting the batsman out. Which is the bowler I always hoped to be. The other type constantly worries about where the ball is going. This is not a category you want to be in. It is where bowlers in bad form tend to dwell. You certainly don't want to be there as a Test cricketer. Then again, I needn't have worried about where the ball was going because I was clueless about its destination, and it was a nice surprise when one landed in a decent area and posed the batsman a question. When I ran up I wasn't sure if I was going to be serving up a Steven Harmison special to second slip or an absolute jaffa. Not a nice experience.

Hopefully those who accused me of deserting a sinking ship as soon as the Ashes were lost will now understand that this was not an overnight decision. Such was my concern that I had gone to see Alastair Cook before the third Test at Perth, which started on 13 December. He persuaded me that I needed to keep going. That he needed me for the match.

'Mate, you know I'll do my best for you,' I replied, 'but we both know I shouldn't be playing.'

With three Tests to play, the Ashes were still alive at this point and I thought the team would be better off without me; with another bowler in it. But Cookie was a mate and so I agreed to carry on, and I gave it my best.

For a short period, when I got a couple of wickets early on the first day of the match at Perth – Michael Clarke caught at short midwicket and David Warner slapping a long hop straight to point – I dared to dream that Cookie was right and everything would be fine after all. Of course, I'd taken five wickets at Lord's the previous summer when three were complete flukes. Over a career, you earn slices of luck at times for all those occasions when you bowled well and didn't taken any wickets. Was this redressing the balance? Unfortunately not.

As a group we were bowling quite well, and we should have bowled them out relatively cheaply, but it was my bowling at one end, this floaty filth, that was releasing the pressure. The seamers were trying their backsides off at one end and I was offering up the equivalent of throw-downs at the other. It just felt like I was preventing any chance of us winning that game. Not only had I lost the ability to be the banker within the England attack; I had actually become the complete opposite. I was the liability allowing a position of strength to drift away from us, and I felt helpless. Australia posted 385 all out, after being 143–5, and were in control of another match.

It's important to say I don't regret answering Cook's call. If I had to go back in time I would do the same thing again because I have always been an 'it'll be all right on the night' kind of guy. Just turn up, perform and stop worrying about things. This simply confirmed my worst fears.

Things didn't get any better in the second innings and my final over in Test cricket cost 22 runs. The surprising thing for me when I reflect on this is that it was an over that contained two dot balls. I was bowling on a pitch that was turning lavishly and Shane Watson, who was always a decent player of my bowling but someone who could be tied down, kept smashing it out of Perth. It wasn't even being hit for big sixes that bothered me most. It was the anaemic nature of the stuff leaving my hand. It was everything that I hate about bad spin bowlers, those bowlers who don't try to turn it but just land it on a spot and hope for the best. To see those farewell deliveries of my professional career on video makes me shudder. Unfortunately, at the end that was the best I had to offer.

Of course, I was immediately removed from the attack and replaced by Joe Root, and the fact he was about 20 times better as a bowler told me what I had to do now the Ashes were conceded. My right elbow wasn't allowing me to engineer enough revolutions on the ball to get the dip necessary to trouble Test batsmen, and the tail-enders were tonking me too. To carry on in those circumstances would have been the most selfish decision imaginable. Anybody playing for England must be physically up to the job.

So after a couple of days soul-searching and an episode where my arm gave way and I dropped our baby Charlie (luckily onto a couch) we relocated to Melbourne and I called Andy Flower, and asked to see him face to face. When we met, I told him I could no longer do it, that I had begun to lose feeling in my hand and was not the bowler I had been. I had to retire. We deliberated for a while together and then he asked me: 'Are you sure you want to do this?' I told him that I had been left with no choice. At that point he told me the management had been looking at footage and comparing it with how I bowled in the past. They knew I had a problem. Therefore the one thing that upsets me about the whole episode is that afterwards Andy suggested that it was me who desperately wanted to go home. But it was Andy who told me: if you've finished playing, you'll have to leave Australia. Effectively, I was sent home immediately. People were critical that I quit and headed home when I could have stuck around and helped the young spinners. I can tell you now that I would have loved to have done just that.

Not least because I had my wife Sarah and kids Wilf and Charlotte with me, and it meant I had to organise getting the four of us back home. To be frank, as someone who had had everything done for him by the ECB for the previous five years, I was utterly clueless trying to organise long-haul flights.

I was informed I could stay for three more days and then head back. It should have felt like the biggest disappointment of my career to know that my England career was over, and in one way it certainly was, but I also felt a great sense of relief that I would be letting the team down no more. Some journalists would later write that a half-fit Swann was better than anyone else we had in the spin-bowling stocks. That was their judgement call. All I can say is that I would never want to play half-fit or at half-capacity. It would not be fair on myself or my team-mates.

The way my departure was reported made it look as if I had demanded to go home and some of the other players remained critical of my departure. I remember Matt Prior saying: 'You shouldn't have left, mate,' during a chat months later. The message couldn't have got through to the squad that I couldn't carry on.

I could see from the team's perspective that having an extra body around – someone not selectable because he's not physically up to the job – only serves to clog up the dressing room. I could see why a team management would want a player like that to be sent home. But on the other hand, I was the best spinner England had had since Jim Laker, and they could have used me in some capacity to help whoever was coming in. That's how I viewed things.

The abuse I got on social media for returning to the UK was quite extraordinary. Did people really doubt that I loved every single minute of playing cricket for my country? That I didn't enjoy earning £1.5 million a year as an England player? That I would want to turn my back on all that? Of course I wouldn't. Anyone who could think such a thing is an idiot and clearly reads the wrong newspaper.

The one thing that really irks me about being forced into premature retirement is that I was desperate to go past Derek Underwood in England's leading Test wicket-takers' list. The number 297 had been in my head for quite some time, in fact, and I was of the opinion that I was going to breeze it. If I had remained healthy, in an ideal world I would have passed that target the following year, and I could even have been looking at the 2017–18 Ashes as my final series. Physically, I believe I could have played on until I was 38. The rest of my body was fine – or at least good enough. It was just that darned elbow.

When it all stopped so abruptly, one of the things I struggled to get my head round was how this fairy-tale international career – which didn't take off until I was 29 – had come to an end. I would have done anything to carry on playing Test cricket, the finest game in the world. You are handsomely remunerated, get recognised in the street for being good at your job and your kids are proud of you. I'd have given up one-day cricket in a heartbeat, but even now whenever I see Test matches I realise how much I still adore it. It gives me the pangs of wanting to play again. Occasionally, I even get the sinking feeling that I am better than a guy they've just picked to follow in my footsteps. Then, I plop out a couple of hopelessly venomless deliveries in a charity match and remember I am not.

Perhaps that is why I could not watch a ball of the remainder of the 2013–14 series. In fact, the first England Test match

I watched after the defeat at the WACA was the last-ball loss to Sri Lanka at Headingley the following summer. I didn't find watching easy at all, and not only because my mate Jimmy Anderson was last man out.

No, it was OK when England were batting, but when they were bowling, and in particular when Moeen Ali was bowling, it was horrendously hard. Even on commentary for *Test Match Special* when people were talking about the job that I could potentially still do, it was upsetting. I've always enjoyed Moeen doing well. Not least because every time he does, no one is speaking about me. Whenever he does badly or England struggle in spinning conditions, my name still gets dragged up.

Moeen tends to have hot streaks and barren spells because he doesn't really believe in himself. He's a bloody good bowler but has a confidence issue, and that's why, at the start of the 2017 summer, he made such a big thing about wanting to be England's second spinner. It created a stupid situation whereby they picked Liam Dawson just to make Moeen feel better about himself. As far as I am concerned he can call himself the number two as much as he wants, even when there are no other spinners in the team, as long as he is doing the bulk of the work. When they claimed Dawson was the first-choice spinner it was so condescending. I was uncomfortable with it from Liam's point of view because he would have known he was not as good a bowler as Mo.

To be honest, since retirement I have wanted to help Mo – but I've only ever talked to him once. After I finished, and

Andrew Strauss got the job as director of England, I got in touch with a jokey text: 'Now, let's talk about that highly paid consultancy spin role.' Aside from a couple of 'ha ha' responses, nothing more was said. Then at the back end of the 2016 summer, Mo was getting hammered by the Pakistan batsmen and someone wrote in a newspaper article: 'What is Graeme Swann doing in the commentary box when, blatantly, he should be in the dressing room helping our spinners?' Shortly after this, Strauss phoned me up.

'Look, Graeme, it's about time we spoke about this off-spin position,' he said.

I was sitting in the living room with Sarah at the time and my face lit up. Of course, there had been that text exchange, but I hadn't put a great deal of thought into being a coach. I didn't know whether it was something that would suit me. But in those few seconds I felt a sense of purpose returning.

'Yes, mate,' I said. It's about time you phoned, I thought.

'What do you think of Saqlain Mushtaq?' he said.

I was crestfallen.

'Are you serious?'

'Yes: Saqlain, what do you think?'

'I think he'll be great, mate,' I said, and put the phone down.

That was the moment I thought I was being asked to bring on the next generation of England's spinners – and they'd gone for Saqlain instead. The fact I'd had a couple of glasses of wine meant I could see the funny side of it. In fact, I thought it was hilarious. But the laughter on the outside masked the hurt I felt inside. It was like an old-school rejection letter. Like I had just stormed an interview but walked out of the room to reveal a huge hole in the back of my trousers.

In a way it was an echo of the end of my playing career. I'd imagined walking out for the fifth Test in Sydney on 3 January 2014 with a chance of winning or retaining the Ashes. When I'd left home in October, I thought it might be my last tour for England. During the second Test, less than two months later, I knew it would. People always say sportsmen instinctively know when the time is right to retire. When I made my Test debut in India in 2008, I considered it entirely possible I would not feature beyond that very tour. Everything afterwards was one giant, gorgeous bonus.

Undoubtedly, waiting almost eight years between my international debut, in an ODI in South Africa in 2000, and my second one-day appearance in 2007 always made me appreciate playing for my country that bit more. I consider myself one of the privileged few. Although I confess to an addiction to being the centre of attention, I didn't need a big send-off from the Barmy Army. I had the memories to take with me. I hoped theirs would be of a bowler who took wickets and won matches.

Of course, the end came in one of England's most emphatic defeats – only the third Ashes whitewash, following those in

1920–21 and 2006–07. I have to dismiss the notion that this came about from an inability to cope with pressure. International cricketers combat pressure all the time. But it was a product of the environment in which we found ourselves. In Australia you are a very long way from home, very isolated, and so if the home team gets on top of you it fits their modus operandi perfectly.

Australia had a good team, were developing under Darren Lehmann and maintained a really positive outlook throughout. But their X-factor was a left-arm bowler called Johnson swinging the ball at 90 miles per hour, operating at the absolute peak of his powers. We just couldn't admit we were struggling against him. Australia took a more aggressive approach to their cricket that winter because, in their own view, they had become a bit soft. Johnson was at the heart of this toughen-up policy. He wasn't trying to get people out, he was trying to knock them out, and it was a tactic that undoubtedly worked.

For us, this series was a bridge too far. It was a case of one or two people hanging on. Selfishly, I went thinking: 'I'll get another Ashes win here.' When I look back, the signs were staring me in the face. Matt Prior was knackered by that stage, to the extent that when he tried to return the following summer, pretending the pain he was suffering didn't exist, he couldn't even run 10 yards to take a catch against India at The Oval. To be fair, the doctors had been telling him there was nothing wrong for a year. Then, at the end of the 2014 season they were warning that his badly frayed Achilles was ready to snap. And Jonathan Trott should never have got on the plane. Don Bradman missed the first bodyline Test in 1932–33 because he wasn't mentally right, heading to the seaside instead, and in hindsight Trotty should have done something similar.

Meanwhile, Kevin Pietersen had given up on contrition and turned into Machiavelli again. While I was in Australia, I knew nothing about the whole episode that would lead to his sacking in February 2014. Like the rest of the country, I only found out when the breaking story flashed up on Sky Sports News. I tried to get hold of the lads and Matt Prior told me: 'You will not believe the way he's been carrying on. It's been remarkable.'

Kev and I never liked each other. But we had to form a professional relationship to make things work within the team. Basically, we rubbed along because it was in both our best interests to do so. I wanted him in the team because he was a brilliant player, and I think he recognised I was a good bowler. Furthermore, on this particular trip I had made a real effort from the start, knowing that team unity was always vital to any team's chances of winning in Australia.

At my retirement press conference, I made some comments about certain players being 'up their own backsides', a something-and-nothing comment that caused a lot more fuss than I intended, but I promise you this was not aimed at

Kev or any of my international team-mates. In fact, at that point, I truly believed England's short-term future should include Pietersen. Since his reintegration in 2012, his attitude had been fine from what I had witnessed. There was no reason to discard one of the best players in the world.

As I didn't want to leave on bad terms with anybody, I actually went out of my way to be friendly towards Kevin, and to be fair he was extremely generous ahead of our departure, putting me in touch with a friend of his in Dubai who owned a hotel, so that Sarah, the kids and I could have a holiday on the way home. I didn't expect such a lovely touch, so when I left I sent him a thank-you email in which I told him that although we hadn't always got on I appreciated the gesture and wished him all the best for the rest of his career.

A few weeks later, after I had written a column in the *Sun* on KP's removal from the England team, I received a screaming telephone call from Andy Flower. As a columnist I had revealed what I knew of the drama, which was limited, and provided an honest reflection that I had been witness to no problems with Kev on the tour.

'What the hell are you supporting that bloke for?' Andy now demanded. 'Have you any idea what he was doing on that trip?'

I hadn't, but Andy was intent on telling me. Sadly, there was no reason to disbelieve it. The whole England career had always seemed to be a big game for Kev. He has very good

PR. His supporters argue he got the rough end of the deal in the end. I am not too sure he did.

However, Andy Flower was a whole different kettle of fish. When I saw him a few months later, to my own surprise I felt no lingering bitterness. I actually gave him a hug.

Kevin's portrayal of Flower as a miserable control freak, dubbing him 'the mood hoover', is completely different from the man I know. Kevin had a poor relationship with Andy because Andy doesn't take any nonsense. He's a hard-nosed bloke and a brilliant coach, England's most successful of all time, and I can reveal that he did smile. He laughed a lot, in fact. Maybe just not with people he didn't like.

Yes, he was fundamentally a serious bloke, totally dedicated to his job. But when you have a drink with him you discover another side to his personality: the old-school Rhodesian, open, friendly and a bit mad. Not that we saw it on this particular trip, when the pressure got to him.

The reason we had been so successful as a Test team for so long was his no-nonsense approach. He encouraged us to find the way to score runs and take wickets and go out and do it. In Australia we just couldn't do it. Normally on a tour one or two players are out of form. We had nine or ten, and although rare, it was a recipe for disaster.

The fault lay at the door of the playing squad, yet when we lost Andy was vilified in the media for being like a headmaster, for being too strict. There were claims he'd engaged too many management and backroom staff. Utter nonsense.

Contrast this with when we won in 2010–11 and he was hailed as a genius because of his attention to detail.

When Europe won the Ryder Cup at Celtic Manor in 2014, Paul McGinley, as captain, went to great lengths in terms of preparation, which included ordering blue and yellow fish for the tank in the team room; the seams on the trousers were made of the finest Egyptian cotton. He was lauded as a hero because his players turned up and played amazing golf. Tom Watson was the exact opposite: old-school, laid-back, and there was nowhere near that attention to detail. It was 'turn up, relax, have a drink'. The United States played terribly and lost. Watson was seen as a dinosaur coach. Phil Mickelson played badly and blamed Watson. All a load of nonsense, to be honest.

When you stand over a static white ball on the tee it doesn't matter what colour the fish are, or what colour your trousers are; it is just about you and the ball. Had Watson won, he would have been presented as someone who was able to simplify things, to free the players' minds by getting them to relax and play their best, whereas Paul would have been accused of over-complicating everything – being too zany.

We get very fickle about coaches in this country. Andy got labelled as some kind of control freak, but he was doing everything in his power to make us the best he could. Yes, he called meeting after meeting on that trip, and some of them were the most boring meetings on earth. But he wanted us to get the best out of ourselves, and fundamentally he's a caring, nice man. I have no hard feelings towards him whatsoever. I just wish things could have ended on a happier note.

Date	Venue	Team	Scores	Team	Scores	Result
21/11/2013	Brisbane	Australia	295 & 401-7d	England	136 & 179	Australia won by 381 runs
05/12/2013	Adelaide	Australia	570-9d & 132-3d	England	172 & 312	Australia won by 218 runs
13/12/2013	Perth	Australia	385 & 369-6d	England	251 & 353	Australia won by 150 runs
26/12/2013	Melbourne	England	255 & 179	Australia	204 & 231-2	Australia won by 8 wickets
03/01/2014	Sydney	Australia	326 & 276	England	155 & 166	Australia won by 281 runs

17

SWINGING TO VICTORY

EVEN though the 2013–14 series was a car crash from an England perspective, I still fancied a home win heading into 2015. The cricket ball itself plays such a part in the outcome of Ashes cricket these days, I think, and in our own conditions we have the wood over the Australians.

Over here, their batsmen aren't used to the ball swinging like the Dukes does, and equally their bowlers don't know how to bowl with a swinging ball. So when faced with the Dukes the Australians struggle. They don't seem to be able to handle the lateral movement in either innings. Conversely, in Australia, the Kookaburra ball just doesn't swing and so the Australian bowlers, in contrast to English counterparts relying on the skill of moving it around, aim to get it down the other end as quickly as possible.

From the very first Test match at Cardiff in July 2015, when the atmosphere was encouraging some serious boomerang, the differences between the skill levels of the two bowling attacks were obvious. Mitchell Starc was getting it down at 90 miles per hour and the ball was going for him; he just couldn't get it on target. He was way wide of the off stump to the left-handers all the time, and he had probably never bowled with a ball that had swung as much in his life.

Now, I am not pretending it's an easy skill to master. It's actually very difficult to adjust when it's like that. You almost need to aim for fine leg when you let go of the ball, and that is not something that feels natural to a fast bowler. However, just consider what Jimmy Anderson would have done in the same scenario. If the first one he lets go in a bowling spell swings big, the second one will be close to unplayable, and that is why I thought England would be in with a good chance.

Yet it was Anderson's new-ball partner Stuart Broad, a man who epitomises the big-game player, who landed the most decisive blows with the Dukes in this particular series. In the fourth Test at Trent Bridge in August 2015, everything just happened so spectacularly fast.

Ever since I have known him, when a team has really needed him to pull a performance out of the bag, Broad has managed it. From out of nothing he will conjure up a ridiculous spell, and he has done so often enough in his career for it to feel quite normal. He is one of the great streak bowlers of all time. Think of his five versus Australia at The Oval in 2009, his seven-wicket ransacking of New Zealand at Lord's in 2013, or the 6–17 – including a spell of 5–1 – to win the pivotal Test in Johannesburg in early 2016.

This one, though, topped the lot given the circumstances and the execution of his skills in perfect conditions. England, 2–1 up in the series, were without Anderson due to injury and Broad was simply phenomenal that first morning. I was working for *Test Match Special* and, out on the ground, looking at the wicket before play there was a decent grass covering. It looked like a good morning to bowl. Then there was a squall of rain about 15 minutes before the start. They didn't get the covers on quite quickly enough to stop the smattering juicing it up further. I actually predicted it would be a good day for him there and then, although I suggested he could have three or four wickets, not the incredible 8–15 he ended up with.

So what's the secret to such hot spells? Well, quite simply, he just puts the ball in good areas and is considerably quicker than he looks. He is fit and strong, someone who doesn't lose his pace, and add that to the incredible belief he has got and it makes him an awesome performer.

Straight away people will say: 'Well, why can't he do that every time?' However, in sport not everything is on a plate for you, things are not always in your favour. Sometimes you get lucky, sometimes you don't, but the really good players cash in when everything is laid out for them. In this kind of situation Broady cleans up.

I can think of no one I played with during 15 years with

Northamptonshire, Nottinghamshire and England to compare to him in this regard, to be quite honest. Back in the early 1990s there were a couple of overseas pace bowlers who made a habit of running through opposition batting cards. Waqar Younis was deadly as soon as the ball started reverse-swinging, and, with his tail up, seemed to be guaranteed five wickets in such conditions. Curtly Ambrose had a couple of famous darts too – like his 7–1 versus Australia in 1993, and his half-dozen haul when England were sliced and diced for 46 in Trinidad in 1994.

Ambrose had a couple of similar attributes to Broad: he was very tall, blessed with good pace, perhaps a bit quicker, but devoted to banging a good length and giving the batsman nothing. Stuart has never done anything out of the ordinary during his most prolific times. It just happens that when things are in his favour he becomes almost unstoppable.

Like Glenn McGrath he is at you all the time, bowling a lot to hit the top of the stumps, so that means lbws, bowleds and caught-behinds are all possible. In fact, it is because they have repeatable actions that he and Jimmy Anderson are so good. Their bad days are never that bad. Get them on a flat wicket, with the batsmen on top, and they can look ordinary, sure, but so does everyone else in the world in those circumstances. To me, though, the definition of a world-class player is someone who, the second the odds tilt in their favour, guarantees results.

Inheriting that leader-of-the-attack label for the penultimate Test of the 2015 Ashes could have brought undue pressure for the wrong kind of character. In the absence of Jimmy Anderson Stuart was the senior bowler, and people looked to him to set an example. He revelled in the responsibility. When he is on fire things happen all the time, and I know exactly what it's like to be on the field during these times: as a slip fielder you expect a nick every ball.

That's one of the reasons Ben Stokes was able to take what I reckon might be the best catch I have ever seen live – the full-length grab, low down, at fourth slip to dismiss Adam Voges and leave Australia 21–5. Stokes catches flies as a pastime but even by his standards it was an absolute worldie. And I would put that down to the fact that in those Broad streaks, you are prepared for exactly that happening – for batsmen being forced to play at deliveries and edges flying into the cordon.

Of course, you can argue a top slip fielder should expect an edge every ball. But most of the time you are braced rather than expectant. When Broad has his dander up it's almost like your feet are on springs ready to push off in anticipation of a diving catch.

Voges's dismissal was the fourth of Broad's five – the fastest five-for in Test history, spanning just 19 deliveries. The fourth, fifth and sixth wickets had never fallen at such an early stage of a Test match. Australia's 60 all out was their lowest in an Ashes Test since 1936. Such was the batting calamity that extras were the top score. By the end of the first day, England had a first-innings lead in excess of 200 and Joe Root had doubled the Australian total on his own.

The Ashes were well and truly alive when the players took the field that morning, and I am not sure they had slipped through a team's hands so quickly in more than 130 years of being contested. It was the kind of freaky bowling display that occurs about every five years in county cricket. You just don't expect such a thing in a Test match, do you? As soon as the demise started, you could almost anticipate what was coming. It follows that every new batsman that walks out is going to struggle more because he's not as good as the batsman one place ahead of him. The best Australian batsmen were all at sea, so what hope had the tail? It was actually a bit of a surprise when England went 20 minutes without taking a wicket at one point.

Stuart Broad's name found its way into another chapter in the annals of the Ashes – and also onto a local Nottingham tram to commemorate his achievement. I wonder whether the Aussie newspaper that had refused to acknowledge his existence in 2013, scrubbing him from their match reports following his previous Test appearance against Australia in Nottingham, could remember him?

Things might have been so different, of course, had Root not been dropped on nought by Australia wicketkeeper Brad Haddin in the first Test of that 2015 series at Cardiff. As it was, Root went on to make 134. It was a reasonably tricky chance but one you would expect to be taken as often as spilled, and its significance stretched beyond the immediate effect it had on the scoreboard.

Root had arrived at the crease with England 43–3 and the difference between being four wickets down and him contributing as he was able to thereafter was immense. When you have someone playing like he did in that counter-attacking way, it instils confidence in the rest of the team. You can imagine the thoughts in his team-mates' heads: 'Yes, we can beat this lot. Just look what Joe's doing to them.'

Had he been out for nought, you'd have had the complete opposite – the sense of being unmanned by them getting your best player out cheaply. Sport can be like that sometimes. It can swing violently on single moments, and I would argue that England began developing a real feel-good factor at that point, when it so easily could have been doom and gloom. The best players in the world seem to have the ability to create ripple effects in their team. Not only is it their air of calm, it is the pressure that is taken off the other people. A good performance increases confidence and makes everyone else look that little bit better when it's their turn to contribute.

I know Joe also viewed this series as a chance to address his biggest career disappointment – being dropped in the previous Ashes series. I actually thought him being left out of the final match in 2013–14 was harsh because he made a really good 87 in Adelaide and his statistics were not that much worse than any of his top-six rivals. So scoring hundreds at Cardiff and Nottingham in 2015 when the odds were in the favour of the bowlers proved to be a fine riposte.

Joe seems to have the complete all-round game. He plays spin well; he plays fast bowling well. He doesn't seem to have any obvious flaws, and he has played enough Tests for me to be confident that no one has found him out, and no one will. When you are sitting yourself on the naughty step because you keep getting out in the 70s and 80s it suggests you are in a good place. He's averaging 54 in Test cricket and I expect, a bit like Ricky Ponting experienced, his statistics will only dip a touch once age starts to kick in. As he still looks about 15 at the minute, let's hope that is some time away.

Root's two hundreds were compiled in bowler-friendly conditions. Contrast that with the returns of Australia's superstar batsman Steve Smith. In the three Test matches when the ball swung around, England romped to victories. He was all at sea as soon as there was some lateral movement because he doesn't have a technique against the swinging ball. Whereas in the two Test matches that were played on flat pitches, in much more Australian-style conditions, he got big hundreds and England lost. Hence the final score: England 3 Australia 2.

Smith emerged as an international batsman in the making back in 2010–11, and although he has maintained an idiosyncratic technique, the one thing that I noted when up against him was that whenever he struck the ball, his head was as still as anything. When we had Australia on the ropes he held firm, and a couple of good pull shots in Melbourne gave off a bit of a message. I made a mental note: this lad's not too bad. But I won't pretend I thought he would turn out quite like he has. These days he's mustard, and the reason I like him is because he has progressed while keeping his unorthodox technique – he appeals to my maverick side.

He is either very thick-skinned or very thick. Throughout his entire career he must have had nearly every coach saying to him: 'No, you don't stand like this, you don't touch your pad like that, you don't move so much in your stance.' All coaches try to turn young batsmen into a clone of Geoffrey Boycott. He must have just nodded: 'Yeah, yeah, yeah,' and ignored the lot. He drives with a braced front leg, he doesn't get his head over the ball and he is often on the move before the ball's even left the bowler's hand. It's almost as if he has said: 'Sod you lot, this works for me.' He watches the ball and hits the ball.

In the two London matches, at Lord's and The Oval, the conditions felt slightly more Australian than English and the balance of power between the two sides switched round. In the capital, Australia posted first-innings totals of 566–8 declared and 481 all out; in the Midlands, their all-out-for-60 Trent Bridge shambles followed Jimmy Anderson's masterclass at Edgbaston in the third Test, when they scrambled to 136. When you have a protagonist as expert as Anderson in lateral movement, there really isn't a lot of blame you can heap at the batsman's door. There just didn't seem to be anyone in the Australian team able to adjust to it.

Had the ball not swung for five Tests, it could so easily have been 5–0 to Australia. Equally, if it had swung all the way through it would not have been hard to envisage a 5–0 result for England. It is rather bizarre, really, to consider such a drastic switch between one end of the spectrum and the other, based solely on atmospheric conditions and the state of the pitch, but this series really was like that, and world cricket is becoming a bit like it too.

Home conditions can prove so influential these days. When things are going well on home turf most of the big four Test teams of India, South Africa, Australia and England are nigh-on unbeatable. India now pretty much trounce everyone at home. Whether this is a condemnation of the modern player's lack of resourcefulness – outside their comfort zone – I am not sure. But there aren't many players who go anywhere in the world and clean up in the way that used to be common. I know I am talking about someone of rare class, but Brian Lara, for example, had the game to adapt to all kinds of conditions.

Whenever a team cannot cope with a set of conditions, and the quality of the opposition in those conditions, the scapegoat is usually the captain or the coach. They are the ones left carrying the can for an inability to get the best out of their own players, and so it was for Michael Clarke in this instance.

I considered Clarke to be a brilliant player, one of the best I ever bowled at, and a consistent performer in international cricket. Sure, he was susceptible against the short ball, but if you didn't get him with the bouncer early on he would more often than not be set for big runs. I also thought he was phlegmatic on the field, and that made him a good leader. Not necessarily the best captain Australia has ever had, but a fairly shrewd tactician, and someone they were lucky to have after Ricky Ponting's time was up.

Every now and again teams do need a change of leader out on the field, and a lot of Australians had had an easy ride for some time because of the good players they'd contained in their teams of the past. Ponting felt the brunt of that when people like Matthew Hayden, Justin Langer, Glenn McGrath and Shane Warne retired around the same time, and Clarke's team did not have the star quality to work with. In some ways he was the star quality of his own team and so when his own form dropped off he was susceptible to the axe.

With the Ashes gone, an average of 16 after four matches led to its own inevitable conclusion. Clarke announced his resignation at the end of the Trent Bridge defeat. Steve Smith would take over the leadership the following winter.

England had already signalled their own intention to move in a different direction with the appointment of Trevor Bayliss at the start of the series, and I had absolutely no problem with the appointment of an Australian coach. As a football fan I was very used to having managers and coaches from abroad, who bring different ways of looking at things and challenge the English way. Bayliss suits this England team; an aggressive one that has grown up in the Twenty20 era, believing that anything is possible. To get a coach whose views clearly promote the same sort of ideas was ideal. He's a very similar character to Eddie Jones, who has had such success with the England rugby team. He clearly likes players to express themselves.

For quite some time, English cricket was seemingly guilty of being overly stats-based, constantly looking at what had happened in the past, whereas the new outlook seems to focus on what can be achieved in the future. They want to embrace what is possible rather than what has been possible previously. So it was a right-time-right-place fit for all concerned.

Personally, I think the Ashes remains the crown jewels of international cricket. The world audience for it is phenomenal, the pinnacle of anything the world stage has to offer, and the increased hype and build-up associated with 24/7 sports reporting doesn't take anything away from this.

My only concern is that it is increasingly becoming a series won by the home team, although I would like to think that might change over the next decade or so because England will develop into a unit that can stand up to different challenges, just as the England team I played in did. It will be a worry if the home teams continue to drub opponents every single series and as a result the Ashes becomes less of a spectacle, more predictable. Let's face it, if you know who is going to win before a ball is bowled, it stands to reason you are not going to get as excited. You need that jeopardy, that surprise element, to keep it special.

Amid all the talk of a Test World Championship, aimed at adding context to the longest format, I have reservations about whether such a scheme would motivate players. Money is obviously one form of motivation for modern players, but do not underestimate the draw of tradition. I used to love individual Test series, and I tended not to pay much attention to the world rankings. Which team was ranked number three or four had no bearing on my thinking. I just threw myself into trying to help England win each series. It was a real attraction to play Test series home and away, and I am not sure a World Championship would have made me feel any differently.

Thankfully, English and Australian players still view Test cricket as the ultimate, drawn in by the prestige that goes with playing in such a revered historical rivalry. So, although in other parts of the world where Test cricket is not as prominent there will be a generation who grow up ignorant about its rich history and focused entirely on Twenty20 – which is obviously a danger to the global sport as we have known it – the Ashes' high profile should see it continue to prosper in the short to medium term.

Beyond that, however, it will need players and administrators to protect Test cricket in general. When I broke into the professional ranks I saw it as a really important career goal to play for my country. I always had an affinity with the England team and I felt really passionately about wanting to break into it. These days, a lot of cricketers play for countries that they weren't even born in, and that mercenary element is the biggest threat. Cricketers now move so freely and frequently around world cricket's changing landscape that they do not necessarily care which badge is on their caps.

The current England side appears to have the balance right. All the star players are clearly focused on England as their primary concern, but people like Ben Stokes still command huge Indian Premier League fees too. If you are a superstar, playing for England every game, you are earning a load of money as it is, without chasing it elsewhere.

A bigger concern for me is the prospect of having to be subjected to a four-day Ashes Test. Quite simply, Test cricket is special because it is the ultimate examination of your endurance and skill over five days, and I would not want to see anyone meddle with the traditional format. To the argument that so many matches reach a result by the end of the fourth day anyway, it's a two-finger response from me.

If you limited all Test matches to four days I fear you would either see a lot more draws or, alternatively, result pitches being prepared, as we witnessed in Division Two of the County Championship before the toss rule was changed to allow the visiting team the option of bowling first. When I hear people say that four-day cricket would be better for sponsors and the finances of those hosting matches, that saddens me. I understand that money provides the spectacle, but the game has to be bigger than worrying about the balance sheets.

Cricket is played on grass not paper, and if a match naturally finishes inside four days, great, but equally so if neither team can force a result by the end of the fifth. Having played in a couple of classics that have gone all the way to the final evening, such as the Cardiff match in 2009, it would horrify me to think that kind of Ashes drama might be denied us in future.

Date	Venue	Team	Scores	Team	Scores	Result
08/07/2015	Cardiff	England	430 & 289	Australia	308 & 242	England won by 169 runs
16/07/2015	Lord's	Australia	566-8d & 254-2d	England	312 & 103	Australia won by 405 runs
29/07/2015	Birmingham	Australia	136 & 265	England	281 & 124-2	England won by 8 wickets
06/08/2015	Nottingham	Australia	60 & 253	England	391-9d	England won by an innings and 78 runs
20/08/2015	The Oval	Australia	481	England	149 & 286	Australia won by an innings and 46 runs

ENGLAND v AUSTRALIA in ASHES SERIES

	Played	Australia	England	Drawn
All Tests	325	130	106	89
Tests in Australia	162	82	56	24
Tests in England & Wales	163	48	50	65
All series	69	32	32	5
Series in Australia	34	18	14	2
Series in England	35	14	18	3

All Ashes Series between England and Australia

Season	Winner	Margin	Season	Winner	Margin
1882/83	England	2-1 (3)	1953	England	1-0 (5)
1884	England	1-0 (3)	1954/55	England	3-1 (5)
1884/85	England	3-2 (5)	1956	England	2-1 (5)
1886	England	3-0 (3)	1958/59	Australia	4-0 (5)
1886/87	England	2-0 (2)	1961	Australia	2-1 (5)
1887/88	England	1-0 (1)	1962/63	Drawn	1-1 (5)
1888	England	2-1 (3)	1964	Australia	1-0 (5)
1890	England	2-0 (2)	1965/66	Drawn	1-1 (5)
1891/92	Australia	2-1 (3)	1968	Drawn	1-1 (5)
1893	England	1-0 (3)	1970/71	England	2-0 (6)
1894/95	England	3-2 (5)	1972	Drawn	2-2 (5)
1896	England	2-1 (3)	1974/75	Australia	4-1 (6)
1897/98	Australia	4-1 (5)	1975	Australia	1-0 (4)
1899	Australia	1-0 (5)	1977	England	3-0 (5)
1901/02	Australia	4-1 (5)	1978/79	England	5-1 (6)
1902	Australia	2-1 (5)	1981	England	3-1 (6)
1903/04	England	3-2 (5)	1982/83	Australia	2-1 (5)
1905	England	2-0 (5)	1985	England	3-1 (6)
1907/08	Australia	4-1 (5)	1986/87	England	2-1 (5)
1909	Australia	2-1 (5)	1989	Australia	4-0 (6)
1911/12	England	4-1 (5)	1990/91	Australia	3-0 (5)
1912	England	1-0 (3)	1993	Australia	4-1 (6)
1920/21	Australia	5-0 (5)	1994/95	Australia	3-1 (5)
1921	Australia	3-0 (5)	1997	Australia	3-2 (6)
1924/25	Australia	4-1 (5)	1998/99	Australia	3-1 (5)
1926	England	1-0 (5)	2001	Australia	4-1 (5)
1928/29	England	4-1 (5)	2002/03	Australia	4-1 (5)
1930	Australia	2-1 (5)	2005	England	2-1 (5)
1932/33	England	4-1 (5)	2006/07	Australia	5-0 (5)
1934	Australia	2-1 (5)	2009	England	2-1 (5)
1936/37	Australia	3-2 (5)	2010/11	England	3-1 (5)
1938	Drawn	1-1 (4)	2013	England	3-0 (5)
1946/47	Australia	3-0 (5)	2013/14	Australia	5-0 (5)
1948	Australia	4-0 (5)	2015	England	3-2 (5)
1950/51	Australia	4-1 (5)			

ACKNOWLEDGEMENTS

Thanks to Richard Gibson for cobbling together my incoherent ramblings, Roddy at Hodder and Stoughton for his guidance, patience and knowledge of the London restaurant scene. Also, my agent Mark Brodie of Stellar Management for working tirelessly. My wife Sarah and kids Wilf, Charlie and Jessica for the odd occasion of quiet to enable me to get on with this book, and finally Rob Lee for being my all-time favourite right midfielder for Newcastle. Well, one of them anyway.

Photographic Acknowledgements

The author and publisher would like to thank the following for permission to reproduce photographs:

Section One
Hulton Archive/Stringer/Getty Images, Popperfoto/Getty Images, Paul Popper/Popperfoto/Getty Images, Hulton

Archive/Stringer/Getty Images, Bob Thomas/Popperfoto/ Getty Images, Paul Popper/Popperfoto /Getty Images, Paul Popper/Popperfoto/Getty Images, The Sydney Morning Herald/Getty Images, Popperfoto/Getty Images, Hulton Archive/Stringer/Getty Images, topfoto.co.uk, Popperfoto/ Getty Images, Colorsport/REX/Shutterstock, Daily Mail / REX/Shutterstock, Popperfoto/ Getty Images, Central Press/ Stringer/Getty Images, Central Press/Stringer/Getty Images, Trinity Mirror/Mirrorpix/Alamy Stock Photo, Lordprice Collection/Alamy Stock Photo

Section Two
Hulton Deutsch/ Getty Images, Popperfoto/ Getty Images, Popperfoto/ Getty Images, Popperfoto/Getty Images, Topical Press Agency/Stringer/Getty Images, Central Press/Stringer/ Getty Images, Central Press/Stringer/Getty Images, Topham/AP, Associated Newspapers/REX/Shutterstock, Hulton Archive/Stringer/ Getty Images, Colorsport/REX/Shutterstock, topfoto.co.uk, Dennis Oulds/Stringer/Getty Images, Adrian Murrell/Staff/Getty Images, Patrick Eagar/Popperfoto/Getty Images, Patrick Eagar/ Popperfoto/Getty Images, Phillip Jackson / Associated Newspapers/REX/Shutterstock, Adrian Murrell/Allsport UK/ Getty Images, Patrick Eagar/Popperfoto/Getty Images, Adrian Murrell/Allsport UK/Getty Images, Bob Thomas/Getty Images, Adrian Murrell/Getty Images, Getty Images, David Munden/ Popperfoto/Getty Images.

Section Three

Patrick Eagar/Popperfoto/Getty Images, David Munden/ Popperfoto/Getty, Patrick Eagar/Popperfoto/Getty Images, Graham Chadwick/Getty Images, Adrian Murrell/Allsport UK/Getty Images, William West/Getty Images, David Munden/Popperfoto/Getty Images, Philip Brown/Popperfoto/ Getty Images, Hamish Blair/Getty Images, Philip Brown/ Popperfoto/Getty Images, Tom Jenkins/Getty Images, KIERAN GALVIN/REX/Shutterstock, Clive Rose/Getty Images, Tommy Hindley/Professional Sport/Popperfoto/ Getty Images, Andrew Romano/Getty Images, Andy Hooper/ Daily Mail/REX/Shutterstock, WILLIAM WEST/AFP/Getty Images, PHIL BROWN/AFP/Getty Images, Hamish Blair/ Getty Images, Stu Forster/Getty Images, WILLIAM WEST/ AFP/Getty Images, IAN KINGTON/AFP/Getty Images,

Section Four

Gareth Copley/PA Archive/PA Images, Hamish Blair/Getty Images, Paul Gilham/Getty Images, Tom Shaw/Getty Images, Mike Hewitt/Getty Images, Gareth Copley/Getty Images, ANDREW YATES/AFP/Getty Images, Mitchell Gunn/Getty Images, Gareth Copley/Getty Images, Ryan Pierse/Getty Images, Chris Hyde/Getty Images, Andrew Fosker/REX/ Shutterstock, Shaun Botterill/Getty Images, Stu Forster/Getty Images, Andy Hooper/Associated Newspapers/REX/ Shutterstock, Ryan Pierse/Getty Images, Gareth Copley/Getty Images, Stu Forster/Getty Images, Philip Brown

INDEX